REGNUM STUDIES IN MISSION

Charis and Charisma

David Yonggi Cho and the Growth of Yoido Full Gospel Church

REGNUM STUDIES IN MISSION

A full listing of all titles in this series appears at the close of this book

By Way of Introduction...

It is by the grace of God that Yoido Full Gospel Church has grown to be the largest church in the world. For the last 45 years I have ministered in obedience to the calling of God. Many people have talked about and have analyzed my leadership. In fact, my leadership is leadership by the Holy Spirit. Without the inspiration and guidance of the Holy Spirit, I would not have been able to exercise the leadership to inspire and influence people.

I am pleased that this book, which analyzes the growth of Yoido Full Gospel Church, has been published in English. I am also delighted that the Institute for Church Growth has begun its ministry to serve the world churches as well as the Korean churches. This is the first book in English to analyze the growth of my church in a systematic form. The story of how God has worked in the Yoido Full Gospel Church should be an ongoing topic for analysis, and church growth a subject for theological reflection, because theology deals with who God is and what He is doing.

The Church should grow healthy, and lost souls should be won, nurtured in faith, and transformed to serve society through the ministries of churches. I hope that the contents of this book, especially the insights on church growth and leadership, will be a challenge and an inspiration to all of you. I hope that every reader of this book will be captivated and inspired by the vision of God. May God bless you.

The Reverend Dr. David Yonggi Cho

REGNUM STUDIES IN MISSION

Charis and Charisma

David Yonggi Cho and the Growth of Yoido Full Gospel Church

Editors:

Hong Young-Gi
Myung Sung-Hoon

Institute for Church Growth

regnum

First published 2003 by Regnum Books International

Regnum is an imprint of the Oxford Centre for Mission Studies
St. Philip and St. James Church
Woodstock Road
Oxford, OX2 6HR, UK
www.ocms.ac.uk/regnum

09 08 07 06 05 04 03 8 7 6 5 4 3 2 1

British Library Cataloguing in Publication Data
A catalogue record for this book is available from the British Library

ISBN: 978-1-506475-10-3

Distributed by 1517 Media in the US and Canada

Contents

Contributors

David Yonggi Cho

Dr. David Yonggi Cho, is the senior pastor of Yoido Full Gospel Church, the largest church in the world. Located in Seoul, Korea, the congregation is comprised of over 760,000 members. The author of over 100 books, Dr. Cho received in 1985 the 'Gold Medallion Book Award' from the Evangelical Christian Publisher's Association for his work, *The Fourth Dimension*. Dr. Cho, a graduate of Full Gospel Bible College (Seoul), received honorary doctorates from Bethany Bible College, Scotts Valley, Calif.; California Graduate School of Theology, Glendale, Calif.; Oral Roberts University, Tulsa, Okla.; and Regent University, Virginia Beach, Va. Dr. Cho's wife, Grace (Kim Sunghae) Cho, is an accomplished composer and pianist, and is the president of Hansei University. She and Dr. Cho have three grown sons.

John Han Hum Oak

Dr. Han Hum Oak is the senior pastor of SaRang Community Church in Seoul, Korea, which he planted in 1978 and which has grown through the use of discipleship training. At present there are more than 30,000 members at SaRang Community Church. He is the developer of Call to Awaken the Laity Seminars, which have trained more than 6,500 pastors in Korea, Japan, Taiwan, and the United States; 5,500 in the Korean church alone. His publications include *Call to Awaken the Laity*, now available in Korean, English, Japanese, and Chinese; plus a three-volume curriculum based on this book; the Upper Room Bible Study Curriculum in eighteen volumes; and numerous others.

Peter Wagner

Dr. Wagner is the founding President of Global Harvest Ministries, a ministry that brings together prayer networks for the purpose of focusing prayer power on world evangelism. He is also the founding President of the Wagner Leadership Institute and Wagner Publications. Dr. Wagner, in conjunction with George Otis Jr., of the Sentinel Group and Ted Haggard, Pastor of New Life Church, have joined together to found the World Prayer Center in Colorado Springs. He was the former professor at Fuller Theological Seminary Peter Wagner has written over three dozen books. Peter and his wife Doris, have three children and seven grandchildren.

The Wagners make their home in Colorado Springs, Colorado, where they are members of New Life Church, pastored by Ted Haggard.

Cecil M. Robeck

Dr. Cecil Robeck is associate professor of church history and ecumenics at Fuller Theological Seminary in Pasadena, California, and an Assemblies of God minister. He belongs to both the WCC and NCC Faith and Order Commissions, co-chairs the Pentecostal/Roman Catholic and Pentecostal/World Alliances of Reformed Churches dialogues and the Los Angeles Catholic/Evangelical Committee. He also represents the worldwide Pentecostal movement with the Secretaries of Christian World Communions. His works are *Prophecy in Carthage: Perpetua, Tertullian, and Cyprian, Charismatic Experiences in History*, etc.

Myung, Sung-Hoon

Dr. Myung, Sung-Hoon, is a church growth expert, who encountered numerous ministry fields and church growth theories. After he graduated from Sogang University, he finished the curricula at Full Gospel Theological School (presently, Hansei University) and Methodist Graduate School of Theology (obtained Th.M. degree). He was further educated and was conferred of the degrees, M.Div., Th.D., and Ph.D. from Fuller Theological Seminary in the United States. He served as a professor of Hansei University and the director of Church Growth Institute for 10 years from 1993 to 2002, serving Korean churches and pastors of all denominations. Currently, he is the senior pastor of the second sanctuary of Yoido Full Gospel Church and makes unsparing effort for the healthy church growth. He has written numerous books and articles including *Church Growth 10 Commandments (Korean), Diagnose Your Church, Church Growth Mind, Leadership Growth Mind*, etc.

Joel Comiskey

Dr. Joel Comiskey was a missionary at Ecuador of South America. Currently, he works as a church planting pioneer and church consultant as well as a professorship at Columbia International University. He graduated from Long Beach City College and obtained the degrees of M.A. from Alliance Theological Seminary and Fuller Theological Seminary, M.Div. from Columbia International University, and Ph.D. from Fuller Theological Seminary. He is the author of *Home Cell Group Explosion* and *Groups of Twelve*, etc.

Ma, Won-Suk

Dr. Ma, Won-Suk is a Philippine missionary, sent out by the United States Assemblies of God, a world-class Pentecostal Old Testament scholar and a scholar of mission studies. He works currently as a professor of Asia Pacific Theological Seminary located at Baguio of the Philippines. After he graduated from Full Gospel Theological University (presently, Hansei University), he obtained the degrees of M.Div. from Far East Advanced School of Theology at Manila, Philippine and Ph.D. from Fuller Theological Seminary in the United States. He is also an editor of Asian Journal of Pentecostal Studies and Journal of Asian Mission currently and presented numerous international research papers. He is the author of *Until the Spirit Comes: The Spirit of God in the Book of Asaiah*, etc.

Park, Myung-Soo

Dr. Park, Myung-Soo is a professor of church history at Seoul Theological University and a director of Holiness Church History Research Center currently. He completed the requirements for Th.M. and Ph.D. at Seoul Graduate School of Theology. Furthermore, he majored in church history at Boston University in the United States to be conferred the degrees of STM and Ph.D. He was also a visiting research associate at Harvard Graduate School of Theology. He also serves 'Good Church' located at Gangnam-Gu (ward) of Seoul city as a preaching pastor. His main authorship includes *Modern Evangelical Theory on Holiness, The Main Flow of Modern Evangelism, Parables in Church History, History of Early Holiness Church*, etc.

Hong, Young-Gi

Dr. Hong, Young-Gi is a consultant on church growth and leadership area as well as a scholar of mission studies in this globalization age. After he graduated from Sogang University (B.A.) majoring in English Literature, he worked as an executive secretary of CAM (Christ's Ambassador Mission) for a campus ministry He finished the requirements for M.Div. from Hansei Graduate School of Theology and was anointed for a pastorship from Yoido Full Gospel Church. Additionally, he studied at Oxford Centre for Mission Studies in England and was conferred of Ph.D. degree in Theology from Wales University. He is serving Korean churches as the president of Church Growth Institute and the General Secretary of CEN (Church Equipping Network). He also teaches missiology at Hansei University. He is the author of *24 Hours Christian* (1995), *Korean Mega-Churches and Charismatic Leadership* (2001), *Project for the Vision of Kingdom of God* (2002), *Project for Prayer Revival* (2002), and published a number of international papers.

Institute for Church Growth

The Institute for Church Growth (ICG), which is an incorporated body, provides various information for the benefit of the Korean Churches and the pastors. It was founded in 1993 by Rev. Dr. David Yonggi Cho with the directorship of Dr. Sung Hoon Myung in order to activate church growth and to cultivate church leadership. Its Ministries are Monthly Magazine (Church Growth), Publishing, Research Project, Seminar, Internet Service, Church Consulting, Church Networking, etc. At present Dr. David Yonggi Cho is the chairman of the board and Dr. Joshua Young Gi Hong is the president of ICG.

Preface

The body of Christ, the church, must grow. The characteristics of a growing church is that the leaders and lay Christians are equipped with church growth mind. Rev. Cho, who has grown his church to be the world's largest church, possesses this mind. Reverend Cho has relied on the power of the Holy Spirit everyday and has dreamt a magnificent growth of his church throughout 45 years of his ministry.

The vision and principles of Reverend Cho's church growth deeply inspired all the churches throughout the world. There are numerous cases of church growth by inspired students of Reverend Cho. Reverend David Cho is also our spiritual mentor, and he has influenced us greatly in establishing theories on church growth. Without such unselfish support of Reverend Cho, who is serving also as the chairperson of the Board of Directors of the Institute for Church Growth, this Institute could not handle the ministry of serving the growth of all Korean churches regardless of denominations.

This book is the result of reorganizing systematically the church growth of Yoido Full Gospel Church and Reverend David Cho. It is organized in three parts. The first part attends to the interviews of international pastors and theological scholars on the growth of Yoido Full Gospel Church. The second part is concerned with the principles of church growth that Reverend Cho has lectured. The last and third part considers research papers contributed by international theological scholars on Reverend Cho's church growth.

This book will serve as a practical guidebook to provide a deep insight on church growth to pastors, theological students and lay Christians. By all means, we pray in the name of the Lord that the body of the Lord, the church, grows and the kingdom of God expands.

August 2003
Rev. Dr. Myung, Sung Hoon
Rev. Dr. Hong, Young Gi

PART 1

INTERVIEWS ON YOIDO FULL GOSPEL CHURCH GROWTH

1. Church Ministry, Taking Steps with the Holy Spirit
   Interview with the Rev. Cho

2. Message of Hope
   Interview with the Rev. Oak, Han-hum

3. Leadership and Communication
   Interview with Dr. Peter Wagner

4. The Influence on the Churches in the World
   Interview with Dr. Cecil Robeck

CHAPTER 1

Church Ministry, Taking Steps with the Holy Spirit

Interview with Reverend Dr. David Yonggi Cho

The following interview was conducted in an interviewing suite of Yoido FGTV (Yoido Full Gospel Broadcasting) for an article to appear in a monthly journal, *Church Growth*. The interview was taped and distributed nationally. The interview focused on Reverend Cho's self-professing principles of church growth and his insights. The interviewer was Reverend Myung, Sung-Hoon.

Good morning, Reverend Yonggi Cho.
Reverend Cho: Good morning.

We appreciate your making time to talk with us this morning. I am sure that you have been asked numerous times the same question over and over, but how would you summarize your vision for your ministry?
Reverend Cho: Church ministry is to let people know of Jesus Christ, God's one and only son, so that people can receive the salvation by believing in Him. It is also to help and guide the saved people to serve the Lord faithfully and then to serve the neighbors by Godly love. I believe there is no room for a human wisdom to be used in the ministry. The purpose of God's calling is to preach the good news all over the world. Since this is God's command, obeying this command is the most fundamental mission of the church ministry.

You have stated that the nature of the ministry is to preach the good news to all people and to serve others. What do you think is the key or the factor to grow to be the world's largest church?
Reverend Cho: One might be mistaken that I am saying this out of my humility but, in fact, building a mega-church strictly belongs to the Lord's absolute sovereignity. I can say it as the first premise that God has had His plan and will, and the Lord has chosen me presently to serve as a chamberlain of a mega-church. During my

ministry, I have come across so many God's servants who are better educated and talented. I am less educated and talented, then why has God chosen me to minister in the world's largest church? It can only be explained by God's absolute sovereignity and not by me or by any human reasons. I can personally say the following as significant factors that contributed to building such a mega-church.

Firstly, a definite message to let people know of Jesus Christ and to let them know that Jesus Christ provides all their lives' needs necessary for church growth. Our reformed churches without such message would face an impossibility to build a large church. After the Korean War, this country was devastated. People of this nation were in a state of anxiety for the lack of necessities in life such as food, clothes, and housing and for not having much hope for tomorrow. I started my ministry with these people to deliver Jesus' gospel for salvation, to encourage them to have a hope for the future, and to fulfill their inner needs.

Jesus' gospel is the message of eternal salvation that remains the same beyond any certain period of time, but the instrument in which to fill the gospel can vary. It was the message of hope, faith, love, and encouragement and vision for life to these people who were hungry, poorly clothed, and despaired. Consequently, a large number of people flocked to the church.

Secondly, praying is absolutely necessary for church growth. Church growth can never be realized without praying. It is because we can talk with the invisible God and experience His presence through praying. I myself was devoted to praying with a do-or-die desperateness. I also emphasized the importance of praying with the congregation members. The Friday all-night prayer and fasting movements were all started in our church for the first time in Korea. Thus, prayer contributed greatly to our church growth.

Thirdly, it is the experience of the Holy Spirit. We receive God's grace from reading and hearing God's words. When we apply God's words in our lives and experience God's dispensation, we are empowered by God. Christians who believe in Jesus receive the Holy Spirit. However, not all of them are filled with the Holy Spirit. Thus, we began the campaign to encourage them to experience the fullness of the Holy Spirit and to receive the nine charisma of the Holy Spirit. Through this campaign, the congregation members began to experience the Holy Spirit in their lives and to have fervent faiths, and this collective love for the Holy Spirit contributed greatly to the growth of our church.

Fourthly, the vitality of small group activities contributed to the church growth greatly. Humans have many desires. The most fundamental ones are the desire for clothes, food and housing. After that, it is the desire to be safe, to belong, to be recognised and to fulfill ones dreams, follows these fundamental desires.

People, who come to the church, invariably want to have a fellowship and to be recognized in a group, once they receive God's blessing to hear God's words and to be stabilized in life, and to be free from the problems of clothes, food and housing. The most terrible enemy in one's life is the loneliness. Loneliness makes a person sick in mind and body. Thus, Sunday Christians, who come to the church on Sunday only to hear the sermon and hurry out the door, can not have their inner desires satisfied in the long run. Thus, our church exerted all-out effort to organize, stabilize, and vitalize the small groups by the residential zone since the days of our ministry at Seo-Dae-Moon area (West gate area of ancient Seoul).

The organizational structure, that our church opted, is similar to parishes of Catholic church except that it is organized in small groups by the zone in a much smaller scale. These small groups enable the congregation members to be away from the mother church and to form a small group in a local society for the fellowship and recognition. People wander about and drift away from a church, in which they do not receive the fellowship and recognition they deserve. The reason, that our church became the internationally renowned church and was able to retain our congregation members for 10 years or 20 years, is because they could belong to these smaller organizations.

Lastly, the reason for the growth of our church can be attributed to our gospel mission and our service to the society and the world. When a church cries out, 'Give blessing to my church and myself,' such church members soon feel despair and discontent. Church should embrace higher ideal and vision. As Jesus commanded His disciples, 'Go into all the world and preach the good news to all creation', (Mark 16:15) we should embrace the dream for the world mission. Then, the congregation members feel the value of coming to a church to pray, make an offering and serve others.

With this mind-set, many independent missionary organizations were formed in our church. I fully supported the movement to establish such missionary organizations as Businessmen's Missionary Coalition, Young-San Missionary Association, and Success Missionary Society, to gather Christians of similar missionary orientation in order to spread the gospel to the neighbors and to go out for world mission. Our congregation members do not just return home after receiving the grace of God, but they actively fulfill their dreams by participating in such church organizations. I provided the place for these Christians with similar talent and occupation to gather in one place to worship and to serve the society. Due to these laymen ministry, our involved congregation members feel greater satisfaction to achieve their higher Christian cause. I believe that Yoido Full Gospel Church has grown to be the internally well known church as it is today by the combination of all these factors.

Reverend Cho, you have stated, that 'World's largest church is the result of God's dispensation by His absolute Sovereignity.', and I believe God's dispensation by His sovereignity is revealed through people as the instrument. God has used Reverend Cho as the leader for the Holy Spirit ministry. Could you share with us what is the Holy Spirit ministry as you understand it?

Reverend Cho: I believe the church was born when the disciples were filled with the Holy Spirit on the day of Pentecost. Therefore, the beginning, growth and completion of the church can never be realized without the Holy Spirit. Thus, I started the ministry of emphasizing the Holy Spirit from the beginning. Some people had serious misunderstandings about me and our church order. They claimed that our church asserted 'a Christian, who was not baptized by the Holy Spirit, did not receive the Holy Spirit.' This is a misunderstanding. We receive the Holy Spirit when we believe in Jesus Christ.

Without the Holy Spirit, One can not call Jesus Christ as the Lord, and how can one believe in Jesus? Thus, we receive the Holy Spirit when we believe in Jesus.

What I am saying here is to be filled with the Holy Spirit, not just receiving the Holy Spirit. I use the words, 'filled with the Holy Spirit', more often than the words, 'baptized by the Holy Spirit', in order to avoid being misunderstood. When a person repents, is broken from the worldly desires, and devotes himself to God wholeheartedly, he is filled with the Holy Spirit. Thus, charisma of the Holy Spirit is received naturally when one is filled with the Holy Spirit.

However, the most important thing in my life is to have a deep relationship with the Holy Spirit, more important than charisma (gifts) of the Holy Spirit. One of the serious mistakes that today's Christians make is they expect to receive the charisma of the Holy Spirit while they spend little time having daily encounters with the Holy Spirit. It can cause serious problems if one regards the Holy Spirit as the means and not as the purpose.

The Holy Spirit is a person with knowledge, feeling and will. Being personal means being recognized as such. The Holy Spirit is the Counselor. The Counselor is written as *paracletos* in Greek. *Paracletos* means being called by God to be near us and to help us. So far we have experienced and understood that the Holy Spirit is with us. If we repeatedly disregard the Holy Spirit, He disowns us eventually.

The early Christians recognized the Holy Spirit as the absolute senior partner of the Apostles. The official announcements of the Jerusalem General Assembly, which were sent out after discussing such issues as the Law and circumcision concerning the Gentiles, started with the sentence, 'The Holy Spirit and we have decided as follows'.

We can see the Holy Spirit personally accompanied the Apostle Paul during his three missionary trips. I experienced the Holy Spirit, for the first time, when our church reached a congregation of 3,000 members in 1964. God's inspiration was revealed to me when I was praying for a the revival of our church. Since then, I have recognized, welcomed, invited, and relied on the Holy Spirit, and I have started the ministry of serving the Holy Spirit as my senior pastor.

I pray every morning, confessing, 'The Holy Spirit, I recognize you. I welcome you. I invite you. I rely on you. Please take my hands and lead me with the grace of Jesus Christ and the love of God!' When I write the sermon prayerfully, and stand up to deliver a sermon at the pulpit, I pray, 'The Holy Spirit, please be with me. I can not do a thing by myself. Please hold my hands and accompany me!' After the sermon I thank the Holy Spirit always, 'The Holy Spirit, I thank you. Because you anointed me, held me, and led me, I could do this work.' I have continued doing the ministry in this manner with a deep sense of partnership with the Holy Spirit.

There are some who denounce me. 'Reverend Cho disregards the Trinity. He overtly relies on the Holy Spirit to the extent that he disregards God the Father and God the Son. Hence, he disregards the Trinity.' However, this is a wrong accusation. Emphasizing the Holy Spirit nowadays does not mean disregarding Jesus Christ or the Father. Jesus said He would be with us when the Holy Spirit comes to our spiritual minds. Whose spirit is the Holy Spirit? The Holy Spirit is the Spirit of God and Jesus. Thus, although the emphasis on God thè Trinity may differ, God the Trinity remains the same always.

There are reasons why one can not expect a church growth without a deep relationship and partnership with the Holy Spirit. The church was built by the Holy Spirit during the New Testament times. The church grows in the embrace of the Holy Spirit, and the church is perfected in the Holy Spirit. European churches have a long history of 2,000 years and boast magnificent buildings. There are many churches, ministers, and excellent facilities in Europe. However, many people have left the European churches. One only finds empty pews in many European churches. What caused it?

The reason is that the European churches have betrayed the Holy Spirit. They have tried to build a human-centered church without the Holy Spirit. People can not meet Jesus Christ and God the Father in it. So they naturally wither and die out. For the revival of European churches, one should invite the Holy Spirit again and begin a new relationship with Him. Even if we try to strengthen our church system or hold profound theological discourses, we can not achieve a church growth without the essence of the church, the Holy Spirit.

There are many ministers who would like to serve the Holy Spirit as their senior pastor/partner. Nevertheless, they often face the obstacle of not knowing the detailed know-how. What kind of practical advice would you give to them?

Reverend Cho: I personally pray and pray in tongues many times. Of course, I pray in worldly languages, but I pray in tongues also. When I pray in tongues, the Holy Spirit indwells me. I can not help but experience that the Holy Spirit is working through me.

Thus, praying in tongues is very important to me. Praying in tongues sometimes makes me wonder about the meaning of prayers. I feel strongly the personal indwelling of the Holy Spirit and my prayers are the prayers of the Holy Spirit through me.

I live with the mind-set of a servant working for the Holy Spirit. I pray several times daily, 'The Holy Spirit, I recognize you, welcome you, invite you, and rely on you. Be with me, the Holy Spirit!' When I consider a matter of faith, I also pray, 'The Holy Spirit, I do not know how to solve the problem with human wisdom. Please help me!' After all, the Holy Spirit is the Lord of the Harvest, and I am His servant. The Bible reads, 'As the eyes of slaves look to the hand of their master, as the eyes of a maid look to the hand of their mistress, so our eyes look to the Lord our God till He shows us His mercy.' (Psalm 123:2) When I am in the position of a servant, I always look to the Holy Spirit. The Holy Spirit accompanies us, and He works through us.

Many people wonder how you prepare a sermon after having seen you delivering a powerful message despite a busy ministry

schedule. Are there any special methods for preparing a sermon?

Reverend Cho: There is no special method. I live praying for God's message 24 hours a day. A message loses its power if it is taken from somebody else's book or sermon. It may be flawless in terms of its structure and biblical knowledge. However, the message, which has not been received personally by me, does not exercise its power on me.

An analogy would be a parrot. A parrot can repeat words without knowing the meaning, but it does not have the power to persuade. I receive God's message directly from Him and come forward believing firmly that this message is given for my people at this time and place.

Many people ask me to provide the sermon text days ahead of the time for the conference or revival meeting, but I have never been able to do so. The reason is, I do not know what message God would like me to deliver in advance. If I use the message written ahead of the time of delivery, I do not receive the power of the living Holy Spirit. Thus, I pray at the place of a sermon and try to deliver God's message that is given by the Holy Spirit of God there.

God has given me His message whenever I pray for it. As a messenger of His message, I wait until the master of the message gives His words. So, when I am asked presently, 'How long did it take for you to receive God's message?' I reply that it has taken 40 years. I have lived the life of praying and crying out everyday for His message since the day I started my ministry.

God has given me His message at different times and places, sometimes while I am walking, listening to other pastor's sermon, sleeping or reading the Bible. I have a habit of carrying a notepad and pen in my pocket always to write an inspiration of God. This inspiration is hard to come by again if it is missed and not noted.

After receiving the inspiration, I logically organize the message in the form of an introduction, body and conclusion. With this structural organization, deductive and inductive reasoning is used after the message has been 'cooked' (treated) so that the readers can understand it well.

Even if the message is 'cooked' by an excellent 'cook', it's no use to have a message without the content. So, receiving the essence of a message, the content, is most important. After receiving the content, the messenger should be able to deliver the message in the most meaningful ways.

I have intend to deliver a message that even a preschooler can understand. Many people, who came and listened to my sermons, have said, 'Reverend Yonggi Cho's message is too easy', 'Reverend Cho's message is too simple for sophisticated people', and 'It does not have the depth.' Nevertheless, whoever has said it, a message is only as effective as it is understood.

The livelihood of a minister is to create God's message. As a married woman has an important calling to give birth, a servant of the Lord gives birth to the message from God. People often say they compose a message, but I don't compose a message. I give birth to the message. I experience the birth pains whenever I give a sermon. There is nothing harder than receiving the Holy message. When God grants me two messages a week sometimes, I feel it is a feast. I don't have to suffer the birth pains for the next week. However, such occasions are rare. God usually grants one message a week, and I make a desperate effort to receive it.

Receiving a Holy message and delivering it in a sermon has been the biggest burden and the most difficult task for me. I would not be exaggerating if I said I spent 90 percent of my ministry work on receiving and delivering a Holy message. The remaining 10 percent of my ministry is spent on counseling and calling on the homes of our congregation members of this world's largest church.

In trying to deliver God's message well, I have to read the Bible more, meditate more, and read a variety of books. Our mind has to be stimulated to come up with new ideas. Thus, I have to pray and study always for a message of the Holy Spirit.

Reverend, you have been doing the ministry of training, giving the vision, and challenging many ministers around the world not only in Yoido Full Gospel Church. What is your view on the trend in the churches around the world? And what are your thoughts on how churches of Korea have to react or take proactive measures against the trends in the churches around the world?

Reverend Cho: I think many churches around the world are generally in a slump. On the other hand, new history of revival is being made. I have a calling for overseas mission and have been to many countries around the world. Churches in Africa are booming with remarkable vitality, and churches in South America are also very revitalized. While some churches in America are in a state of decline, other new churches are experiencing revivals. Churches in former USSR were so suppressed that they became almost extinct, but they are now in a state of revival. Southeast Asia and Northeast Asia have been predominantly under the influence of Buddhism and Islam, and the revival in these area has been slow but steady.

The churches around the world have begun to experience the dynamic vitality of the Holy Spirit, having just awakened. Where does this power come from? Invariably, it originates from prayer and Holy Spirit movement. It does not come from any theological system or institution.

Through the personal experience of meeting God and being changed by the Holy Spirit, prayer movement, the Holy Spirit movement, and small groups movement, churches are beginning to rise again.

Korea had a great revival when the prayer, the Holy Spirit and the divine healing movement at Jang-Dae-Hyun church in Pyungyang began in 1906. The Reverend Gil, Sun-joo's grand repentance movement or Reverend Kim, Ik-doo's grand divine healing movement, etc. were the foundations for the first revival of Korean churches. However, during the Japanese colonization, Koreans were forced to worship the Japanese Emperor's shrine. The Communist North Koreans persecuted Korean churches during Korean War. Although all these are past, Korean churches have been going into a state of inertia because of the materialism that is widely permeating Korean society, and the widespread institutionalization, systematization, and secularization of Korean churches since the 1960's.

The revival of Korean churches can be acheived again: firstly, there needs to be a grand prayer movement leading to repentance from the past secularism. Secondly, the churches of Korea need to look beyond and outwardly. It is understandable for the poorly-clothed and the hungry to cry out, 'Help me'. However, after receiving the blessings, we have to be more mature. Churches need to wake up from hibernation and move forward to be more patriotic, cosmopolitan, and altruistic.

Lastly, the churches of Korea need to urge on the Holy Spirit movement based on traditional theology. There is no revival of churches without the Holy Spirit movement. Therefore, we should rekindle the Holy Spirit movement and actively participate in it to manifest the charisma of the Holy Spirit. Korean churches need to eschew bravely minster-centered churches. Each individual church should promote small group movement to involve lay Christian leaders in the ministry.

In order to rescue the churches of Korea from the slump, churches should train lay Christians and advocate their involvement so that they can have the mind of being called to build the church of Christ.

Lastly, what is your thought on the future plan and vision for Yoido Full Gospel Church?

Reverend Cho: Because the vision of the minister is so important for a church, I have always been praying. When I turned 60 years old, I prayed, 'God, two thirds of my ministry life has passed, and one third is left. Please help me to obey the will of God for the rest one third of my ministry time!' My future is not planned by me but is determined by God. Thus, I prayed and prayed to ask the way of God. The Lord is an earthenware maker, and I am just clay. As long as I am the clay on my Lord's hand, I have to accept what the Lord makes.

I have had several clear callings. Firstly, God has called me to be a pastor. Thus, I will spend all my effort for my life to nurture the congregation members as the senior pastor of Yoido Full Gospel Church. Secondly, God has called me to be an overseas evangelist. The Lord has not called me to be just an evangelist for Korea. So, I have been to the 5 oceans and 6 continents so far. As long as God allows me the strength to do so, I will make every effort to do the missionary work as an overseas evangelist.

Thirdly, God has called me as a Christian businessman. Thus, I have founded a university and I take an active part in its operation. I have been engaged in many social works projects to help children, orphans and widows. Our Elim welfare town has been at the forefront of these endeavors. I have been planning to build a silver town for the elderly who believe in Jesus. We continue to publish the Kookmin Daily News paper. I continue to support our auxiliary organizations such as the theology research centers or the Institute for Church Growth, which help many churches regardless of the denominations. Many disciples of our church have gone for the pioneering mission in remote areas of Korea or abroad, and I will support them fully. To these three callings, a pastor to the world, an overseas evangelist, and a Christian businessman, I wisely work, distributing the time and material resources prudently. The budget of our church programmes will be distributed equitably for these works.

Thank you for your insightful comments made during this long interview. I pray for your continued health in the Lord and great success in your world mission.

CHAPTER 2

Message of Hope

Interview with the Reverend Oak, Han-hum

The following interview was conducted at the Church of Love in December 2002. The Reverend Oak, Han-hum has been widely known for his expertise in discipleship training and is regarded as one of the most respected pastors in Korea. He attributes the Reverend Cho's powerful and incarnate messages to be the foundation of his powerful and effective ministry.

Reverend Oak, Han-hum, Glad to see you. How have you been?

Reverend Oak, Han-hum: I have been doing great. How about yourself, Reverend Myung?

I have been doing well. First of all, I would like to thank you for accepting our interview on the occasion of the publishing of 'Charis and Charisma' on the 10th year commemoration of the Institute for Church Growth. I believe it was so significant and wonderful that the Church of Love and Yoido Full Gospel Church exchanged the senior pastors for the sermon last April. I believe it was a significant achievement for the union of the churches of Korea. Would you please comment on this?

Reverend Oak, Han-hum: Exchanging senior pastors of the two largest churches in Korea for the sermon was very meaningful and mutually beneficial. In retrospect, I wish such an occasion like that happened sooner. The Yoido Full Gospel Church is huge, and our church is small, relatively speaking. Thus, some common ground for contact would seem hard to find. Apart from the size, I believe we should understand the Holy Spirit movement and such an exchange is desirable in order to understand the traditional Korean churches. I think such relationship should have been actively promoted and encouraged sooner.

I see. What was your image when you were delivering the message at Yoido Full Gospel Church? Were there any special feelings when the Reverend Yonggi Cho was preaching at the

Church of Love?

Reverend Oak, Han-hum: When I was preaching at the Reverend Cho's church and was listening to the Reverend Cho's sermon here at the Church of Love, I felt that there was no wall among lay Christians. It would be almost impossible to have such hospitality even 20 years ago. However, seeing that the lay Christians are accepting one another with such open minds, understanding one another and feeling mutuality with one another I thought there is less barrier among lay Christians than among pastors. I was impressed how similarly the congregation members responded to the sermons. They demonstrate the maturity of traditional Korean churches and Full Gospel churches. When we are immature, we have the tendency to fight, argue and disregard each other. However, when we mature as Christians we can forgive and accept one another. I felt that I was at home when I was preaching at Yoido Full Gospel Church. I also sensed that the Reverend Cho was not stressed when he was preaching at the Church of Love.

I heard many testimonies about receiving the grace through your sermon at Yoido Full Gospel Church. I think there was a spiritual rapport between the two pastors of the mega-churches as expected.

By any chance, are there any facts about the Reverend Cho that you misunderstood? Could you please comment on it if possible?

Reverend Oak, Han-hum: It can be regarded as a collective misunderstanding by Korean churches as a whole rather than my personal misunderstanding. There were many churches that showed allergic reactions to the Reverend Cho's Holy Spirit movement even 20 years ago. It seems to me the traditional churches had some theological belief that prohibited accepting the ministry of the Holy Spirit back then. Especially, the theological belief of the Presbyterian churches understood that the baptism by the Holy Spirit happened only once historically, and they could not be receptive to the idea of the baptism by the Holy Spirit and the ministry of charisma. As a matter of fact, I myself consented to such ambience. Also, there was a criticism of the Reverend Cho's message, that emphasized the threefold blessing of divine healing, blessing in all matters, and having all go well to beginning Christians, being undulating faith. I was influenced by such an atmosphere. However, this misunderstanding was not just my personal feeling but a shared feeling in Korean churches for a while.

Is there any new impression made when you met the Reverend

Cho in person and exchanged the sermons?

Reverend Oak, Han-hum: In my case, most of the unilateral misunderstandings in the past had been resolved before we exchanged the sermons. We have become mature, and uncooperative behaviors from the theological point of view have been corrected. In my case, I listened and attended fully to the Reverend Cho's lecture tapes and began to have a new understanding of his ministry.

Thus, because I had maintained a new conception and understanding of the Reverend Cho's ministry already, I had no new impression of him since I met him last.

I also believe that you were receptive to the idea of exchanging the sermons because you had such an understanding. The Reverend Yonggi Cho mentioned you several times to his junior partners before inviting you. The Reverend Cho said then that he had read all your books. He also stated that we should have an open mind on the discipleship training program, which stressed the raising and nurturing of new Christians to be disciples of Jesus and was a rather underemphasized aspect of the Pentecostal Holy Spirit movement. Reverend Ock, you once said that you responded very positively to the Reverend Cho's emphasis on the absolute sovereignity of God in his message or the preaching ministry. Could you please give us a word on it?

Reverend Oak, Han-hum: I was also among those who criticized the Reverend Cho's message being undulating. Then, afterwards, I widened my theological point of view and began to notice some weak spots in the theological view of the Presbyterian churches. As a result, I started listening to the Reverend Cho's message with a new perspective. Soon I realized that the Reverend Cho's message had a very important meaning in some respects. The reason is because the Christians, to whom the Reverend Cho ministered in the beginning, were not traditional, typical 'Christians' and were not accepted fully by the existing, established churches at that time. The Reverend Cho centered on these hopeless people, who were in despair, while the existing churches overlooked them.

It was crucial for the Reverend Cho to find a contact point with these people, whose souls were overlooked by existing churches and lingered as outsiders of these churches, in order to preach the good news. What is this contact point? Tell the sick that they can be cured. Tell the poor that they can be wealthy if they are blessed by God. The contact point was these hopes. These contact points became a channel to lead them eventually to salvation and hope in the Kingdom of God. The message of the Reverend Cho uses the inductive approach. It is an approach that starts from life's concerns and leads to the gospel of the Kingdom of God gradually.

People could see, feel, and experience the gospel. This point makes the message of the Reverend Cho very meaningful. In one respect, he wrote a new chapter in the history of messages of Korean churches. Nevertheless, others have tried to copy and exaggerate messages of this pure and genuine intent and caused the downfall of these messages to be a cheap gospel.

We have to understand the pressing context under which the Reverend Cho could not help but deliver these messages. The time was right after the Korean War, and the country was devastated far from the sight of rebuilding the country. What would be the message that these people of despair would heed to? In some respects, the Reverend Cho showed an aspect of Jesus, who associated with prostitutes, the sick and the needy, in order to give them hope. One thing that makes me feel being at a loss is that no one else but the Reverend Cho can deliver the message of the Reverend Cho.

Many pastors deliver similar messages, but they lack the power as great as the Reverend Cho's. The reason it came to be like this is that the Reverend Cho has the sense of pressing duty to deliver this kind of message, and that he demonstrates the signs and the power of healing when he delivers his message.

However, the other pastors, who deliver similar messages lack the power. The Reverend Cho's message loses its strength if it lacks the power to impact people. The message of the Presbyterian churches, which deductively introduces its dogma or preaches the hope for the Kingdom of God, may not impart the power or the bodily experience at the moment, but it retains its life to a certain extent. However, messages like the Reverend Cho's are pragmatic, and the power of these messages are manifested outwardly. Only then, a change in people occurs.

Thanks for the insightful remarks. Aren't those two facts related – the fact that the Reverend Cho is a praying servant and his allegiance to the absolute sovereignity of God and the fact that only the Reverend Yonggi Cho can deliver his message? The Reverend Cho admits that he is very much influenced by Calvin's theology. What is your thought about it?

Reverend Oak, Han-hum: I was very impressed by it. The Reverend Cho himself told me that he is a Calvinist. The reason for the Reverend Cho's conversion and the process of his church's growth can only be explained by the sovereignity of God. I believe, because he kept a God-centered faith, which professes the absolute sovereignity of God, the ministry of the Reverend Cho has not been led astray and he has walked the right path.

If faith in the absolute sovereignity of God is not deeply rooted in his faith, there is a good probability that a man of such position as the Reverend Cho's can go astray. There can be signs of incorrect theological belief, being treated as if he is God, or becoming a heretic. I believe the main factor, that prevented this from happening, is the Reverend Cho's allegiance to the sovereignity of God and the fear of God. On that account, we can see that the message and ministry of the Reverend Cho have been well balanced.

This is the 45th year of the ministry of the Reverend Yonggi Cho. Presently, Yoido Full Gospel Church is praising and glorifying God as the world's largest church in terms of the number of congregation members. What do you think are the factors that significantly influenced the growth of Yoido Full Gospel Church?

Reverend Oak, Han-hum: The factors for the growth can be seen clearly. It is after all the charismatic leadership and message of the Reverend Yonggi Cho.

Message and leadership, right?

Reverend Oak, Han-hum: Yes. Without those, all other factors are auxiliary. We can see that the revival of Yoido Full Gospel Church could not have been possible without the Reverend Yonggi Cho.

You are seeing the revival not as a result of a general principle but as an exceptional phenomenon.

Reverend Oak, Han-hum: Yes, it is an exceptional phenomenon. Accordingly, it is also the reason for my worry about Yoido Full Gospel Church. When a big tree falls, there is nothing left under it. A small tree can not grow under a big tree. Historically, the ministry of an excellent pastor ended with the pastor, not being able to pass on the ministry. I speculate that there is a special dispensation of God. The ministry of a less famous or talented pastor can be passed on to the next pastor within the church. Pastors of similar caliber can pass on the ministry a lot easier. However, if the predecessor is so great, then it can be a problem to find a suitable successor.

Then, how do you think Yoido Full Gospel Church should prepare for the succession of leadership in the future?

Reverend Oak, Han-hum: Obviously, the second Reverend Yonggi Cho should emerge. However, it is almost impossible.

If so, what are other possible alternatives?

Reverend Oak, Han-hum: The next best alternative has to be found. For example, a man of great stature like the Reverend Moody died a long time ago. However, his influence succeeded him for over 100 years. We have to study those factors that made this possible. There were capable people, a strong organization, and a systematic safety net, which could succeed the spirit. The Moody Bible Institute is an example.

Isn't the situation of Moody similar to Wesley?

Reverend Oak, Han-hum: I will say it is so. Wesley was an excellent organizer. The style of Wesley was systematic, which concentrated on dispersed small communities rather than on one mega-church. In that respect, it could last longer. If we speculate on the times after the Reverend Yonggi Cho, it is very important for the next generation to reap the reward of the emerging leaders who have been growing under the grace of the leadership of the Reverend Cho. I believe it is very important to prepare leaders. In the case of the Reverend Charles Spurgeon didn't the church under his leadership head downwards when he passed away due to the fact that the next leaders were not prepared? To recapitulate, it is very much needed to prepare the successor of the ministry, power and spirit of the Reverend Yonggi Cho. It can not be achieved in a couple of years. It needs 5 to 10 years, at the least.

Jim Collins' book, *Good to Great,* gained much popularity recently. In that book, Jim Collins states that there are many good enterprises but only a few great ones. One of the characteristics of a great enterprise is a successful leadership transition.

In dealing with the succession of CEO of a company, it is said that the company, which trained systematically and promoted a self-development for many years and chose a successor within the company, performed much better than the counterpart. It seems your remarks coincide with this observation. I would like to ask you another question. Would you please assess, on a personal level, the influence of the Reverend Cho on the churches of Korea?

Reverend Oak, Han-hum: The positive influence of the message and ministry of the Reverend Cho on the churches of Korea can be summarized by his contribution of instigating the Holy Spirit on them as aforementioned. Another is that he has found the contact point and has preached the good news to the people, who needed it desperately, by incarnating the gospel. And there are many people in Yoido Full Gospel Church, who have been cured of critical diseases and have become wealthy not only just escaping the poverty. One thing that I would like to point out reluctantly is that the message of the Reverend Cho is viewed as lacking an emphasis on discipleship. Among the believers in Yoido Full Gospel Church, there are stories of some congregation members who have become less devoted to the Lord after becoming healthier and wealthier. I think these are unintentional side effects. I believe it would be a good opportunity to make the churches of Korea healthier if new theological and ministerial endeavors are undertaken to remedy these side effects.

Professor Donald McGavran, who is often called 'the Father of Church Growth Studies', states in his book, *Redemption and Lift,* that people become less devoted to the Lord after their quality of lives improves, having being saved and blessed.

I construe that he meant shifting the emphasis to the devotion of God rather than to being blessed.

Reverend Oak, Han-hum: Yoido Full Gospel Church has a great potential in that respect. There are many people in the church who are being blessed, regardless of the worldly or spiritual blessings. Now these people have to be taught to live the life of obedience and devotion ethically according to the Word of God. If the believers in Yoido Full Gospel Church turn to this direction, there will be an explosive power of the church for others to follow. This could be a turning point for the ministry of the Reverend Cho.

I believe a mentality is needed to regard the blessing as a means not as the goal. I think such a training to regard the blessing as a wonderful means to worship the Lord completely is in need.

Reverend Oak, Han-hum: I believe Yoido Full Gospel Church will have an enormous potential to do God's work even after the Reverend Yonggi Cho if it continues to promote the gospel of blessing.

Thank you. At least, please give us a word of encouragement for the publishing of the book, 'Charis and Charisma'.

Reverend Oak, Han-hum: It has been already 10 years since the Institute for Church Growth was founded. Time flies.

I would like to appreciate your Institute's efforts in suggesting a new vision for church growth to all churches of Korea regardless of the denominations during the past. I wish a continued blessing for many churches to grow qualitatively and quantitatively through the Institute for Church Growth for many years ahead. I am glad to see that a book, that has systematically organized many writings of the

Reverend Cho on church growth, is being published. I hope that many pastors learn the principles and insights of the Reverend Cho on church growth.

Thanks a lot, Reverend. I wish your good health.

CHAPTER 3

Leadership and Communication

Interview with Dr. Peter Wagner

The following interview with Dr. Peter Wagner was conducted by the Reverend Hong, Young-Gi in an interviewing suite of Manhattan Hotel at Yoido on September 2002. The interview was supplemented by email afterwards, and it focused mainly on the theme of the Apostolic leadership of the Rev. Cho. A world renowned guru on church growth, Dr. Peter Wagner has studied and published numerous books on the world mission and church growth for his life. He believes that the strong leadership of the Rev. Cho stems from the spiritual authority, that is revealed in his vision and messages.

Hello, Dr. Wagner. I am glad to meet you.

Dr. Peter Wagner: So am I. Thank you for doing well the precious ministry of studying the church, the body of Christ.

Dr. Wagner, You have retired from the professorship at Fuller Seminary's New School of World Mission and Institute of Church Growth and now lead the Wagner Leadership Institute. How are you doing?

Dr. Peter Wagner: God has prepared a ministry operating a research center for the world mission and leadership development before my retirement. Presently, there are about 40 research associates devoted on the research ministry, and I feel a great fulfillment. My research has the prime interest in developing the leadership of church leaders and is prospering gradually with the leading and blessing of God. I am preparing leaders, who can succeed and continue this work for continuous development, even after I step down.

Leadership is also my research interest area. You have studied the leadership extensively so far. Do you have any emphatic thing to say to Korean church leaders, perhaps?

Dr. Peter Wagner: The important thing in leadership development is to strengthen the strong point. Everybody has some weaknesses. However, it is more important to focus on your strength than to improve on your weakness. The leader should know, develop, and apply his/her gift. Working without a gift of the Holy Spirit is very difficult.

Leaders should know their gift and should develop their strength more. Then, what strong point and gift does Reverend Cho, Yonggi have in your opinion?

Dr. Peter Wagner: The important quality of Reverend Cho, Yonggi that I found is his gift of excellent leadership. The reason that he could have the world's largest church was he was one of the greatest leaders in the world. What I wanted to learn from Reverend Cho, Yonggi in our fellowship was how he manifested his leadership. Along with the leadership, the strength of Reverend Cho, Yonggi is his communication ability. Reverend Cho, Yonggi has an excellent communication skills. I was deeply impressed by Reverend Cho, Yonggi, who wanted to learn about many things happening around him and had a strong desire to learn by reading as many books as possible. He has the ability to communicate what he realized and learned to people clearly.

I know that you have a specially friendly relationship with Reverend Cho, Yonggi. How did you get to know him?

Dr. Peter Wagner: I heard about Reverend Cho, Yonggi for the first time because of Yoido Full Gospel Church's explosive growth. I was a professor of church growth studies, and naturally Reverend Cho, Yonggi and his church drew my attention. I wanted to visit the church. However, I did not think I would meet Reverend Cho, Yonggi personally. When I visited Korea in the 1970's, I lectured at a theological school on church growth studies. I indicated my desire to visit Yoido Full Gospel Church in my free time. However, the leaders of the theological school did not regard the church as traditional, and they did not want me to visit the church.

This made me very upset, but I did not have a choice. I have never thought that Reverend Cho, Yonggi had some problems in his faith. Thus, I made up my mind to visit Yoido Full Gospel Church when I visit Korea the next time. Then, a friend of mine told Reverend Cho, Yonggi that I was in Korea. Soon enough, Reverend Cho, Yonggi invited me as a member of the board of directors of Church Growth International, and I accepted his offer.

We became friends right away, and Reverend Cho, Yonggi instituted Reverend Cho, Yonggi scholarship for two students, who participated in Church Growth International Conference annually.

This was one of the most important contribution of his to Fuller Theological Seminary. And his contribution became the important factor for many student recipients of the scholarship to have a successful ministry afterwards.

Dr. Wagner, you have observed Yoido Full Gospel Church for a long time. Could you summarize the growth factors of the church? And what do you think is the most important factor?

Dr. Peter Wagner: As I have mentioned already, the growth of Yoido Full Gospel Church was due to Reverend Cho, Yonggi's excellent leadership and his communication ability. I believe this is the most important factor. Along with these points, it was also important that Reverend Cho, Yonggi had a special concern for lay church leaders such as the elders around him to gather them and to make them devoted for church ministry and mission. Reverend Cho, Yonggi's Full Gospel Businessmen's Union is the exemplar case. And the successful development of cell groups provided an infrastructure for a limitless growth. It prepared a system to deliver Reverend Cho, Yonggi's pastoral philosophy and message.

You regard Reverend Cho, Yonggi's leadership and message and the structural foundation as the important growth factors. You also consider that the spirit is more important than the system as a growth factor.

Dr. Peter Wagner: That's right. A system such as cell groups is a structure to be filled by the spirit. One could see that Reverend Cho, Yonggi's ministerial spirit and message were the important factors in implanting life to the system.

Then, what is your thought on Reverend Cho, Yonggi's sermons? Do you think they are related to the church growth?

Dr. Peter Wagner: Reverend Cho, Yonggi's message of salvation, healing and blessing is very important for church growth. His sermon did not overlook the realities of people's lives. His preaching focused on equipping people to have the image, that God wants. His teaching is powerful and touches people's hearts. People experience God amidst realistic problems. Thus, many people have come to the church to favourable affect the church growth.

You have suggested a 'new apostolic movement' recently. Lyle Schaller proposed a 'new reformation movement', and Donald Miller asserted a 'new paradigm movement'. Who are the Apostles and what are their characteristics according to the new apostolic movement?

Dr. Peter Wagner: New apostolic movement is a church revival paradigm upon the authority of the apostles. 1 Corinthians 12:28 reads, 'And in the church God has appointed first of all apostles, second prophets, third teachers, then workers of miracles, also those having gifts of healing, those able to help others, those with gifts of administration, and those speaking in different kinds of tongues.', and we have to carefully observe God's spiritual order; the first- apostles, the second- prophets, and the third- teachers.

The apostles have many characteristics, and the most important are the following two characteristics. Firstly, the apostles have a spiritual authority different from other church leaders. The authority of the apostles is not an authority by some kind of religious title. It is not given by human but by the spiritual authority of Christ. All apostles have apostolic gifts, and each apostle does the work of the ministry having various tasks. Secondly, the apostles have a clear vision. They know what God is saying to the church. The apostles receive God's revelation directly from God or from the prophets. Since they receive God's revelation, they can proclaim God's message with courage and firm faith.

Then, Reverend Cho, Yonggi can be regarded as a spiritual apostle.

Dr. Peter Wagner: That is so. Reverend Cho, Yonggi can be regarded as an apostle. The word, apostle, may sound unfamiliar in Korea. I can understand it fully. Whether Reverend Cho, Yonggi is called an apostle or not, it is clear that he is acting and functioning as an apostle. His apostolic leadership functions very importantly in maintaining and growing the spiritual order in the church.

Then, what kind of apostleships are there?

In general, it can be classified into four kinds. Firstly, there is vertical apostleship. They are of the most common and special apostleship and work in various tasks above the other apostles. The Apostle Paul is a typical example of vertical apostles. Timothy and Titus were team members of the Apostle Paul. Secondly, there is a horizontal apostleship. They call other Christians for a certain purpose. A typical exemplar case would be James from the Jerusalem church. He persuaded the Jerusalem Council and was one of Jesus' brothers. His main function was to call all the other apostles and to preside over the meeting. The horizontal apostleship carried out an effective leadership through this network.

Thirdly, there is a hyphenated apostleship. These carry out more than one duty. For example, the Apostle Paul was appointed a herald and an apostle and a teacher (2 Timothy 1:11) and Timothy did the work of an evangelist and an Apostle (2 Timothy 4:5). Fourth, there is a market place apostleship. The above three types of apostles worked in the church. However, the market place apostles work outside the church. The kingdom of God is not limited inside a local church only. The kingdom of God is the place, where God's people are working. We have to recognize the apostleship to reform the world and society. The Biblical example of marketplace apostleship is Lydia, a dealer in purple cloth from the city of Thyatira, and Luke, the doctor (Acts 16:14, Colossians 4:14).

If so, what kind of apostleship does Reverend Cho, Yonggi belong to? And what is his Apostolic characteristics?

Dr. Peter Wagner: First of all, He is basically a congregational apostle. He has a powerful spiritual authority in Yoido Full Gospel Church. He is a leader of the church and not an employee of the elders. I think many Christian leaders, who pioneered and built a mega-church, belong to this category of congregational apostleship. He is also a vertical apostle because he pioneered and built so many churches in need of his caring. Under a vertical apostle, a network of many individuals, missionary organizations, and churches exists to obey the spiritual authority of the vertical apostle. Looking at many churches and Christian leaders, who work under the spiritual authority of Reverend Cho, Yonggi, he is definitely a vertical Apostle. I heard Reverend Cho, Yonggi started building many pioneering churches from several years ago. I think this is a very important project. In addition, observing so many people attending and participating Reverend Cho, Yonggi's international conference, Reverend Cho, Yonggi has been anointed powerfully for the apostleship of convocation. Reverend Cho, Yonggi's spiritual authority, vision and desires are very important characteristics that show he is an Apostle.

As you have mentioned, the apostles have a spiritual charisma. However, wouldn't there be some difficulties when the charisma is institutionalized? Didn't Margaret Poloma, an American scholar on politics and religion, assert that excessive development of a system could choke the charismatic spirit using the analysis example of the United States Assemblies of God? Although an apostle can lead with excellent character and ability in the church, wouldn't it be difficult to preserve the vivacity of the apostle's apostolic calling and spirit with time (for example, when the apostle passes away)?

Dr. Peter Wagner: I agree. Dr. Hong, you are the expert in this area, aren't you? The institutionalization of a charisma is inescapable. The charisma does not last if it is not institutionalized. On the contrary, excessive institutionalization results in choking the charismatic spirit. Thus, a creative balance between the charisma and institutionalization is important. I believe it is very important to cultivate a network to preserve the life of apostolic calling. The apostles should cultivate new charisma. And, they should develop it in their apostolic network. Then, more apostles can grow.

You are saying that the apostolic and spiritual authority of Reverend Cho, Yonggi needs a creative institutionalization. Don't you think that these issues you just pointed out have important consequences on the future of Yoido Full Gospel Church? What is your view on the future of Yoido Full Gospel Church?

Dr. Peter Wagner: I am one of people, who have a deep concern for the future of Yoido Full Gospel Church. Up until now, Reverend Cho, Yonggi has carried out an excellent ministry. One point is that Reverend Cho, Yonggi should have a deep concern to create a system, which can produce an outstanding disciple or a successor. In my opinion, it is important for Reverend Cho, Yonggi to deal with the public responsibility of selecting future leaders, guiding them personally as a mentor, and preparing for the succession of his spiritual authority systematically. Although the balance between charisma and system is not easy, it is very important.

Yoido Full Gospel Church will be recorded in the history of world churches. Thus, I have a praying mind for the continuous growing of the church. I hope that Reverend Cho, Yonggi's accomplished ministry will continue in the future.

I would like to ask you for a word on the book, 'Charis and Charisma'.

Dr. Peter Wagner: I am glad that a systematic book on Reverend Cho, Yonggi's church growth is being published. I believe this will become an important book. I hope many Christians including the lay Christian leaders in Korean churches gain deep insights through this book.

Thank you for your great comments. I wish you a good health to carry out the great ministry of God to the last.

Dr. Peter Wagner: Thank you. I wish the continuous development of Institute for Church Growth and the healthy victory of Yoido Full Gospel Church and Reverend Cho, Yonggi.

CHAPTER 4

The Influence on the Churches in the World

Interview with Dr. Cecil Robeck

The following interview with Dr. Cecil Robeck was conducted by the Reverend Younggi Hong in a cultivation center at Gwanglim on November 2002. Professor Cecil Robeck has taught church history and ecumenism for a long time at Fuller Seminary and is a representative scholar of the Pentecostals. Professor Robeck believes the mind of the Rev. Cho for church growth and ecumenism have greatly influenced the churches in the world.

Hello, Professor Robeck. I am glad to see you again after our meeting in Germany. How have you been doing?

Professor Cecil Robeck: Yes. I am glad to see you again as well. I have been busy doing research, writing papers and books and conducting seminar lectures as well as the ministry of striving for the consolidation of churches. But with the grace of God, I have been healthy.

What made you come and visit Korea again this time?

Professor Cecil Robeck: I have come to represent the Pentecostal theologians and lead a regular conference between Ecumenical theologians and Pentecostal theologians. The conference is being held in Korea this time, so I have come to participate. I had discussions with theological scholars of the Assemblies of God (Full Gospel). And you (Dr. Younggi Hong) also participated in the discussion, didn't you? I was deeply impressed by the discussion.

Have you visited Yoido Full Gospel Church?

Professor Cecil Robeck: Yes, I did. Our party was impressed by the church, I think Yoido Full Gospel Church inspires many people.

You have observed Yoido Full Gospel Church for a long time, and I wonder what you believe are the factors for its growth?

Professor Cecil Robeck: Well, that's a difficult question. Especially, since I have only been to Korea twice. but I have heard about pastor Cho for many, many years. In fact I first heard him preaching in 1960s. I have watched the church with a great deal of interest and with a great deal of satisfaction, and I think there are a number of factors I suppose that fit into this. If I may say, the most influential factor for the growth of the church is Pastor Cho's powerful inspirational message. Of course, I think korean people have the mindset to take spirituality seriously, and there are people, who in this country have been looking for answers to real spiritual questions. Pastor Cho has been able to bring those. He's been a charismatic articulate spokesman for providing answers to real problems that people face in everyday life. I think his emphasis on the supernatural has been incredibly important, especially in the culture that takes supernatural seriously on the issue of healing, benediction, exorcism, and confronting the demons, I think these have played an important part in making this particular church grow within the korean context.

I would also say that Pastor Cho's message of blessing is a positive message that the people need to hear. it's not just a positive thinking but it goes much deeper in that it has more meaning than positive thinking. But it seems to me that people hear enough bad news all week long. That's fine, it's good, if the church can be a source of good news. Pastor Cho proclaims the good news of God's life to people.

You seem to view that the main growth factor is Pastor Cho's gospel, which is well suited in the Korean context. Powerful in spirituality and yet practical messages move the people's mind more readily. Do you have anything else to point out as another factor?

Professor Cecil Robeck: Yoido Full Gospel can be regarded as the most orderly organization among Pentecostal churches. I would have to say that this is probably the most hierarchical church I have run into within the pentecostal movement. It is clear who is in charge and responsible when things go wrong. This is a patriarchism in a positive sense. As anyone can see, Yoido Full Gospel Church is an enormously huge church. Pastor Cho has shown his fatherly concern to nurture the church. This orderly spirituality can be construed as another secret for the church growth.

I would also say that, as I have looked at the church, the structure of small groups, that are superintended by pastors at a whole range of level, has been absolutely critical to the church growth. I can give you an example of my own church, not the church that I have been in for the last 25 years but the one prior to that where our pastor suggested an experiment with small groups. We had about 25 people coming on Wednsday nights for the Bible study.

However, within 6 weeks of establishing the small groups, we were running a hundred and twenty five participants. By the end of the year, we were running over two hundred. Then we hired a new pastor, and the new pastor came and said, 'I don't like small groups. I'm gonna stop them,'. And we went back to 25 people on wednesday night. The threat, that these small group have or hold for some people, don't have to be a threat if the leader train them properly. And I think Pastor Cho has done a wonderful job of training those people and organizing this in such a way that the communication is clear and leadership is clear.

To recapitulate, Professor Robeck, you believe the spiritual messages and authority of Pastor Cho and the effective small group ministry are the major factors for the church growth. Then, how Yoido Full Gospel Church contributed to world Christian movement, and especially what is the contribution of Pastor Cho?

Professor Cecil Robeck: Well, obviously, Yoido full gospel church has become a center piece for Christians as a whole but also for the pentecostal movement, specifically. I think it has grabbed the attention of many people around the world in ways, nobody else could. It talks about the most vital message, that a church can have, and it is the message of the power of the Holy Spirit in the daily lives of individual believers. As I ponder on the changes in world religion, especially changes in the Christian world, Pastor Cho's proclaimed message on the power of the Holy Spirit is the source of empowerment for many missionaries sent out to the mission field as well as the church itself.

It seems to me that the future belongs to churches like Yoido Full Gospel that they are having such an impact worldwide. Such churches which influence the world by preaching the redemption by Jesus Christ, the power of the Holy Spirit, and the empowerment of laity, raises the ministry to a new level. All of these kinds of things are the kinds of things that the newer and the younger churches should hold as vital. So I think it will have a continued contribution. Yoido Full Gospel Church will have a continued contribution to the churches in the world through establishing new churches, releasing the literature, and broadcasting. It is a wonderful idea in this age of technology to be able to download the Sunday sermon and to have people watch all over the world. On any given Sunday, millions of people in every corner of the earth can have an access to the sermon from Yoido Full Gospel Church. Pastor Cho continuously adapts himself to the changes to adjust not only his message but his ministry direction. I believe this is an important influential quality that gives challenges to the churches in the world.

That's right. Reverend Cho's message and ministry have remarkable adaptability to modern technical and societal changes. That is to say it has the leadership for the future churches in times of modern cultural waves. It has a phenomenal impact in this world of technological changes.

I mean you are riding on the forefront of the wave if you would in leading the church into the future. Yoido Full Gospel Church keeps the delicate balance of dynamic modern technology and traditional Christian spirituality. Grant Walker once said of the Pentecostal movement, which balances modernity and spirituality, 'the garden of Eden equipped with the satellite dish'.

Professor Cecil Robeck: Yes, Yes, right that Grant Walker. I think there is a lot of truth to it if you think about the history of Pentecostalism. We've been never afraid of technology. I think it is true of the Pentecostal churches, too. A lot of churches, especially the historic and traditional churches have been very slow and very reluctant to step into the communications or broadcasting program. But you know in the 1920s, 1930s, 1940s, we were already involved in the radio ministry. Aimee Sample McPherson, who made the Four Square Gospel Pentecostal was the first women in the united states, I believe, who held the license to a FM station. That broadcasting station is still on the air. Well. I can't remember the call letter, perhaps it's a Full Gospel station. What is certain is that that is a Pentecostal station. Secondly. when we got into the 40s and 50s, we moved to TV ministry. Oral Roberts' ministry was broadcasted via television since the 1950's. Trinity Broadcasting Station uses videos and TV broadcasting as well as having satellite campuses all over the world.

Now the use of internet. I think we were never afraid of using the internet. We've seen that as a tool, which we can use to proclaim the gospel of Jesus Christ.

So I think of another thing Grant Walker said. He said Pentecostalism was very pragmatic. Yes, we have always been pragmatic. Pentecostal churches are fast to give up on tools that are not helpful in spreading the gospel. On the other hand, if it works, we continuously use it for the heavenly cause. I think that's true of Yoido Full Gospel church as well, if not the foremost runner in this respect.

Professor, you are known as an expert or a guru in Ecumenics. How did you become devoted to the Ecumenism?

Professor Cecil Robeck: I never thought about being involved in Ecumenism in the past. Then in the early 1980's. while I was sleeping, the Lord woke me and said,'Cecil, You will take on the Ecumenism movement for me. You will go around the world and teach the body of Christ the importance of Ecumenism.' I studied Ecumenism and headed straight to the field by the calling of the Lord. As I was involved in Ecumenism more and more, I soon realized the significance of this ministry more and more. The ministry of Ecumenism is to make the body of Christ realize the identity of the mission and focus on building and extending the kingdom of God through network and partnership. The Fuller Seminary sent me out as a special emissary to participate in a theological communications with Roman Catholics, Presbyterian, and WCC, etc. The Pentecostal movement had the vision of Ecumenism from its inception. The Pentecostalists have the most awareness and support for the Ecumenism now than ever before.

Do you think Dr. Cho has also contributed to Ecumenical movement?

Professor Cecil Robeck: I know Dr. Cho has contributed to Ecumenical movement. I have been very proud of him especially recent years, when he and Korea Assemblies of God have attempted to move into the Korean National Council of Churches and then have become a member. Yoido Full Gospel Church has become a member of that council. I think it is a very important progress within the Korean context, in which you have roughly 28% of your population now as christians and still 72% who are not. This fact provides in a sense a reconciled diversity, or if you would, a vision of consolidation of Yoido Full Gospel Church within this country.

It provides a vision of diversity for the peace and reconciliation at the same time, and Pastor Cho has been on the forefront there.

From what I know, he has taken a good deal of criticisms from fellow ministers in the Assemblies of God in the United State, but I have to say that I think he's right and they are wrong about Ecumenism. Let me explain just briefly that the history of the Ecumenical movement in the united states is very different from the history of the Ecumenical movement in Korea. But most of our leaders in the United States do not understand cultural differences and national differences and so forth. They tend I think to look still at korean Pentecostalism as a kind of missionary outreach of what is taking place in the United states, which means they then transplanted often too much the culture of the United States.

I think one of the things I would love to see is for our leaders in the United States to say it is OK to have Pastor Cho show us the way. I think he is in a unique position probably the most unique position except for perhaps a few churches in Latin America that have already been actively involved in Ecumenism to lead the way and to develop in a sense the protocol for how the Pentecostal can interact ecumenically. I believe that, because of his unique and important position in the history of world churches right now, his ecumenical ministry can greatly contribute to the coalition and development of world churches.

Can you say more about the impact of Reverend Pastor Cho Yonggi's leadership or his church growth on the world church in general?

Professor Cecil Robeck: Well. I guess I have to say that even the World Council of Churches (WCC) people are very aware of Pastor Paul Yonggi Cho. They know the story of Yoido. They wonder about it if they don't understand how it can be. And I know many of them, many of the leaders in the World Council. They made trips to Korea simply to observe what's going on here and to see what it is. I know other church leaders have done so. and that means it is a challenge to many churches in the world to think or rethink what it takes seriously in terms of 'evangelization and church growth'. The most natural ministry of a church is to focus on the rebirth of life, which means to save the lost soul. Pastor Cho's ministry let the fundamental mission of a church known to world churches once again.

What do you think is the strength of Pastor Cho Yonggi's leadership in church growth?

Professor Cecil Robeck: Well, I think there are two parts to it. One is I think his personal integrity, and the other is his spiritual charisma that goes a long way in this. Excellent leadership stems from reliable personal integrity and authority. I suppose that the place where I worry about the most is not that he will lack integrity – he will always have integrity – nor he will ever lack of his charisma but that I worry about what will happen when Pastor Paul Yonggi cho retires. I worry about that. I think it's a matter of prayer. I think it's probably a matter of prayer here in Yoido. too.

Yes. Many people are interested in the future of Yoido Full

Gospel Church. Can you suggest any ideas or alternatives in this respect?

Professor Cecil Robeck: Well, that's not an easy question to answer. A careful preparation is needed indeed in order to succeed Pastor Cho's excellent leadership for the future of Yoido Full Gospel Church. I think Pastor Cho has an excellent gift in running and managing at organizational level. In that respect, I believe Pastor Cho is planning for the successorship as well. If a person is to succeed Pastor Cho, he has to be clearly the person whom God wants. He has to be a leader to lead these people to a new, higher spiritual level. We can explore together many positive challenges that Yoido Full Gospel Church is facing. The solution to these challenges may be simply found by focusing on the positive ways of how to lead more people to Christ. The new successor will need the charisma to lead people. On the organizational level, the new successor would need the organizational administrative structure of the church in place that could make the transition fairly painless.

It's about the time to close this interview. Do you have anything to say to Pastor Cho?

Professor Cecil Robeck: Keep up the good work. I think clearly you are a pentecostal leader who has very few peers anywhere close to you. You are the person to be reckoned with, and that means clearly you have a message, a positive message, to give not only to the Pentecostals but to the world. If I have any encouragement for you to say, it is 'be the prophet, be the prophet.' Stand firm on your ground and use your base to open all of us up to what God has for us.

Thank you very much for all your insightful comments, Professor Robeck.

Professor Cecil Robeck: Thank you. I earnestly pray that Pastor David Yonggi Cho and Yoido Full Gospel Church will take on the ministry of God greatly even more in the future.

PART 2

YOIDO FULL GOSPEL CHURCH AND REV. CHO'S PRINCIPLES FOR CHURCH GROWTH

1. Church Growth and Leadership
2. Church Growth and the Holy Spirit
3. Church Growth and Prayer
4. Church Growth and the Sermon
5. Church Growth and Cell Groups
6. Church Growth and the Mass Media
7. Church Growth and the Kingdom of God

The contents of Part 2 summarize the 7 principles of church growth that the Rev. Cho has been emphasizing during the past 45 years of his ministry. For this publication, the lectures, books and other various writings of the Rev. Cho on church growth have been excerpted from and reorganized.

CHAPTER 1

Church Growth and Leadership

Leadership is the Key to Church Growth

Pastors assume the leadership position to lead the faith of the congregation members whether they want it or not. However, this way of the leader requires a great responsibility and endurance for a hardship. On the other hand, as great the responsibility is, it is also the way of joy to feel a glory and fulfillment. Looking at a nation, if a wrong leader is chosen, it heads to downfall. On the other hand, if a right leader is elected, the nation is headed to success. As we can see, the success and failure of a nation depends on its leader. Thus, pastors in a leadership position should continuously pray and do their best in every endeavors.

The followers take after the image of their leader. Not only the way to speak and act, they also take after the way to think. Thus, pastors should have an absolute sense of being a leader and cultivate well the pastures, that God has entrusted in them. The pastures develop in various shapes in accordance with the leadership. Actually, observing a cell organization, the cell will prosper if the leader is capable. In contrast, if there is a lack of a leadership in a cell organization, it heads to downhill. It is the same for a church growth. The most important concern for a church growth is the leadership of the pastor. In all respect, it can not be overemphasized to speak of the importance of a leadership. Leadership determines every outcome.

The Leader's Requirements for Church Growth

Then, how can you become a leader, who can be complimented by God, can nurture the congregation members well, and can grow the church healthily? I would like to suggest four requirements to be a leader of growing church type, especially to help in leadership development.

Firstly, the leader of the growing church type should find out the needs of others and fulfill them. For example, entrepreneur should be able to quickly assess the supply and demand during the process of market distribution between the supplier and consumer in order to succeed. In world trading, it does not guarantee a success to expand the production capacity. The supply and demand of other overseas market should be analyzed scientifically and quickly in order to react properly in planning the production. Only then, the enterprise operation could succeed. Likewise, a leader loses his/her qualification if he/she can not implement the plan to fulfill others' needs based on the needs analysis. In that respect, the pastors should be more diligent than others in order to find out the present needs and requirements of the congregation members and to satisfy the needs and requirements.

Secondly, the leader of the growing church type should make others successful. Making others succeed does not mean hiring an incapable person and doing everything possible at any cost to make him/her successful. The leader, who makes others to win, delegates the appropriate tasks based on their aptitudes and helps them to develop themselves joyfully through such tasks. It is a duty of a leader to assign the right man in the right post. Doing so requires a constant concern and effort to do the best for the followers. Hence, the capable and talented individuals are encouraged to use their talents fully.

When those individuals, who are not fit for the task, are found, they should be guided to work on appropriate assignments while supplying any deficiency and encouraging and training them. The leader should be able to show such leadership at will.

Thirdly, the leader of the growing church type should have the spirit of a pioneer and move forward constantly. Most people are preoccupied to maintain the status quo. The reason is people prefer stability over venture. However, when a leader only pursues stability and leads his organization indolently, the leader loses the qualification as a leader. A capable leader should be adventurous and aggressive. There will be many new burdens when the leader is constantly developing new ideas and tries to implement them. Nevertheless, an organization can not prosper and develop without taking the risks.

Fourthly, the leader of the growing church should make every effort for self-development. We have to make every effort for self-development, comparing myself of today against myself of yesterday. There are no Biblical leaders or leaders of the century, who were idle in their self-development. Look at Moses. The 40 years of time in the wilderness was a precious time for his self-development. The 3 years of time in Arabia was a time for self-development of the Apostle Paul. Also, look at the world leaders. Sometimes in a prison. sometimes in a hospital, they were struggling between the survival and death in numerous times. However, they never ceased from working on their self-development.

I have explained four requirements to be a leader of the growing church type so far.

Pastors are leaders regardless of their church size. Thus, pastors should study and practice constantly to satisfy these four requirements in order to demonstrate the leadership of the growing church without any regret. When doing so, you would surely be an excellent leader, and the congregation members of your church will enjoy the lives of success. Moreover, the church will continue to grow.

The Attitude of a Leader of the Growing Church

For a church to grow, the attitude of the leader is absolutely important. If the leader thinks he can not grow his church, the church growth can not happen. For the church growth to take place, a firm faith and a positive attitude are utmost important. Therefore, the leader should have a positive faith as scribed in the Bible, 'I can do everything through him who gives me strength.' (Philippians 4:13)

When I graduated from a theological school in 1958 and began to build a new church at outskirt of Seoul, the Holy Spirit always led me to have a positive attitude of 'I can do.' My situation at the time was so pessimistic. All the people around me were struggling with poverty, and the church was very operable financially. As a matter of fact, it was these times when I learned to fast and pray. That is, it was more due to the fact that I was in a desperate situation of not having enough to eat than due to the fact that my faith was so deep and passionate.

However, in retrospect, it was a time of spiritual blessing. Looking at me suffering from hardships, many colleagues have made these discouraging remarks;

> Do you believe that you can build a church in this slum while suffering from poverty? Give it up! Why don't you fold down your tent right now and come to our church to serve as a Sunday school pastor?

In any event, whenever I knelt to pray, my heart's desire was burning within me fiercely. Although there is nothing to be seen in my eyes, to be heard in my ears, and to be held in my hands, I had a long cherished wish, which was certain and intense. Thus, I have said to myself many times. 'I will build the largest church in Korea. Yes. With the help of the Holy Spirit, I can do it.'

Others mocked at me, believing that my dream was a vagrant fancy. People, who were not inspired by the Holy Spirit, could not have understood my dream, which seemed impossible to achieve in reality. The reason is because they never experienced such inspiration. However, I believed that it was possible to build a large church by the work of the Holy Spirit and that my dream would come true certainly. For church growth, it is the most important for the leader, the pastor, to have an attitude of conviction or an assurance of achieving the dream above all.

Pastors should have a positive attitude on church growth constantly. I have thought of church growth for 40 years, and I still have this burning desire for the continued growth of the church. Since the Holy Spirit is still working on the Gentiles and nations of nonbelievers even today, the church will continuously grow. God has anointed all those, who believe in Jesus Christ, with the Holy Spirit, and is working through them. Now, if the pastor does not have a firm conviction of his/her church growth, it would not only disappoint God greatly but also make it impossible to expect a church growth.

It is now the time of church growth by the work of the Holy Spirit. Hence the pastor should expect and firmly believe in church growth wherever his/her ministry is located. Then, church growth will surely happen. Now the attitude of the leader of church growth type can be explained in five points.

Firstly, have a philosophical basis for church growth

I ask myself personally these questions. 'For what do you wish your church growth? Isn't the reason your bodily desires?' Of course, there is no one who doesn't wish to succeed in his/her work. The reason is, in most cases, the fame, wealth and the fulfillment from the self-achievement follows the success. However, the pastors should not use their ministry as a means to obtain these worldly things. When I first started my ministry 40 years ago, I began building my church with wrong motives. As the consequence, I had to endure many ordeals because of the wrong selfish purposes. However, nowadays, I have a sound philosophical basis for church growth to answer clearly those people, who ask me 'why do you want your church growth?' The answer is 'I am serving currently 700,000 congregation members, but I have still this burning desire to continuously grow our church even more.'

The Lord has said, 'This is to my Father's glory, that you bear much fruit' (John 15:8). Here, the fruit that the Lord mentions is not the fruit of the Holy Spirit nor the fruit of the Christian life but the fruit of the spiritual salvation of the soul. Thus, in order to glorify God even more, we have to lead more people to the Lord and pray in Jesus' name that these fruits will not fall to the ground but grow continuously -fruit that will last (John 15:16).

One of the reasons that I desire church growth so much is to redeem a greater number of neighbors from the ruins of eternal hell. Truthfully, it is so natural and necessary to have the desire to lead even one more soul to the Lord, if one knows for sure that there is heaven for everyone to attain and that there is a hell for everyone to avoid at any costs. Furthermore, my reason for wishing for church growth is to acquire the human and material resources for various missions. From my personal experience, I could not even think of doing any missional work to preach the gospel to the unreached, when my ministry was struggling to provide me with enough clothing, housing and food during the hard times at the tent church.

Compared with the past, I now, through so many congregation members and abundant resources, can preach the gospel at much greater scale and do things that I could only dream of in the past. There must be a philosophical basis for whatever one is endeavoring to do. Likewise, pastors, who wish church growth, should have firm philosophy to drive forward church growth resolutely.

Secondly, wish for church growth fervently

Those who wish church growth should have their minds all preoccupied with the work to make it happen. In the same context, Plato, a Greek philosopher, asked the youths, who came to be his disciples, 'Can you fall in love with philosophy madly?'

It is as foolish as expecting to reap grapes from a brier for the pastors to wish for church growth, when they are satisfied with their ministries status quo or they take the inattentive attitude of having the 'job'. I have seen so many ministerial partners, who take the ministry as a 'job' and lead the ministry indifferently while I have been working on the ministry. Needless to say, their church was dying. Church grows only upon the heartfelt tears longing for its growth.

Reverend Jashil Choi, who accompanied my ministry for 26 years, longed for the growth of Yoido Full Gospel Church, that I am ministering, with all night praying, fasting prayer everyday as well as ceaseless gospel preaching and home visiting. I thank God for making our church grow as it is today as the result. Therefore, if you sincerely want church growth, be burnt with the passion to grow. Then, the church starts to live and grow.

Thirdly, have the hope for church growth

There may be some, who don't understand and mock the relationship between the hope and church growth. Nevertheless, it is a mistake. Whatever the task is, if we do not have our heart throbbing at achieving the task, it does not happen. We remember the days on the Christmas Eve, New Year's Eve or our birthday when we could not go to sleep easily with some anticipation of hope. It is this hope and throbbing that is needed for the ministers today.

It was the time when I was leading a crusade at a public assembly hall with the capacity of 5,000 people in Karlsruhe of Germany. At that time, Reverend Müller was organizing and leading the congregation as well as being the senior pastor of the fastest growing church in the city. He said repeatedly to me, 'Reverend Cho, I have been losing sleep many times lately because of my heart throbbing. My heart throbs just with the thought of the hope of growth of my church.' When I heard this, I realized that he had a very important element for the church growth in his life.

It was 1958, when I started my first year of ministry at a 'church' in a tent donated by U.S. Army soldiers laid out with several straw mats at Daejo-Dong in Seodaemoon-Gu after graduating from a theological school. During the first year, I experienced all the joy and sadness of ministers. When I was suppressed so many times by the despair that I was doing a fruitless work because of my volunteering instead of God's calling, I trembled with the regret for the meaningless hardship.

During this hardship, I collected and read all the success stories of world famous ministers as much as I can. Then, I would be surrounded by a deep illusion that I became one of them and felt a breath-taking emotion. As this illusion and hope filled in my heart, I felt greater self-confidence that 'I can do in the Lord'. My heart throbbed with the hope. I remember then spending days and nights on studying to cultivate the capability as equal as the image of such great pastors.

It was a Sunday. My heart was in captivity with the illusion that I was preaching in front of several thousand Christians while only about 100 Christians were having the worship service at the tent church. So, I burst out loudly.

> All of you, although right now I am having the worship service with only 100 Christians on straw mats in a tent church, soon I will be worshipping with over 3,000 Christians.

At this unsuspected comment, all the congregation members laughed without malicious intent. In retrospect, I think that they felt some sympathy and compassion for this poor first-year minister. Nevertheless, it was not the case for me. My heart was fluttering in anticipation and hope. It was 1959. Then, in 1964, after 5 years, 3,000

Christians were worshipping with me indeed. Thus, if you want church growth, do not feel ashamed of having the heart throbbing with anticipation. Soon the dream will come true.

Fourthly, have a firm conviction for church growth

The world famous guru on church growth studies, Dr. McGavran, made this statement at 'The First Research Seminar on Church Growth', which was held at Yoido Full Gospel Church in July 1976. 'Church growth happens only to those minsters, who hope and believe in it.' This statement was so sharp that it pierced to the core. In whatever endeavors, without the faith that it will be accomplished, it would not bear the fruit. Looking at the Gospels, Jesus left so many precepts on the power of faith to us, 'Your faith has healed you'(Matthew 9:22, Luke 18:42, so forth), 'It will be done just as you believed it would' (Matthew 8:13), 'If you can? said Jesus. Everything is possible for him who believes'(Mark 9:23) and so on.

A pastor ended up in a big city, being worn out after failing his ministry at several places. He did his utmost, thinking that it is the last chance.

However, his ministry achieved only so little, and he began to lose his confidence gradually. Then, suddenly, a great change came upon him one day. When he came home after delivering a powerful message of painful preparation with all his strength, his wife said something very touching for the first time in their marriage. It was only a few words, but it was as precious as thousand pounds of gold to him. She said, 'Honey, I received so much grace of God from your sermon today.' It may be regarded as a trifling compliment; however, these words gave the pastor a new faith and courage for church growth.

Thus, pastors should constantly read books that boost the faith for church growth. The human mind is like a sponge, and it absorbs the words filled with the faith to make it his strength. I fill my faith with books of faith. And then I read such precious books several times repeatedly. Moreover, I befriend many successful people and make effort to have the opportunity to converse on faith and success.

In 1969, when I was moving my ministry for the third time from Seodaemoon Full Gospel Church to Yoido, it was so testing time that I could not bear alone on my personal power. A total of 1 billion won was required to build a church that could accomodate 10,000 people. If this was not enough, countless changes in construction design (blue print) were required to build it with a special construction engineering method. And whenever there was a change in construction plan, there was a big tension on the relationship with the construction company. On top of that, the congregation members, who were pressed with economic burden, began to leave the church, and new congregation members made their intention to register after the church was constructed completely. In addition, at that time, Yoido was a desolate island of sand with no trace of buildings nearby, and there was hardly any means of public transportation.

My close partners and friends advised me that it was a big mistake for me to go out to Yoido and warned me that a mass of congregation members would soon desert the church.

At this time, it was the faith that I needed the most. It was not just a belief but the conviction to bring forth a miracle. So I lived with the Bible and the bibliography of the famous apostle of faith and the father of orphans, Reverend George Müller, placed on top of the headrest. The reason that I could overcome so many feelings of despair creeping on me can be attributed to the conversation with the Word of God and a man of great faith. I had a firm conviction that Yoido Full Gospel Church will grow beyond any imagination. As the result, the church has grown to be the home of over 700,000 congregation members.

The church of Jesus Christ is bound to grow. Jesus likened the heaven to planting a mustard seed. A mustard seed is smaller than other seeds; however, when it grows, it becomes a bigger tree than other trees to be the nest for many birds. The church may start out as small as a mustard seed, but we should not forget that there is a growing life in that seed. The ultimate responsibility for the growth of a church falls upon the minister. The 'fruit of continuous growth' will certainly be granted to those pastors, who are firmly convinced for the church to grow and have the throbbing heart with anticipation and hope moment by moment.

Fifthly, think church growth whenever awakened or sleeping

A stone thrown into a calm lake makes small or large waves on the water surface in proportion to its weight. Likewise, the mind of a man/woman makes waves of thought in accordance with his/her environment.

Pastors, who think their churches can not grow, can find easily the negative reasons why it is so. Likewise, those pastors who believe their churches can grow, can find as easily the positive reasons why that's the case.

There is a law of the flock in this world. Sparrows gather together to make a flock, and ducks gather together to form a pack. If a minister continuously thinks about the reason why his/her church is not growing, the wave of his/her thought will gather negative things wherever he/she goes putting the law of the flock into action. However, when a minister continuously sends out the waves of church growth to surrounding environment, they attract concentric waves from the surrounding environment to make the sound of the throbbing heart heard all over.

The waves of growth, that overflow from a minister's mind, echo within the minds of all Christians in the church regardless of their duties in the church. Consequently, the entire church transforms into a massive movement for growth, demolishing all the walls of impossibility and moving forward with amazing power. Likewise, the source for this massive movement for growth, that is the wave-making stone, must be thrown from the mind of the minister verbally or non-verbally. Thus, the minister should fill his/her mind with the possibility of church growth day or night in order to make his church-growing mind the power of a full impact.

I have never forgotten even for a moment the passionate and concentrated thinking on church growth during my 40 years of ministry. I have focused on the absolute condition that my church can grow and should grow.

As the result, before too long, all elders, deacons/deaconesses, and lay congregation members began to side with this thought. Moreover, the invisible waves of church growth mind brought numerous elements for success from the environment, putting the law of the flock into action, and new ideas on church growth sprung to my mind. After all, in 1974, the congregation increased by the vast number of 7,000, and it increased by another 3,500 despite the fact that I was on the overseas mission for almost 6 months off and on. Now, it has 700,000 congregation members.

From outside the church, all this growth may be looked upon as a miracle; however, in reality, the principle of church growth was applied. Any minister can use this principle. And achieve growth. Once the church passes the threshold of growth, it gains the momentum to grow as a rolling snowball grows bigger and bigger. Focus the energy of all thinking on the goal of church growth. Then, it will achieve an explosive growth.

Creative Life of a Leader of the Growing Church Type

A leader of the growing church type lives the life of creativity. Here, the creative life means to have the vision and dream for church growth. The premise for having these dream and vision is to proclaim that 'I can do it in the Lord'. In Mark 9:23, 'If you can? said

Jesus. Everything is possible for him who believes'. Thus, whatever the circumstances, if the minister thinks 'I can', he/she already stands in the procession of success.

The reason is because once we begin to think 'I can', the belief sets free the creative power of the Holy Spirit to have many ideas occur to us and to bring forth the reasons and circumstances for the possibility.

For example, if you determine that 'our church can not grow anymore', then many conditions that make it true occur to prevent the growth any further. Moreover, it is often the case that the church experiences a decline. However, if you think 'our church can continue to grow' and drive forward, then ideas, that make it happen, sping up to make it grow continuously. God does not work with negative people, who assert the impossibility and dwell on the difficulty. The Holy Spirit uses the mind of people, who have the mind to look for the solution first even at difficult situations. The Holy Spirit gives ideas to those people, who say 'There is a solution to everything. Let's find out the way'. Then, what is the attitude that we should have in order to work with the Holy Spirit after having the creative ideas and dream?

Firstly, we should avoid traditional thinking pattern. There is no such word as perfection to us, humans. We have to renew ourselves always. We must have a revolutionary mind, free from the bondage of traditional thinking. If we stress on traditional values too much, we get stopped and become stagnant. It is the same for the leaders of growing church type. If we continue to dwell on traditional custom and mind, we get satisfied with the status quo to stop progressing. We have to break the old shell with a revolutionary idea.

Secondly, we have to incorporate new ideas in our mind always. When someone suggests a new idea, we should have the attitude of listening carefully before delving into judging its practicality. Then, we can be said as people of creative mind and dream.

Thirdly, we should maintain the attitude to try out first courageously. If we withdraw even before trying out, believing in its impossibility, we can not expect to see the creative progress.

Fourthly, the mind to march forward continuously should be maintained. Only those, who have the progressive mind for continuous development and advancement, can be ahead in every aspects, whether it is politics, economics, education, culture, business, etc.

It makes sense for those ministers, who wish to be of the church growing type, to apply the above methods for the development of their ministerial life. Humans can not be perfect. The more advanced next generations incessantly spring up. I contemplate on an epochal approach for my ministerial life. I have the firm conviction that 'our church can grow continuously'. Looking at the present situation, our church does not have the capacity to accomodate any more congregation members. However, if we escape from this traditional constraining mind, there will be many new ideas for further church growth.

Brainstorming is necessary in order to develop ideas unceasingly. The Holy Spirit gives ideas to whoever He chooses. Thus, ideas of every people are worth looking into. After examining the ideas of anyone, those, that lack the practicality, are to be discarded whereas those, that are practical, are to be accepted. If someone believes something can not be done without trying, then he/she can not accomplish anything.

The Holy Spirit does not work with a minister, who does not take the same creative attitude as the Holy Spirit. The Holy Spirit continually marches on. The Holy Spirit develops new ideas and makes it to progress toward better direction. The Holy Spirit leads toward tomorrow than today, the next month than this month, the next year than this year. Therefore, ministers should never say 'I can not do'. Contemplate on the way to make it work. The act of giving up easily by thinking 'it can not be done' is an act that prohibits the work of the Holy Spirit.

As such, the life of a leader of church growing type should never give up easily in whatever circumstances and drive forward with a progressive mind. Let's escape from traditional indolence and incorporate new ideas to try out anew incessantly. This is the model for the creative life of a leader of church growing type.

The Self-Development of a Leader of Church Growing Type

In order to be a leader of church growing type, one should set an example for the congregation members in public or in private life. One should continually make an effort for self-development. Then, how should one embark on his/,her self-development?

Firstly, the leader of church growing type should develop himself/herself spiritually before everything else.

Before Jesus was crucified, He prayed to God, 'For them I sanctify myself, that they too may be truly sanctified'. (John 17:19) Because Jesus was one and only son of God, He did not have the need to sanctify Himself.

The reason He sanctified Himself was to make His disciples sanctified. The relationship between a pastor and a herd of sheep can be likened to the cause and effect of waves. In other words, the wave from a pastor reaches its effect on the herd of sheep. Thus, when the pastor sanctifies himself/herself, the herd of sheep also get sanctified.

A pastor set about a pioneering church in Latin America. Even if the pastor emphasized prayer no matter how at the pulpit, the congregation members did not pray. So, the pastor reprimanded and implored, but it was no use. Feeling great pains, he came across this Jesus' prayer, 'For them I sanctify myself, that they too may be truly sanctified'. (John 17:19), and an idea struck him. 'That's right. Not just by the words of preaching to demand prayer from the saints, but by setting the example of praying myself. Then, will the saints not follow and pray?' Hence, he began to pray earnestly knelt in front of the pulpit. Soon, praying saints added in number, and the church became a praying church.

As we can see in the aforementioned event, the spiritual wave emanating from the mind of a pastor reaches to the heart of the saints to effect them deeply. But the wave from the character of the pastor exerts greater influence than that from the words of the pastor's mouth. If the servant of God lives the life of sanctification, the saints will soon follow and live likewise. If the servant of God devotes himself/herself to God, then the saints will follow and devote themselves to God. Jesus said, 'if a blind man leads a blind man, both will fall into a pit.' (Matthew 15:14)

Thus, the leader of church growing type should first of all devote himself/herself to God wholeheartedly, live the sanctified life, and have the attitude of obeying God's will entirely. Only then, the pastor can transfer the grace of God to the saints and change their lives. The saints can change only as much as the pastor changed himself/herself and grow. When a pastor always looks into himself/herself as the leader and makes effort for self-development for the spiritual growth of the saints, the church will undergo the spiritual growth as well as growth in numbers.

Secondly, the leader of church growing type should have the training to think clearly.

We can see that every successful people had a clear thinking. Those, who do not think clearly, can not succeed in any field. Many people, who come to me for spiritual advice, often make unfocused remarks. They say this thing and that thing, and I can not determine what exactly they are saying. Then, I suggest 'please clearly state to the point what brought you here'.

There are many reasons why ministers fail in their ministry. One of them is a failure to communicate clearly. Often when we listen to a pastor's sermon, we can not understand what he/she is saying because the pastor has not thought in through clearly. Most of the sermons, which do not convey the preacher's thinking clearly, have many words and long sentences to make an ambiguous point. However, the sermon of a preacher, who thinks clearly, tends to have fewer words, shorter sentences and clear points. Pastors, who reiterate and mumble, end up in failing to communicate God's message clearly.

When I, myself, do not pray enough on a Saturday and prepare the sermon adequately and go on standing in front of the pulpit, it clearly shows immediately.

The sermon gets longer because of grumbles and prattle, and the message does not get through because of the lack of focus. Then, I am exhausted and tired even I am the one, who is preaching. At home after the service, my wife will then certainly say 'Today's sermon was so desultory'. But when I put everything else and go up to the prayer mountain for praying to prepare the sermon, I can concentrate on the main point as well as logically developing the introduction, body, and conclusion of the sermon. The the flow of the sermon becomes so clear. Them the next day, I will deliver the sermon effectively, and the congregation members feel the grace of God through my sermon. Thus, the servants of God, whether it is the cell organization or Sunday worship service, should always train themselves to communicate their ideas clearly.

Hence, the leader of growing church type should have the training to think clearly firsthand. Then, be ready to have a resolute mind to have clear ideas by reading the Bible, contemplate and pray as much as possible.

Thirdly, the leaders of growing church type should utilize their time wisely.

If a pastor does not plan well and runs in every direction, he/she can not accomplish anything. Thus, pastors should work with a plan and make the most out of time as short as 10 minutes or 15 minutes. If one does not utilize his/her time wisely, he/she can not expect any self-development. Most ministers, who work at in the fields, go to work at church early in the morning, pay home visits to congregation members all day, and come home very late. Then, they go to bed right away being dead tired. Such a schedule most of the time does not permit any spare time for reading the Bible and inspirational books, praying, and studying for self-development.

Thus, it is important to use any spare time for self-development.

For the last few years, after waking up early in the morning and reading the Bible as well as the morning prayer, I have been studying foreign languages before breakfast. During the day at church, I value any time even as short as 5 minutes or 10 minutes and try to use it effectively. I will set books to read on my desk or carry and read the books whenever there is time to spare. If I can not continue to read, I will mark the place to read the next time. Then continue reading at the next spare time. After for a while, I realize that I have read so many books.

I go home about 7 in the evening. Then, I would have dinner with my family, take a few minutes of rest to study again for an hour with concentration. One can spend this hour reading newspapers or watching television. However, this is not desirable. Although it may be a small segment of time, it becomes a significant chunk of time when they accumulate. I have been using this method for my self-development. And because I have been studying at every chance, I could minister effectively.

Although a pastor may be of church growing type, he/she will get behind if he/she is content with the status quo and does not make efforts for self-development. I myself would not have been able to keep my position if I failed continually to improve myself. When we improve ourselves always, we develop incessantly. I of tomorrow should be different from I of today. The leader of growing church type is the person, who utilize even a small faction of time to research new ideas and study continuously for self-development.

Leadership is the key

If the thinking of the leader of an organization or a nation changes, that of the followers changes as well. When the language of the leader changes, the language of the followers also changes. When the act of the leader alters, that of the follower also gets modified. When the habit of the leader changes, that if the follower also changes. Finally, if the fate of the leader takes a different twist, then that of the follower also takes a different turn. The church is the same. When the leadership of the minister changes to church growing type, the followership of the congregation members will also take the form of church growing type. Therefore, leadership is the key to church growth.

CHAPTER 2

Church Growth and the Holy Spirit

Holy Spirit is the Leader of Church Growth

The Holy Spirit is the initiator and the leader of church growth. The Acts clearly testifies to the Holy Spirit movement, Pentecostal Advent of the Holy Spirit, and the marvelous growth of the early churches. Before the Pentecostal event, the disciples of Jesus were very much afraid to bear witness to the Good News. However, after receiving the baptism by the Holy Spirit on the Pentecost, they spread the Gospel with explosiveness. This Holy Spirit movement of the early church became stagnant during the Middle Ages and Pietism of the 17th and 18th centuries. It then went through the Methodist movement led by Reverend John Wesley, the Revival movement in America, and Holiness and Purity movement to develop into the Pentecostal Holy Spirit movement of the 20th century.

At this time of the early 21st century, most fast-growing churches in the world are the leaders of the Holy Spirit movement as we can see in various statistics and newest information. Not just through the paradigm of church history, Korean churches are true leaders of church growth based on the words of the Bible, and as such they should realize that the senior partner of church ministry is God, the Holy Spirit. Thus, anyone, who works with the Holy Spirit, can achieve an amazing church growth. Then, Let's look at who is the Holy Spirit and how we can achieve church growth along with the Holy Spirit?

Who is the Holy Spirit?

The Holy Spirit is a persona, a senior partner, and a counselor. This is based on the awesome work of the Holy Spirit, that I experienced during my ministry. In other words, it explains the characteristics of the Holy Spirit movement, which made a clear and a distinctive mark in my ministry.

The Holy Spirit as Persona

We can not expect church growth without the presence of the Holy

Spirit as a living person of God. During early days of my ministry, I did not know clearly that the Holy Spirit was a person. Of course, on the knowledge level, I knew God, the Trinity, but I regarded the Holy Spirit as some kind of a power or a force.

Let's suppose that I was invited to your home and was treated indifferently as if I was not there, would I remain there for long? I will leave with a huge disappointment. The Holy Spirit, who descended from Heaven on the Pentecost about 2000 years ago, is still remaining within Christians. However, I neither welcomed nor received the Holy Spirit as a real person of God and treated Him as a certain mysterious power or force. I cried out His name only when I needed Him. God made me realize it deeply within me. I had the fear that I committed a great wrong against the Holy Spirit.

The Holy Spirit was dismayed that I regarded Him as a power or an instrument. The Holy Spirit made me realize that the relationship between Him and me was surpassing that between me and my wife.

The Holy Spirit was with me from the moment I was saved. I did not realize and committed a great wrong to the Holy Spirit. He is a person and wants to be treated and served as a person to make Him happy and content.

With this awakening thought, my understanding and attitude toward the Holy Spirit changed entirely. Throughout all my life, I was cognizant of the Holy Spirit as a person, relied on Him, and obeyed His leading. When we know that the Holy Spirit is a person, our life of faith makes a big leap. Our life changes for the better when we share a deep personal fellowship with the Holy Spirit. I realized that the Holy Spirit has wants a deep personal relationship with Christians. Then, I could have a successful ministry by recognizing, welcoming, serving, relying on Him as a senior partner of my ministry.

The Holy Spirit, My Senior Partner

From the turning point of knowing the Holy Spirit as a person, I studied the Acts with a different perspective. Consequently, I was deeply moved by the relationship between the disciples of Jesus and the Holy Spirit during the time of the early church. They held a special meeting to discuss and decide upon the matter of the Gentiles in Jerusalem (Acts 15:6). Then, they had the decision of the Jerusalem meeting known to all churches of the Gentiles. They certainly treated the Holy Spirit as a person, a member of the meeting and the leader among all in the meeting. Paul and Barnabas awaited for the indication from the Holy Spirit before leaving for the mission fields. They served the Holy Spirit as their senior partner.

Accordingly, I made my mind to correct my attitude toward the Holy Spirit. I began to serve the Holy Spirit as my true senior partner.

Afterwards, I began to study the methods to communicate with the Holy Spirit. I found many teachings on communicating with the Holy Spirit in the Bible. 'May the grace of the Lord Jesus Christ, and the love of God, and the fellowship of the Holy Spirit be with you all.' (2 Corinthians 13:14)

The Greek word, *koinonia*, means 'communion or fellowship'. To have a communion with the Holy Spirit, we must have a fellowship with Him. It is impossible to commune with someone indirectly. We must communicate and converse in order to have a communion.

Fellowship with the Holy Spirit

I make confessions to the Holy Spirit, 'The Holy Spirit, I thank you for allowing this good day. I will be led to victory with You.' Then, I open the Bible to pray, 'The Holy Spirit, please lead me to the truth. The Holy Spirit, You know what God wants to say to the saints. Please speak to me beforehand so that I may know Your will'.

Also, when I head for the pulpit, 'The Holy Spirit, this pulpit is Yours. Let's go together'. When I preach with the Holy Spirit in front of the pulpit, it becomes a meaningful time of feeling the grace of God. I feel the anointing and force that springs up from the Holy Spirit within me.

After the sermon or lecture at a seminar, when I sit down, I say, 'The Holy Spirit, Thank you. I am just Your instrument, and You have done all the glorious works. Thank You'.

There should be a sharp distinction between having a fellowship with the Holy Spirit freely and just experiencing the Holy Spirit.

I began to put this style of prayer and fellowship into action. Then I felt a new strength was overflowing in my life through the anointing of the Holy Spirit in a different dimension than previously. I began to feel the presence of the Holy Spirit in my prayer and sermon. The congregation members told me that I changed powerfully. They said they were receiving greater grace of God. From that moment, our church broke the barrier of 3,000 congregation members and started to grow spectacularly. Soon enough, in 1969, the number of our congregation members reached 18,000.

That time, I said to myself, 'Everything will work out alright. I have a good home, comfortable living allowances, a sedan with a chauffeur. On top of that, I have this church, and I am so satisfied'.

Then the Holy Spirit spoke to me suddenly. 'Today is the last day. Leave this church. Delegate all the final decisions to the general assembly. Don't take anything from this church. Then go into a new church to build'.

I was so amazed and perplexed by this voice of the Holy Spirit and said, 'Dear Holy Spirit, haven't You chosen me by a mistake? I have worked so hard to build churches in two places, and at last this church is growing after enduring so many hardships. I am exhausted. Please choose someone else for your plan.'

Nevertheless, the Holy Spirit spoke to me continuously. 'I am the master of this church. Your work here has ended, so go out. Go to Yoido to build a church, that can accomodate 10,000 people, and make a plan to send out missionaries to the end of the earth.'

Nowadays, we can find churches, that can house 10,000, in several countries. However, at that time, it was almost unthinkable to build a church for 10,000 congregation members. I continued to resist, 'Dear Holy Spirit, I can not do it. I can never do it!' After all, I decided to build a church at the place of the present Yoido Full Gospel Church in 1969. Overcoming so many hardships, that can not be expressed here with the help of the Holy Spirit and the cooperation of the saints, we consecrated a new sanctuary at Yoido in 1973.

As you may know well, our church has about 700,000 congregation members at the present time. However, I return all this glory to God. I confess that I could not have done anything by myself. Even now, I make all efforts to know more about the Holy Spirit. The reason is because the Holy Spirit is the God, the Trinity. He works right here with me at this very time. Jesus accomplished His mission, and the Holy Spirit works to apply the grace of Jesus to us. We can not succeed without the help from the Holy Spirit.

I have never decided and endeavored anything at my will without asking the will of God. I ask the Holy Spirit to work before me. Church growth also depends on the hands of the Lord. Therefore, when you make a plan for a goal, I counsel that you pray to let the will of the Holy Spirit revealed to you in detail and let you know of His goal before jumping to make a decision on your own. The Holy Spirit will let you know clearly and in detail.

Then, you should move forward to achieve the goal with prayer in accordance with the way, that the Holy Spirit lets you know, believing that it will be realized. When you do so, the church growth will happen also.

The Holy Spirit, the Counselor

I have been around the world and led numerous Christian conferences, crusades, revival meetings, etc. Sometime ago, I lectured on the theme of 'the fellowship with the Holy Spirit' in Paris, France. After the lecture, a French man came up to me and said the following.

> Reverend, I have translated all of the Hebrew and Greek texts of the Bible in its entirety. I can see through all the original meanings of the Bible as good as anyone else. This morning, I listened to your lecture, and all the words that you said were all correct without any fault. But one thing has been left out. Reverend has explained the meaning of the Greek word, Koinonia, as 'fellowship, cooperation, communication' only. I would like to add one more meaning, Reverend. The Greek word, Koinonia, has also the meaning of 'strong union'.

'Union!' That is you have be one with the Holy Spirit if you want to experience the same feeling as the Holy Spirit including the pain. We are one in Jesus and in the church, which is the body of Christ. But the Bible says that we become one with the Holy Spirit when we receive Jesus as our savior. Our spirit becomes one with the Holy Spirit, and we can not be separated from the Holy Spirit in all processes of our life.

The Holy Spirit lives with us while being in a union with our spirit. We sleep, wake up, eat and work along with the Holy Spirit. It is written in the Bible that '...if anyone does not have the Spirit of Christ, he does not belong to Christ.' (Romans 8:9)

Christ is within us and present in our spirit as the Holy Spirit. During my early days of ministry as a pioneer church builder, I left one chair among the chairs on the platform empty. No one could take this special seat. This was reserved to remind me in my mind that 'The Holy Spirit is in this worship with me'. When I stand on the platform, I always say 'Dear Holy Spirit, please sit on this seat' pointing to the empty seat. Then I would take the next seat. In reality, the Holy Spirit is not taking the seat; however, I had to firmly believe that the Holy Spirit is working on this ministry with me conscientiously. Nevertheless, I do not practice it anymore. The reason is because it became firm that I serve the Holy Spirit in my life.

For a long time, I have been conversing with the Holy Spirit. It is the Holy Spirit, who helps me to pray to God effectively. It is also the Holy Spirit, who helps me to testify to Christ with all my life. I appreciate and love the Holy Spirit. God, the Holy Spirit, has achieved everything so far. I do not fear anything anymore. It is because the Holy Spirit is with me always and I can overcome anything with the Holy Spirit. Our purpose in receiving the power from the Holy Spirit is to live the life of powerful witnesses to Jesus. (Acts 1:8)

Nevertheless, many ministers do not take steps with the Holy Spirit in their ministry and consequently, do not experience the church growth. The Holy Spirit provides everything needed for church growth. Here, everything, I meant, includes not only financial, administrative, and human matters but also the spiritual realm of peace, love, joy, sacred charisma, etc.

We only have the body, experience and knowledge. But the Holy Spirit gives us the vision, dream and the purpose, and strengthens us to carry out the process to achieve the goal with a positive attitude. The Holy Spirit plants a firm conviction within us. The Holy Spirit helps us to pray and reveals the truth of God in our mind and spirit. Thus, we have to work with the Holy Spirit always. We have an amazingly powerful and competent counselor. Because we are serving the Holy Spirit, it is unthinkable even in our dream to have an 'empty church' or 'sleeping church'.

The Bible says, 'But my righteous one will live by faith. And if he shrinks back, I will not be pleased with him' (Hebrews 10:38). By faith, you can paint in your mind the things, that you don't have, as if you have them in front of you. We are not ordinary people. We are the ones, who are united with the Holy Spirit. We are the ones, who have the vision and walk with the Holy Spirit, our Counselor. I implore you that you serve the Holy Spirit with all your heart. I also strongly advise you that you receive the Holy Spirit wholeheartedly. Never make a hasty decision by yourself. If you move in adherence to the guidance of the Holy Spirit, you can achieve your goal through the power of almighty God.

The Holy Spirit and Church Growth

The Holy Spirit is the spirit of the church and church growth. The Holy Spirit builds a church, grows it, and leads the church to evangelize. It is God, the Holy Spirit, who is the main leader in church growth.

The Holy Spirit regenerates people, builds a church, and uses trained people to make the church growth possible. Therefore, a church can not grow without the power of the Holy Spirit. John Wesley said, 'If a church refuses to be under the authority of the Holy Spirit and does not experience the work of the Holy Spirit, then the church is a complete replica, a fake, even if it prides itself on the tradition as a creed and succeeds glorious apostolic tradition.'

The Holy Spirit works within us even today. The Holy Spirit should be the ultimate source of church growth ('This is the word of the Lord to Zerubbabel: Not by might nor by power, but by my

Spirit, says the Lord Almighty.' Zechariah 4:6) The Holy Spirit uses agents, means and instruments to accomplish the task. The Holy Spirit uses the Words of Inspiration, people full of the Holy Spirit, and church of God as the spiritual institution.

The work of the Holy Spirit is the never-changing principle of church growth. The growth of the early churches is unthinkable aside from the power of the Holy Spirit. The early church grew rapidly from 120 people to 3,000, then 5,000, and then several ten thousands amazingly in a short period of time. The Acts lists 34 signs of the Holy Spirit and miracles as the motive for the church growth.

Nowadays, the fact, that the spiritual aspects of church growth is being emphasized, means the work of the Holy Spirit is being observed with full attention. Church growth scholars emphasize that, if a church does not win the spiritual battle and depends only on methodology, then the church can exert only insignificant influence. It is the same principle as a beautifully decorated automobile, which is made to perfection, is useless if it does not have gasoline in it. In spreading the Gospel and church growth, this gasoline is called 'the power of the Holy Spirit.

Church Growth Through Divine Healing

We can easily think of divine healing as a typical example of the power of the Holy Spirit. Through divine healing, God shows His grace and love to His people. Divine healing is a direct and supernatural work of God, and as such it is an essential element for church growth. If divine healing was not needed, why would Jesus heal diseases on the Sabbath withstanding the persecution and threat to His life from the Jews? Many people say that divine healing is not essential in the ministry; however, I believe it is wrong.

When Jesus commanded the disciples to go out and spread the Good News of the Kingdom of God, He also commanded to heal the sick. Healing by the power of God is the fundamental foundation of the Kingdom of God. Thus, if we don't experience the healing in the name of Jesus, we can not truthfully build a church on a solid rock.

Many people say that we could build a strong church because our church initiated a wonderful system of 'cell organization' early enough and utilized it effectively. However, if we did not act on the divine healing by faith in the name of Jesus, the cell organization would have lost most of its evangelizing power. The cell leaders of our church all pray for divine healing. I have collected all case histories of divine healing, that occurred in our church, and there were countless, numerous cases. These works of divine healing are the medical cases that have been verified by famous local physicians, and no one can deny that those were the work of God. The Holy Spirit pours out the love of God and the grace of Jesus upon us even now.

There are some ministers, who denounce and reject the power of divine healing in the Gospel. But they are making serious mistakes. The reason is because God uses divine healing as an instrument for the Gospel testimony. And in Exodus chapter 15 verse 26, God said, 'I am the Lord, who heals you'. Throughout the Old Testament, the healing works of God are shown in many books.

Furthermore, when Jesus, the one and only Son of God, came down to the earth and testified to the Kingdom of God through His words, He used divine healing as the most powerful instrument of His ministry. Two thirds of the works of Jesus recorded in the Bible are divine healings. There is a reason that Jesus would do His utmost to heal the sick. The most effective method to save people by God's love, mercy and grace is the divine healing.

When Jesus preached, 'Repent, for the kingdom of heaven is near' (Matthew 4:17) while sending out His 12 disciples, He also commanded them to heal the sick and told the same to the 70 disciples later on. Jesus included divine healing in His Gospel testimony by saying,

> Go into all the world and preach the good news to all creation. Whoever believes and is baptized will be saved, but whoever does not believe will be condemned. And these signs will accompany those who believe: In my name they will drive out demons; they will speak in new tongues; they will pick up snakes with their hands; and when they drink deadly poison, it will not hurt them at all; they will place their hands on sick people, and they will get well. (Mark 16:15-18)

As such, the relationship between the Gospel testimony and the work of divine healing is inseparable. Therefore, Gospel testimony and divine healing are the duties of a minister.

Looking at the church history, those early churches, which showed amazingly rapid growth, started to dwindle when they were careless about divine healing. During the first and the second centuries, the churches faithfully performed divine healings, and they continued to grow even under fierce persecution.

However, afterwards, the churches were negligent in performing divine healing, and around 600 A.D. the prayer for the sick almost vanished. Nowadays, we can only see the traces of healing in the Catholic ceremony, where the priest anoints the dying person.

Thus, the churches of today should be the first to show the world to drive out the demons and heal the sick in order to make the charisma of God and the Kingdom of God clear among us. Jesus said, 'But if I drive out the demons by the Spirit of God, then the kingdom of God has come upon you.' (Matthew 12:28) In other words, the proof of the coming of the kingdom of God is driving out demons and healing the sick.

Furthermore, one of the evidences, that proves Jesus Christ is the Messiah, is His healing ministry. John the Baptist, who was imprisoned, sent out two of his disciples to ask Jesus if He was indeed the Messiah. When the men came to Jesus, they said, 'John the Baptist sent us to you to ask, "Are you the one who was to come, or should we expect someone else?"' At that very time Jesus cured many who had diseases, sicknesses and evil spirits, and gave sight to many who were blind. So he replied to the messengers, 'Go back and report to John what you have seen and heard: The blind receive sight, the lame walk, those who have leprosy are cured, the deaf hear, the dead are raised, and the good news is preached to the poor. Blessed is the man who does not fall away on account of me.' (Luke 7:20-22) Therefore, we, the ministers, should study divine healing more thoroughly through the Bible and make use of healing as an instrument for preaching the good news. Then, your ministry is ready to leap to another dimension and to be led to success.

Success of our church can be attributed to not only proclaiming strong God's message but also praying for the sick continuously and diligently. From the moment, we started our church in Daejo-Dong, we concentrated on divine healing, and it became the main driving force for the success of our church.

Since this divine healing is manifested through the faith, whoever believes in it can receive it.

For this reason, the testimony for the gospel gets easier. Thus, when a servant of God works locally or goes overseas as a missionary, he/she should not exclude the ministry of divine healing. Especially for the missionaries, the divine healing makes or breaks the success of the whole mission. When carrying out the overseas mission, it is very difficult for the missionaries, who are not accustomed to the customs and habits of the mission country, to receive the trust of natives in a short time. Nevertheless, if the natives experience the healing from sickness and the demons are driven out, they will be much more willing to trust the missionaries, and as a result the preaching of the good news becomes possible. Divine healing is a quick means to penetrate into the minds of people.

Divine healing is not only a sign manifested to the believers but also one of the gifts of the Holy Spirit. When the saints receive the gift of divine healing, a wholesome power of divine healing is revealed through him/her. Even the saints, who received the gift of faith, can reveal the divine healing through his/her faith. Therefore, pastors should pray incessantly, 'Oh, Holy Spirit, please help me with the ministry of divine healing to heal the sick in my life.' This divine healing is the most effective way to let the people know of Jesus Christ's love and mercy.

I go on mission trips to Europe very often, and when I ask the congregation members to raise a hand if they are sick, about half of the people raises a hand even in places with excellent sanitary facilities like the Unites States or Europe. As a matter of fact, there is hardly anyone, who is not sick. Therefore, divine healing is an excellent means to testify to the gospel. There is hardly any deeper divine experience than being healed of a disease in the body. It is much more effective to experience one divine healing than hearing the sermon one hundred times and realizing 'God is living!' Thus, how graceful it is to lead many people suffering from sickness to salvation by healing them in the name of Jesus Christ!

In a special church revival meeting, if there is no prayer for the sick, the number of people attending the event hardly increases. On the other hand, if a special divine healing meeting is held, the number of attendees increase exponentially. Among them, there are some who are healed and some who are not healed. However, we should not be too much worried about those who are not healed, but we should glorify God with thanks for those who are healed.

Isn't it true that, although you have preached the gospel to 100 people, not all of them will believe? It is an excellent work if 50 people believe when you have preached to 100 people. On the average, it is still good if 20-30 people believe when 100 people heard the gospel. You would not give up on preaching the gospel because only 20-30 out of 100 people believe from the result of your evangelism. It is so likewise for the healing prayer. If 20-30 people are healed from your prayer with hands laid on the place of suffering and pain, it is a wonderful achievement. How amazing would it be to heal even one person whom the medical care in a hospital gave up on? Thus, we should not give up on the ministry of divine healing, which is a command of the Lord, because we can not heal all of them.

There is a particularly important point to be aware of in healing prayer. You should refrain from shaking or tapping the body of the sick or hitting with a fist or palm. It should be a simple healing prayer with the hand laid on the head. Principally, the sickness is a spiritual matter. Because our fight is not with the blood and flesh, we should not harm the body of the sick just because we hate the demons. Since our fight is spiritual, we can win the fight with our faith and prayer.

Therefore, we should do our utmost to manifest the work of divine healing by gently laying the hands on the place of pain and suffering and praying for the healing.

Divine healing is a powerful instrument in testifying to the gospel. The ministry of divine healing should be revived in today's church. Are you concerned that your church is not growing? Pray earnestly to empower you with divine healing. And with faith, continuously practice this divine healing. Many people will receive the gospel in their hearts through the work of divine healing, and your church will continuously grow.

The Work of the Holy Spirit for Church Growth

The Holy Spirit equips the saints as holy testifiers to Christ to participate in the ministry of the Lord. When a person is filled with the Holy Spirit, he/she can not stay still and do nothing. The person wants to do something for the Lord wholeheartedly and acts accordingly. The Holy Spirit not only moves people but also equips them spiritually to be powerful testifier to the gospel. However, the ministry of the Lord is not adequate with a desire. The Holy Spirit empowers those, who are called by the Lord, and helps them to do the work of the Lord. As the result, when a saint, who received the gift of the Holy Spirit, preaches the gospel, it is as if the words of God are pouring out through the saint's mouth. And when the saint, who received the gift of the Holy Spirit, carries out a service for the church, it is as if he/she has received a certain power from God.

The Holy Spirit is a person, who changes the atmosphere for the nonbelievers to be non-resistant and receptive to the gospel. The Holy Spirit defeats the work of satan, who has the power in the air, and works for the people to receive the grace of the gospel personally. It is the Holy Spirit, who causes the nonbelievers to be reborn. Without the Holy Spirit, no one can admit Jesus as the Lord.

Jesus himself said to Nicodemus, ' I tell you the truth, no one can enter the kingdom of God unless he is born of water and the Spirit.' (John 3:5) People spread the gospel, but it is the Holy Spirit, who makes people to be born again. Thus, the evangelists should anticipate the work of the Holy Spirit and react sensitively. The evangelism is the means by which to defeat satan's disobedience and impiety with the power of the Holy Spirit, i.e. the power of God's kingdom to resurrect the dead souls. The miracle of miracles is the miracle of regeneration, which makes the dead spirit to live again. This miracle can be carried out only by the Holy Spirit.

Since 1933, 80% of people, who have converted to Christianity, have done so by hearing the gospel from people, who have been filled with the Holy Spirit. People full of the Holy Spirit testify to the gospel with authority. The disciples of Jesus are good examples in this regard. It is for this reason that Jesus asked the disciples not to leave Jerusalem (Acts 1:4). They had to wait for the Holy Spirit, whom God the Father promised. In preaching the gospel, besides from studying the words of God and praying earnestly, it is important to have the power of the Holy Spirit come upon the nonbelievers. This will result in amazing fruits of the ministry.

Sometimes, I hear the rumor that 'When Pastor Yong Ki Cho dies, Yoido Full Gospel Church is over.' However, these rumors are just what they are – false rumors. The reason is because the person, who built and grew Yoido Full Gospel Church, is not me but God the Holy Spirit. Our church has tens of thousands of cell leaders, who are filled with the Holy Spirit and have protected and nurtured numerous lay Christians. Then, how can this church fall overnight? Yoido Full Gospel Church does not belong to any one person. This church is the church of God and the church, which the Holy Spirit protects. It is for this reason that we should welcome and serve the Holy Spirit in our lives everyday and have the desire to be filled with the Holy Spirit.

Having done so, we can live as those who testify to Christ and spread the gospel to the ends of the earth.

Depend on the Holy Spirit

Church growth is a will of God. However, it is impossible with our power alone. It is possible only when the Holy Spirit helps. If we welcome and receive the Holy Spirit as a person, the Holy Spirit will work with us as our truthful senior partner. As the leader of the ministry, the Holy Spirit will guide us. In order for that to happen, we have to ask earnestly for His help. Not with a formal attitude, but with a divine spirit and true heart, we have to recognize the Holy Spirit, the Counselor. Then, the work of the Holy Spirit will overflow, and we will experience the amazing power of healing the sick and driving out of bad spirits. Then, your church will be ready to leap to another higher dimension to grow healthy.

CHAPTER 3

Church Growth and Prayer

Prayer is the Driving Force of the Church Growth

Many people come to me and ask this question, 'How did you build such an enormous church?' People have an interest in our church in that it is world's largest church as a single church unit. Our church can accomodate 15,000 at the main sanctuary alone and has many other subsidiary churches. One of the reasons why our church has grown this huge is because of prayer. Above all, I devoted myself in praying while doing the ministry. My main interest as the senior pastor of this huge church is the relationship between God and myself. Many people think that prayer is to go forward to God and ask Him to give something. However, it is a part of a prayer and not all of the prayer. The most important purpose of prayer is to go in front of God and 'serve Him'.

Prayer Is Fellowship with God

God is almighty and omnipresent. In other words, He can do anything, know everything and is everywhere. What can this great God need? Nevertheless, God needs a very important thing. In 1 John 4:16, 'God is love'. If you love your wife, you will want to have a close relationship with her. And if you love your husband, you would naturally want to have the time for a close relationship with him.

Since God is love, He wants to have an association with His beloved children. That is one of the reasons that God created us humans. God created humans to be glorified through humans and to share the personal fellowship of love. We were created by the image of God. God built humans and breathed in His Spirit, and so we can have a living soul. Thus, humans can have spiritual dialogue and keep personal fellowship unlike other animals. Humans are creatures who were built to have fellowship with God.

Nowadays, not only lay Christians but pastors often say that they are too busy to have fellowship with God. 'When I have a time, I will pray and do what God wants me. However, right now, I have to visit homes of the congregation members and take care of our church. So I am too busy to pray.' This is indeed very wrong. Our ultimate purpose in our lives is to serve God and to have fellowship with Him. God loves all of you. God wants you to come in front of Him and have a dialogue together through prayer. In this respect, God needs us. People often ask me 'How many hours a day do you pray?' Of course, I live with the mind of praying all day, totally depending on the Holy Spirit. Before I go to bed, I always bind the bad spirits with prayer. Jesus Christ wants us to drive out the devils in His name.

I often shout out in prayer that 'You, the hindering satan, be gone without hindering me while I am sleeping, I command in the name of Jesus Christ.' Then, I have a dialogue with the Holy Spirit. 'Dear loving Holy Spirit, I recognize, welcome, serve, worship, and depend on you. Even when I am sleeping, please work on my spirit.' Surprisingly enough, when I wake up, I realize that my spirit was praising God even while my body was sleeping. When I depend on the Holy Spirit wholeheartedly, I apprehend and appreciate that the Holy Spirit is praying with wonderful praise through my spirit all night long. Even when my mind is taking a rest, I feel that my spirit is continuously praising God because of the Holy Spirit. We have to follow the Words of God in Ephesians 6:18, 'And pray in the Spirit on all occasions with all kinds of prayers and requests. With this in mind, be alert and always keep on praying for all the saints,' to make praying day and night our habit.

I also allocate my time to do what God wants me. For this purpose, I make it the first priority to pray to God before I do anything for the saints or the church. Prayer is the most important work for me. Pastors and may Christians should pray at the least one hour a day. I always say to the ministers, 'regularly pray to God everyday, and serve God with praying at the least 3 hours a day.'

I make all-out effort to pray at the least one hour a day amidst a hectic schedule. On a given average day, I pray at the least for 3 hours a day. Especially, prior to an important events domestically or overseas, I pray at the least for 5 hours. During the prayer, I ask no one to interrupt the prayer. So I instruct my secretary not to allow anyone to enter my prayer chamber.

In other words, except for the Lord, no one can enter my prayer chamber. The person, who should be the first in our lives, is God. There is no more important thing than serving and worshipping God.

When you do what God wants you, God will be glad and fill our heart with joy. Because many people do not allocate enough time to have fellowship with God, they do not understand the profound will of God. When I pray at the least for an hour for the needs of the saints, my heart would be throbbing with anticipation for God. If you sincerely want to know God deeper and to serve our Lord, allocate more time to pray to God.

There is a clear distinction between the prayer, asking God to give something, and the other prayer, thanking and praising the Lord for what He has given us. We should thank and praise God before asking Him incessantly to give something. When we pray with thanks and praise wholeheartedly, we are filled with the Holy Spirit and experience the peace from God. And we can experience the thrilling joy of being with God.

When I return to Korea from overseas crusade, documents that are piled up to my neck await me on my desk. And there are many accumulated things to do. However, I am unconcerned and serene. Since I think it is of the utmost priority to have fellowship with God, I pray to God before doing anything else. God is pleased with my sincere serving Him. Doing so, God pours His wisdom, knowledge, power and prudence on me. Then, He gives me an amazing conviction and courage to finish all the tasks that are piled up in the church.

However, in the case that God does not help me with His special grace, no one knows how long these tasks will take to finish. If God helps you, you can finish any tasks rapidly and easily. This is the very reason that I spend so much time to have fellowship with God. I am not concerned with other tasks in humanistic point of view. The reason is because any tasks can be finished appropriately if God helps us.

The Power of Prayer and Holiness

We receive the pardon for our sin by believing in Jesus Christ and justification from God. We do not receive the redemption by our good deeds but by the forgiveness and grace of God. And with the help of the Holy Spirit, we are sanctified. It is very important to be holy and pure in order to take after the image of Christ. We may be able to deceive the eyes of people; however, we can not hide anything from God. Thus, we have to live the life of good behavior always in front of God.

Humans can not assert their innocence on anything or anyone. Even between married couple, there are some secret parts that the wife or husband is hiding. However, we can not hide anything when we come forward in front of God. God knows everything. So, whenever I pray, I open my heart and profess everything that I am hiding from my wife, children, relatives or friends. Then, the Holy Spirit cleanses me with the blood of the Lord, and the process of sanctification begins. Holiness is more important than anything for Christians.

Since our body is a temple of the Holy Spirit, we have to be holy (1 Corinthians 6:19) – 'Do you not know that your body is a temple of the Holy Spirit, who is in you, whom you have received from God? You are not your own;'. We can live the life of holiness by confessing our sins always and depending on the Holy Spirit.

Some time ago very tragic events took place in American Christianity. Several very famous pastors resigned due to their unholy behaviors, making a large black mark in the history of American Christianity. It was a huge shock to many Christians, who were watching this mishap. Even recently, a very famous evangelist resigned from pastorship. One of his close friends worked together with me. He and I made several television appearances while evangelizing in the country circuit. He repeatedly mentioned this to me. 'The saints in Korea really pray a lot.' I asked then, 'well, don't your Christian organizations pray?' He answered, 'Pray? Don't even mention it. We are always occupied with so many tasks. The evangelist, who stepped down just recently, would shed his tears in front of television and pray fervently. However, when the television recording is over, he laughs and jokes with us, completely forgetting what he prayed. Of course, there is hardly any prayer.' I asked again in disbelief, 'then, didn't you people earnestly pray even in front of the television?' I was very shocked while conversing with him.

Those who pray get forgiveness upon confessing their sins right away even if they might sin again and again. With the work of the Holy Spirit, they win over the sins and live the life of holiness. But, hearing directly from their mouths, I found out that they did not pray or care about praying.

If they prayed before working on their ministerial tasks, I believe the evangelist could not be so immoral to have to resign from the pastorship.

I honestly confess everything when I pray. I confess everything that happened in my daily life. Then the process of sanctification begins. I become cleansed of my sins by the precious blood of Jesus Christ, and the Holy Spirit displays every scene in my life to me. Although the Holy Spirit is our Counselor, He admonishes us for our sins as well as keeping account of our righteousness for the judgment day. (John 15:26, 16:8)

Prayer enables us to hear the voice of the Holy Spirit, therefore it is essential to live the holy life in Christ. Christian faith without the righteousness and holiness loses its foundation. Even if we serve with devotion and know the Bible well enough to recite every verse in it, we will lose our Christian foundation if we do not live the life of righteousness and holiness. Thus, we the pastors should stress the importance of holiness and righteous life in our sermons, while relying on the Holy Spirit. This is absolutely necessary. God has said, 'Be holy because I, the Lord your God, am holy.' (Leviticus 19:2) And Jesus prayed, 'Sanctify them by the truth'. (John 17:17) In other words, the Bible tells us that the way for us humans to be holy is not by our cultivation of the mind or morality but by the words of God and prayer. (1 Timothy 4:5) Therefore, we can be holy if we make the words of God as our guide post and act on what we pray. This is the reason why we should pray at the least one hour a day to confess everything.

When you pray more than an hour, you will feel the indwelling of the Holy Spirit. You will feel that wellspring of joy is overflowing causing righteousness and cleansing by the precious blood of the Lord. This experience is only possible with prayer. Many people say, 'I was baptized by the Holy Spirit and speak in tongues.' However, this can only be our outside appearance and cause us to be boastful to a degree of arrogance. Many people, who speak in tongues but have not changed their habits or lifestyle, should repent. The source of the power of the Holy Spirit is 'holiness'. Therefore, if you are reborn and pray in tongues while being baptized by the Holy Spirit, the speaking in tongues can become a very necessary gift of the Holy Spirit for living the sacred life.

I pray in tongues very often. It has been a great plus in my prayer life (1 Corinthians 14:4). When I pray in tongues, I can open my deep thoughts to God. Although it is a wonderful blessing to pray in tongues, the gift of speaking in tongues is not so useful in our life if we lack in righteousness and holiness. Thus, we should take after our Christ and become mature by being filled with the Holy Spirit everyday (Ephesians 4:13).

Prayer and God's Answer

Answering prayers is one of God's principles. God wants to talk with us through our prayer. God would be glad to answer everything we pray in the name of Jesus. The counseling center of our church is staffed with a trained lay counselors 24 hours a day to offer counseling service over the telephone. But even a few years ago, the counseling center was staffed by pastors, who were on call alternative nights for the people in desperate situations. They advised these people who wanted counseling and prayed for them.

My wife was in pain because of an infection in her bosom after having the second child. However, the doctor said he can not cure her. So, I laid my hands upon her and prayed for her healing. Then, my wife burst out with laughter. I asked her, 'why are you laughing?' She answered, 'I don't have the faith that God will heal me through your prayer.' So I told my wife, 'Don't think of me as your husband but as a holy servant of God.' After a while, she answered back, 'I have known you for a long time. How can I think of you as a holy man of God?' And then she continued to laugh.

This is the problem. Many wives of pastors do not regard their husbands as holy men of God. The reason is because they know all about their husband including their weaknesses. Despite the fact that I prayed several times for the healing of my wife, my wife was not cured. No, indeed it was getting worse. Then one night, I called the counseling center to see if the pastors were doing their work alright. Since I realized that they might recognize my voice, I asked my wife to call for me. My wife pinched one side of her nose to disguise her voice and called them. The counseling pastor, who answered the phone, said the following as soon as he answered.

'Sister, what troubles are you having? God is almighty. God can cure you.' Then, my wife earnestly said, 'I have this infection in my bosom, oozing the pus. And, it is not getting any better.' The pastor said, 'Sister, lay your hands on the place of suffering. Then I will pray for you.'

My wife did exactly what she was told. He prayed wholeheartedly for her. I could hear my wife replying with 'Amen. Amen.' to the prayer of the pastor over the telephone. My wife was very serious even after receiving the healing prayer. I said the following, seeing that my wife had a funny look.

> The person you just listened to is my disciple. Furthermore, he just graduated from a theological school and has been appointed to his position of a pastor in training. He is a freshman. He does not even know how he can pray well. You were not cured even though I prayed several times for you. How can you expect to get healed by his prayer?

Then, the next morning, when my wife woke up, her sickness was gone without a trace. I saw with my very own eyes an answer to a prayer. You have to believe that God would answer whenever you pray. If you do not believe, you can not get anything answered. Prayer is for the 'believers'. Most people pray earnestly, but they do not believe in God's answer. Thus, there are many occasions that they do not experience the answer to their prayers. They would be praying for a certain problem. But believing that their prayer has not been answered, they pray the next day, the next day with the same prayer item. Soon enough they would have prayed over a year for the same problem. This praying style should be changed because it lacks the key element of faith in God's answer.

The Bible says, 'Therefore I tell you, whatever you ask for in prayer, believe that you have received it, and it will be yours.' (Mark 11:24) Thus, after praying, you should acknowledge verbally, 'God, I believe you answered my prayer, thank you.' When you believe in what you prayed for, you will experience God's answering.

Prayer and the Authority to Drive out demons

Nowadays, churches have been a little careless in teaching how to drive out bad spirits. Of course, any power of satan has been defeated completely by accomplishing perfect redemption on the Cross by Jesus Christ already 2000 years ago. (Colossians 2:15) However, the satan still tries to lure people like a roaring lion before receiving the final judgment and being thrown in the lake of burning sulfur forever (1 Peter 5:8, Revelation 20:10). Thus, we have to continuously drive out the already disarmed satan.

Jesus Christ gave the church and all Christians the authority and responsibility to drive out satan (Luke 10:19). However, it is not to fight and win over satan's throngs with our power. Since Jesus Christ already defeated satan and his throngs, we can drive out the bad spirits just by confronting them in the name of Jesus Christ, our Lord. (James 4:7) This is the reason that Jesus said before His ascension into Heaven, 'And these signs will accompany those who believe: In my name they will drive out demons' (Mark 16:17).

The task to drive out demons is very important since Jesus, our Lord, asked us to do so along with the Great Commission. Satan spreads out all bad spirits all over the world in order to lure even the believers.

Among these bad spirits are 'luring spirit', 'dirty spirit', 'wicked spirit', 'lying spirit', 'fortunetelling spirit', etc. So we have to confront these wicked hordes and drive them out.

We have to confront them with prayer since these hordes are spiritual. Knowing this, the bad spirits try to hinder our prayer and challenge us. Thus, before we have fellowship with the Holy Spirit, we have to confront and drive out the hindering satan and his throngs. It is for this reason that I emphasize the need to pray at least one hour a day. When I pray, there are times when all my body is itching and my joints are aching for no reason. And then I feel sleepy as well as having the headache as well as having the following thoughts.

> Pastor Cho, why don't you go to bed now. Yes, you can pray tomorrow again. Your body is aching and you are tired. You have spent so many hours praying. So take a rest today, or how about praying a little later?

Satan creeps in my mind with such ideas. Then I pray and pray to defeat the force hindering my prayer. Soon enough many miscellaneous thoughts occupy my mind. Nevertheless, when I push aside such thoughts and pray continuously. I feel freedom at last. The Holy Spirit dwells in me, and a real prayer begins.

Since many people finish praying before the barriers of bad spirits hindering the prayer are broken down, their prayers do not reach the throne of God. Before their prayers reach the throne of God, they wrap up their prayers.

It is much better to pray even for 5 minutes or 10 minutes a day than not to pray at all. However, even in this case, if they pray 5 minutes or 10 minutes for the sake of formality, these people just scratched the surface and can not truly experience the power of prayer.

When I first started out my ministry, I prayed for 5 hours a day always. Doing so, I could defeat the power of satan and achieve the church growth. At that time to start my church on the outskirt of Seoul, many village people were worshipping a guardian God. When I landed there, A female shaman, who was worshipping a guardian idol, approached and challenged me. From that time on, I had a fierce spiritual fight with the shaman. When the shaman surrendered finally, our church began to grow remarkably in that area.

Pastors should pray at the least one hour a day with full concentration. You will be surprised if I strongly recommend you to pray at least 3 hours a day. Thus, I will start with asking you to pray for one hour a day. I myself felt bored when I started to pray for an hour. When I look at the watch thinking that I prayed for a fairly long time, it was only for 5 minutes. So I started to pray again and looked at my watch again thinking that it was clearly past an hour. Well, it was only for 20 minutes. Likewise, it is often very hard to pray for an hour with complete concentration.

Jesus prayed all night long before carrying the Cross to the hill of Gethsemane. When Jesus came down the hill after praying, He found His disciples sleeping deeply. Jesus said, 'Could you men not keep watch with me for one hour?' he asked Peter. 'Watch and pray so that you will not fall into temptation.' (Matthew 26:40-41)

We call this prayer the 'Gethsemane Prayer'. I humbly ask you to pray for an hour a day in order not to fall into temptation. With prayer, you can bind and tie up satan to throw it out. So, when you pray over an hour, you can experience fellowship with the Holy Spirit and true revival in your church.

Prayer for the Neighbor and Nation

We can not realistically expect pastors to visit the saints' homes and pray for them whenever they are troubled. However when you pray for the saints, the work of the Holy Spirit manifests transcending time and space. Thus, you have to pray for relatives and missionaries who are overseas. This prayer has the same effect as if you are praying in front of them. We have to pray for the nation, its people in various positions and fields. Our prayer becomes the main driving force to save the nation and its people.

1 Samuel 7:3-17 speaks about the assembly at Mizpah. Even though Israel had no recourse but was about to be destroyed by the attack of the Philistines, Samuel gathered all Israelites at Mizpah and asked for their repentance with fasting and praying. One characteristic of this assembly at Mizpah was that it was a prayer assembly that a leader called. Considering the fact that Philistine army were armed with steel weapons and Israel had no steel weapons nor warriors, the defeat of Israel was a matter of time.

However, encouraged by Samuel's intercessory prayer, all Israelites gathered, repented, and prayed with fasting, God gave them a great victory.

Our church prays for the salvation of the nation and its people as well as North Koreans, prosperity and development of the nation, society and culture, domestic and overseas churches, and ministers in every worship service. With this prayer theme, we pray on Wednesday, Sunday and every early mornings. In addition, we pray all night on Friday and at every cell meetings for the nation and its people. Our grand-scale unified prayer saved our nation several times during hardships. When Korea was holding the 1988 Seoul Olympics, North Korea was preparing notorious terror schemes. They wanted to unleash terror or guerilla warfare to devastate the Olympic Games. Thus, our church decided to hold a grand-scale prayer assembly and persuaded our congregation members. So we held a grand assembly at Yoido Square just next to our church, and 1 million Christians participated in this assembly. We prayed all day that the Olympics would take place without any tragic incidents. Under the hot sun rays throughout all day, we prayed for the evangelisation of our nation and the success of the Olympics.

As the result, the 1988 Summer Olympics held in Seoul ended with the greatest success in the history of the Olympics. Whenever our nation was in danger due to national security matters, we stood up firm with our prayer. Prayer defeats the power of satan and brings on the peace of God. All the people in Korea, especially we Christians, know the power of prayer very well. Therefore, whenever there is a trouble in the nation, all our churches in Korea gather together in unison to pray.

Then, we see amazing things happening. Prayer is our request to

God to intervene in our matters. Prayer moves the hands of God. Thus, we can experience the power of God working in our personal life, life of the church, and the life of this nation by praying.

Prayer is the Key to Church Revival

Prayer is the most important key to church growth and survival. One of the most distinguished characteristics of early Korean Christianity is that the saints gathered together for praying in every early mornings. All Christians throughout Korean peninsula gathered around a Presbyterian church in Pyeongyang in 1906. When they assembled to pray, the Holy Spirit was upon them and they began to confess their sins. With this turning point, a flame of prayer spread all over the country, and a remarkable history of revival in Korean churches occurred with so many people converting to Christianity.

I started out my ministry at Daejo-Dong, a slum area located on the outskirt of Seoul. Under a donated U.S. Army tent, we had worship services. The memory of spending all night in prayer is still fresh in my mind. More or less careless of the bitter cold winds in the winter, I threw a blanket over me and prayed so many days, kneeling next to the pulpit. Soon enough several Christians joined me in prayer. And again soon enough, 50 Christians joined me in the all night prayer. These praying partners made the root of my ministry very strong and firm.

Presently, our church has thousands of people, who have become believers in Christ and many more are saved every month. Many saints, who were trained well in our church, are serving faithfully in churches of various denominations.

This is another factor influencing the growth of all Korean churches. The reason for the growth of our church in various ways can be attributed not to any human power or means but to our complete dependence and reliance on God and prayer.

I learned the importance of intercessory prayer through the process of church growth. The priority for intercessory prayer was firstly, for the Korean people, next, for the nation, and lastly, for myself. We should not only learn how to pray but also know how to live our lives through our prayer. Jesus told us, 'pray constantly.' This is an impossible command to those, who are not interested in church revival. However, if you long for the lost souls to be saved or desire to lead the people of this nation to the Lord, praying life is an absolutely necessary element.

Like most churches, our church starts with an early morning worship service at 5 am and a couple of hours of prayer time to start the day. Prayer is very important in our lives. Prayer means a fellowship with God. Also, on every Friday evenings, we have a time for praying all night. Many people, who visit our church for all night Friday prayer meeting, are amazed at seeing so many people filling the main sanctuary to its capacity.

We have 7 Sunday worship services, and all saints prepare for the worship service by prayer. When the worship service begins, our glorified and almighty Lord is present with us. So if the saints prepare for the worship service by prayer, they will experience an amazing grace of the Lord.

I ask the saints to confess their sins before delivering God's message. The reason is because, when we confess our sins and pray, the work of the Holy Spirit opens our believing hearts wide open to receive the true words of God.

Our church has the time for all our saints to pray in unison during Sunday worship. At this time, the prayer in unison sounds like a thunder. Revelation 14:2 records, 'And I heard a sound from heaven like the roar of rushing waters and like a loud peal of thunder.' Pastors, who visit our church to preach a sermon, are often caught off guard with the strong power of the Holy Spirit working magnificently during our worship service. A pastor told me how he experienced such a strong presence of God for the first time with eyes in tears, 'Reverend Cho, God is right here. I could feel the presence of God.'

Testifying to the words of God all around the world, many servants of the Lord ask me often, 'What method do you suggest to revive our church like Korean churches?' Before giving my answer to this question, I would like to share a story of a pastor. The pastor spends so much time to associate with his congregation members after Sunday worship service, he is so burn-out that he can not even pray the next morning. Of course, having time for congregation members is also important. However, there cannot be a revival, if our efforts are not supported by prayer. Thus, if you want revival in your church wholeheartedly, you should have more time for prayer. I make our new believers realize the importance of prayer and stress the importance of making prayer their lifestyle.

However, if I don't pray, they would not pray as well. Since most of our new believers came to know Jesus through our cell organization, they are learning the importance of prayer personally through their cell leader.

One thing that I know from the history of church is that once a revival begins through the prayer movement, a prayer for continuous revival should be continued. Nevertheless, once the revival begins most people think that the revival will continue and become negligent in praying. From the revival history of Western churches, after a few years of revival, people took the revival for granted and neglected praying, which they earnestly and religiously performed at the time of initiating the revival. Likewise, when the passionate flame of prayer is put out, the wave of revival retreats and it's back to square zero as before.

Here, 'the wave of revival' can be likened and explained by a driving principle of an automobile. In order to start a vehicle, we press on the acceleration pedal. If we take our foot off the pedal, the car can move for a short while. What is the reason that a car can move even for a short distance after the gas pedal is not pressed on? It is because of the principle of momentum. However, if the pedal is not pressed on, the car will stop. Thus, we have to be careful not to put out the flame of revival, which starts as an answer to our prayer. If we forget about the prayer, that brought the revival, the revival will soon stop like the automobile without a pressed pedal. Thus, our congregation members and I should continue to devote ourselves for church revival and growth until the day of Jesus' Advent with the mind of being one.

For Continuous Flame of Revival

Do you know the reason for the amazing revival in our church? That's because of prayer. Prayer makes the flame of church revival fiery. As long as the saints pray incessantly, the flame of church revival will continue to burn brightly. The work of the Holy Spirit can occur anywhere, and so a revival can happen in any church. However, if we don't prepare instruments for the revival with prayer, the Holy Spirit can not work. Prayer is the most important driving force of church revival. I hope that a flame of prayer will burn continuously in your church.

CHAPTER 4

Church Growth and the Sermon

A Sermon is an Essential Element for the Church Growth

Sermon is like his life for pastors. Sermon is an important key to successful ministry. It is not exaggerating to say church growth depends on the sermon of a pastor. When a pastor delivers a sermon, there is a non-negotiable purpose. That is the task to lead the listeners to receive Jesus Christ as their savior. In addition, it has the objective of leading the believers to a deeper faith in God.

The Importance of a Sermon

A sermon is not a monologue. It has to be aware of the audiences and the circumstances. I can not forget the mistakes I made when I was beginning my ministry. Often the mistake made by the pastors during their first year of ministry is to boast of their sermon skills. Once I wanted to deal with Kierkegaard, a Danish philosopher. I have read his existential philosophical theory and wanted to preach his main points in a sermon. I thought this was an awesome message. However, against my expectation, the responses of the listeners were rather cold. After the sermon, I came into my office with disappointment. Then, a philosophy professor came to see me with a guide of a saint. I hoped secretly to myself that he would compliment me on my sermon. On the contrary, he criticized me severely.

> Pastor Cho, we are living in the age of knowledge specialization. I am devoting myself to studying philosophy as a philosophy professor. When people like myself come to church, it is not to listen to a clumsy philosophy lecture but to hear the specialized words of the Bible.
>
> Pastor, you should be a specialist in the Bible. Then, all other intellectuals will listen to your sermon.

The sincere advice of this professor annoyed me vfor a while, but it beame a great blessing a long time after. Pastors should be specialists of the word of God. In other words, they should be specialists in giving sermons. And they have to devote all their energy in preparing and studying the words of God, realizing that only the words of God can make people's souls alive and lives abundant.

Pastors do not know everything. They should be specialists of God's words. The message of a pastor should not hit the air in vain. A pastor should have a clear purpose for his/her sermon.

Purpose of a Sermon

When the Apostle Paul was passing Miletus for the last time in his days of gray hair, Paul sent for the elders of the church in Ephesus. When they arrived, he said to them,

> You know how I lived the whole time I was with you, from the first day I came into the province of Asia. I served the Lord with great humility and with tears, although I was severely tested by the plots of the Jews. You know that I have not hesitated to preach anything that would be helpful to you but have taught you publicly and from house to house. (Acts 20:18-20)

This words of Paul show a sincere and genuine image of a pastor. Anything for a flock of sheep, the pastor should preach publicly and from house to house.

How wonderful his words are and how honorable is this declaration? Nowadays, many pastors are not delivering useful messages to the flock of sheep because of denominational dogmas or prestige and status. Moreover, it is sad to see them flogging their flock of sheep.

Although I have done my utmost to follow the dogmas and creeds of my denomination during my ministry, if I find some fresh grass to feed my sheep where the dogmas and creeds of my denomination have not reached, I take it and feed my sheep, often risking my neck. When I understood the threefold blessing as the gospel of Jesus Christ first and testified to it courageously to the saints, I received bitter criticism from many people. Some partner in ministry spent a fortune publishling a book of critisism and distributed it among fellow pastors. There was a bitter attack and criticism on the idea of the threefold blessing in that book.

However, after I shed the Biblical light on the gospel that I was testifying and realized the benefit of this gospel without being contrary to the Bible, I testified to it publicly, personally or at the saints' homes without any reservation. Pastors should graze the pastures from Genesis to Revelation to find nutritional grass for their flock of sheep day and night and lead them to green pastures and fresh wellsprings. And if it is useful, the pastor should be open to ideas from any source. Then, he should digest the idea before feeding them to his sheep. The interest of his sheep should be upheld with the life of the pastor. Thus, the purpose of a sermon is to provide spiritual benefits and to save people from spiritual death.

The Contents of a Sermon

The pastors should deliver a message of 'faith', 'hope' and 'love' above all. It is because the most needy things for the people, who live the hopeless life of disbelief, are faith, hope, and love. However, some servants of God proclaim a message of admonishment always. Of course, such messages to make people repent for their sins are needed. However, we have to remember that only a message that brings the light of faith, hope, and love can change a person.

Today, many people are living life in darkness and broken homes without faith, hope and love. We have to give back these people and families the faith, hope and love that come from God so as to recover their original status. Even if a person or family is in deepest despair, we can make the person or family go on the road to recovery and enjoy a new life by planting faith, hope and love in them.

When a servant of God visits a congregation member's home, he/she can easily find that many people are suffering from so much pain due to doubt and fear. 'Will my company go bankrupt?' 'will I be laid off?' 'will I lose the trust?' 'will I be deserted?', etc. People are under doubt and fear. Moreover, some people are suffering from neurotic insomnia. There are many more people, who are suffering from these problems, nowadays because of the instability in just about every aspect of life, politics, economics, society, etc. Thus, the pastor should remove the bomb of doubt and fear that satan plants in people's minds by delivering God's words of promise for abundant life. There is a reason, that I cry out in my sermon, 'God is good. Believe in the good God.'

> Which of you, if his son asks for bread, will give him a stone? Or if he asks for a fish, will give him a snake? If you, then, though you are evil, know how to give good gifts to your children, how much more will your Father in heaven give good gifts to those who ask him! (Matthew 7:9-11)

With these good words of Bible to tell the saints of 'good God' repeatedly, we can get rid of the doubt and fear that satan planted in people's minds. When we testify to the 'good God' among the saints, it becomes the decisive element not only to help your ministry to be successful but also to lead more people to the Lord.

However, there is something that needs to be done first. Before anything else, the pastor himself/herself should get rid of doubt and fear by recognizing the good God. It is impossible for you to help others be free from doubt and fear, if you have fallen in to doubt and fear yourself. Having the good God as the source of your life and solving many problems along with God, you yourself have to be free from doubt and fear before you can help others.

One of the crucial reasons, for the phenomenal growth of the Yoido Full Gospel Church is that it planted faith, hope, and love deeply in the minds of the saints through the gospel. 'Dear friend, I pray that you may enjoy good health and that all may go well with you, even as your soul is getting along well.' (3 John 1:2) Through these words, we can see that God blesses not only our soul but health and every aspects of life. In other words, God blesses us threefoldly. For those people living a desperate life, these words shed a bright light.

For those people, who could not believe in anything, had no hope in life and could not even think of a warm love, these words made them meet the 'good God'. Then, a blue print of hope and love was drawn in their hearts, and they began to lead other people to our church.

The main reason, that Yoido Full Gospel Church could grow so much despite many hardships, is because it changed people's hearts. It is not because of the nice scenery along the Han river. It is not because of its magnificent building. The reason, many people come to our church changing the bus or subway two or three times whether it was snowing or raining, is because there is a message of freedom for them.

The Structure of a Sermon

The pastor is like a cook. Even if there is a lack of an ingredient, an excellent cook can prepare a great dish. A cook needs various ingredients and spices. Likewise, when a pastor 'cooks' his/her sermon, the word of the Bible is the main ingredient and all the things in the nature can be regarded as spices. It depends on the pastor how to deliver a wonderful sermon with these materials. Then, what should we do in order for us to 'cook' the words of God well? First of all, we have to contemplate on the words and catch the main theme of the message while praying. Next, we have to structure our sermon by introduction, body, and conclusion parts so as to deliver the sermon logically and reasonably.

Introduction Part of a Sermon

The introduction part of a sermon is an important part that can determine the success and failure of the entire sermon. When we eat food, we usually have a sip of a soup first before we delve into eating rice. If there is no soup, we would have a taste of a watery source of Kimchi. It is like an appetizer. Western food also has an appetizer like a salad and then the main dish. In a sermon, the introduction part functions like an appetizer such as a soup or a salad. The preacher should draw the attention of the listeners within 5 minutes of his/her sermon. When the preacher succeeds in drawing an undivided attention of the listeners, he/she can keep their attention until the end of the sermon.

Napoleon used this effectively to overcome a dangerous situation. It happened when he was crossing over the Alps. The soldiers were dead tired climbing the mountains. When they reached the summit, they were also very thirsty, but there was no supply of water for them. In this dire situation, soldiers were very reluctant to go down the mountain to do battle. At this time, Napoleon delivered an impromptu speech.

> When we are about halfway down this mountain, there is a world famous peach orchard. This peach is so sour, people, who have eaten this peach, can not have food for several days because their teeth are set on edge from the sourness of the peach.

As soon as the soldiers heard this speech, their mouths began to water. After they heard Napoleon's speech, the soldiers gained new courage and began to climb down the mountain for the next battle. Likewise, the preachers should be able to satisfy the needs of the listeners in a fairly short time. For that purpose, preachers should study the words of God incessantly and heed the voice of the Holy Spirit.

The Holy Spirit watches over the mind of people and gives the wisdom to the preachers to draw the listeners' attention completely.

Body Part of a Sermon

After wetting the mouth, now is the time to have the main course. Food has to taste good no matter what. Although the color and shape may look tasty and very nutritional, people seldom eat the food if it lacks in taste. It is the same for the body of a sermon. No matter how useful the message is and how eloquently the message was delivered, it does not guarantee continued attention of people. A sermon has to contain a deep and meaningful taste.

The body of a sermon is the life of a message. Even if you fail in other parts of a sermon, you should not fail in this part. The body is the essence of the message that you implant on the minds of the listener. Thus, we should place the essence of the message on a cutting board and cut it in pieces that are just about the right size to chew with the knife of the Holy Spirit.

In order to deliver a 'tasteful' sermon, we have to research how to 'cook' the message of the Bible. The three methods can be listed. They are 'expository sermon', 'textual sermon', and 'thematic sermon'. The 'expository sermon' gives a didactic and edifying sermon through explaining the Biblical text in terms of the background, textual meaning and annotation or commentary. The ministers should be prepared to deliver a dynamic and living message to change the life of not only themselves but the listeners.

The 'textual sermon' extracts and preaches the main point from several verses of the Bible. For example, let's suppose we are preaching on one of the most famous verse in the Bible, John 3:16, 'For God so loved the world that he gave his one and only Son, that whoever believes in him shall not perish but have eternal life.' For the body of a sermon on this verse, we have to choose the most suitable message by listening to the voice of the Holy Spirit. Then, afterwards, start with the question of 'who is God?' since the verse also starts with 'For God so loved the world'. We can say that God is omnipotent, omnipresent to create the heaven and earth as well as all the creatures and is our father. Secondly, speaking on the 'world', we can also preach that humans have betrayed the trust of God since Adam and Eve and corrupted by teaming up with satan to pursue the lust of the body and eyes as well as the fame in this cursed land to end up in a total ruin. Thirdly, it is now the time to talk about 'God's love'. God did not spare His son to give the eternal life for us, who deserve to die of sins, and Jesus Christ carried all our sins on the Cross and gave us the redemption by hanging on the Cross. Thus, by the blood of Jesus, we, the humans, can now receive the eternal life and testify how great the love of God is. Finally, we can explain the meaning of 'eternal life' to finish the body of a sermon. As aforementioned the 'textual sermon' extracts certain parts of the Biblical text to explain the Biblical meaning of the text.

However, a 'thematic sermon' is different. The 'thematic sermon' first sets out a theme and expands on it for its explanation. Here, we can use an inductive or deductive reasoning. This 'thematic sermon' can deal with a wide range of problems and adapt to the needs and requests of the listeners easily. On the other hand, it is important for us how to divide the body of a sermon.

Usually, the body part is separated into 3 or 4 main points. If it is necessary, we can expand it to 5 main points. Nevertheless, if there are many main points, the sermon tends to get longer and lose its emphasis.

Conclusion Part of a Sermon

Now, the concluding part of a sermon should finish up the sermon with a refreshing taste. After eating the main meal, we drink barley tea or a piece of fresh fruit for the refreshing taste in the mouth. Likewise, the concluding part of a sermon should be brief and clear, and as if we are gaining our composure again, it should be able to recapitulate the message spoken in the body part of a sermon.

Lately, many pastors, who have expounded and delivered a good message in the body part of a sermon, often fail because they do not explain the relationship between the message content and the listeners in the end. All people love to hear something about what they are involved in and have a relationship with. Thus, the pastors should clarify how his/her sermon is directly related to the life of the listeners. So, a total time spent on a sermon should be between 30 and 40 minutes desirably. It is said that the attention span of an adult is at the most 40 minutes. Thus, a long sermon can backfire.

Illumination by the Bible and the Holy Spirit

Pastors should put their lives on the line to testify to the words of God. It requires a tremendous effort to bring a new, living message, full of spirit, to the listeners.

I spare no effort in obtaining the material for a sermon always in every aspects of life. I have read all the books that I can possibly handle following the guidance of God. There are so many books on the shelves of my study room. However, I can not read all books realistically due to the constraints of finance and time. I subscribe to good Christian weekly or monthly journals and magazines, Reader's Digest, as well as such international news magazines as Time and Newsweek. Especially, I read new books of world famous pastors to make it the food for my mind. Moreover, I record many daily events in my notebook that could be of concern to Christians. I record everything that could be of help in testifying to the words of God.

I think it is most important to ask the Holy Spirit to help. The ultimate shepherd of a flock of sheep is the Holy Spirit, and the master of the Harvesting servants is also the Holy Spirit. The Holy Spirit lives in the church today, is clothed with the church, and works in the church. It is impossible to deliver a useful message to the saints without the help of the Holy Spirit, much like trying to fly over the Pacific ocean without boarding an airplane. Thus, the preachers should hang on to the Holy Spirit like a hungry baby holds on to the breast of his/her mother.

When all the preparation is complete, the message comes finally from the Bible. When we continue the life of studying the words of God, the Holy Spirit brings the message from the Bible. It is a life-long task for the pastors to study and search for a message. One should not be overconfident, saying 'this should be enough.' Just like a woman pearl diver fights the waves and other dangers of the sea with her life, the walk of pastors seeking a good message should not stop at any point.

A Sermon and A Parable

Charles H. Spurgeon, the famous English preacher, explained 'If we use the analogy of a sermon as a house, then a parable is like its window. Too few windows will make the house too dark like a prison cell. Too many windows will make the house so bright that it will lose its coziness.'

A parable has an amazing effect to make the words of God easily understood and prevent the listeners from becoming bored. The more experienced the preacher is, the more he/she uses parables. Although stories like 'once upon a time...' are not so useful anymore, a parable describing a modern life is still very effective. Among parables, a personal testimony of the preacher has a tremendous attractiveness to it as it grabs the listeners' attention.

The most urgent need that I feel in the ministry is the lack of parables as a material of sermons. Sermon materials or parable materials are used as soon as I get a hold of them as if fire woods are burnt and used up soon enough in a fireplace. Thus, a preacher should seek a parable with his/her eyes and ears wide open. One of the reasons that the words of Jesus were so imprinted in the minds of people is because He used the parables, that described common events to common people, to explain the gospel of the kingdom of God.

Requirements of a Preacher

Up to now, I have mentioned several things related to a sermon. Additionally, I would like to state a few things that a preacher should attain. As for a chef, he/she uses not only the taste but smell, vision and even hearing in order to prepare the dishes. In order to make it desirable to eat, a food should taste good in the mouth. and it should look tasty and make a chunky sound as if chewing Kakdoogi (a diced Radish Kimchi).

Likewise, a preacher should keep a tidy appearance as a spokesman of God's words. If the hair is dishevelled and the clothes are wrinkled, people do not regard the message as palatable even if the words coming from the preacher's mouth are good for the soul. Thus, a servant of God should keep a neat appearance in front of the public. However, I do not mean to wear extravagant and luxurious clothes.

Also, one should use standard language when testifying to the gospel. I make a constant effort to use standard language. If a preacher uses a dialect, the listeners, who do not understand the dialect, would be lost in amidst the sermon while trying to figure out the meaning of the dialect. Thus, we should use the standard language and gentle words. This is like using vision and hearing to increase our appetite.

I have been ministering over 40 years, but my mind is burdened on Saturdays. It is not easy to make a dish, that looks and smells delicious with a good nutritional value. Before the sermon, I outline the introduction, body and conclusion of the sermon to practice several times to myself.

Then, it becomes clear to me that this parable is not appropriate here and this word is not proper. It would not be overexaggerating to say that a preacher, who does not preach to himself/herself, does not deserve to stand in front of public to preach.

The most important thing in a sermon is to obey the voice of the Holy Spirit every moment. Although you have prepared the sermon very thoroughly, it becomes harder on yourself and the listeners would experience a difficulty in receiving the grace of God, if you are not with the Holy Spirit in the process of delivering the sermon. Thus, it is important to receive the help of the Holy Spirit while relying on Him entirely.

The most powerful weapon, that a preacher has, is the word of God. If a minister is blundering in 'cooking' the words of God well and feeding the saints with it, he/she lacks the quality required of a pastor. We have to be equipped with excellent spiritual 'cooking' skills to choose the necessary message and deliver the most appropriate message for the listeners whenever and wherever whether it is to visit the homes or cell meetings of saints or at a pulpit of a church on a Sunday. Then, the sheep will be able to feed on green, fresh grass and live an abundant life. Therefore, the pastors should never stop praying to God as well as studying continuously to make every effort to 'cook' the words of God in the most delicious way. Then the pastor will leap to grow into a higher dimension, and his/her church will grow beyond any imagination.

A Sermon Delivered by the Power of the Holy Spirit

The difference between a sermon and a lecture is that a sermon overflows from our hearts whereas a lecture comes from his/her brain. This was an incident happened when I visited a wonderful city of Monterey near San Francisco.

I was to stay with a Korean family while I was delivering a sermon in a special Christian conference. The head of the house was a professor in the United States Army's Linguistics School. This professor did not receive God's grace from pastors and checked out several churches in the area. Fortunately, he was moved by the sermon of a pastor in the Full Gospel Monterey Church and began to attend the church regularly. For the sermon of a preacher to manifest the presence and power of the Holy Spirit, the pastor should have a deep personal relationship with God.

> When I came to you, brothers, I did not come with eloquence or superior wisdom as I proclaimed to you the testimony about God. For I resolved to know nothing while I was with you except Jesus Christ and him crucified. I came to you in weakness and fear, and with much trembling. My message and my preaching were not with wise and persuasive words, but with a demonstration of the Spirit's power, so that your faith might not rest on men's wisdom, but on God's power. (1 Corinthians 2:1-5)

The ministry of the Apostle Paul was the manifestation and power of the Holy Spirit itself. This style of ministry is hard to believe in daily mundane life. If you invite a guest in your house but do not greet nor welcome the guest in the morning and evening, leaving the guest alone by himself/herself, how many days would the guest stay in your house? The guest would leave the house in a fury, saying how could you treat a guest so terribly? If a person would feel so, how sad the Holy Spirit would feel. We do not know how much we are mistreating the Holy Spirit in our life of faith. The Bible says we must keep the Holy Spirit. How can we deliver a sermon if we make the Holy Spirit sad and cause Him to leave? It is the Holy Spirit, who is mainly responsible for a sermon.

> When the Counselor comes, whom I will send to you from the Father, the Spirit of truth who goes out from the Father, he will testify about me. And you also must testify, for you have been with me from the beginning. (John 15:26, 27)

For a preacher to deliver a sermon, that renews the testimony for the gospel and changes the life of saints, the pastor should have a personal fellowship with the Holy Spirit by recognizing, welcoming and serving Him. Many pastors ask me how many hours a day I pray. I feel anxious that I can not answer this question exactly. People, who experienced the baptism by the Holy Spirit, know that the Holy Spirit makes them pray at any time. Whether awake or in sleep, no matter what you are doing, the incense of prayer should be rising to the heaven with the power of the Holy Spirit at the altar in your mind. However, the pastor should feel inadequate with such prayer. Whenever you have time and need during any time in a day, you should pray, entreat and contemplate. From my personal experience, I can experience the work of the Holy Spirit before testifying to the words of God even in a small gathering, only if I pray for half an hour or an hour or two hours before the preaching time.

Thus, the preachers should put aside their personal matters as a gardener cuts the branches off a tree. The church does not necessarily grow if the preacher has many activities. How much grace a pastor receives deeply in his/her heart is the essence of church revival. Generally, personal evangelism and counseling can be delegated to a trained lay Christian. The next secondary tasks can also be left in charge of an assistant pastor. However, the senior pastor should hang on prayer desperately. So a pastor should carry out the ministry unto the Lord first and then ministry unto the people.

A pastor should pray as needed always. Of course, it is a matter of fact for a pastor to have a time to pray to God in the early morning everyday. Standing on the Sunday pulpit is like the life of a pastor.

Therefore, the pastor should pray especially on Saturdays for the Sunday pulpit. Usually, I pray on the Saturday afternoon at my praying chamber for the Sunday worship service. I do not limit any time for this prayer. I pray until I am certain in my mind of the voice of the Holy Spirit guaranteeing the presence of the power of the Holy Spirit at the pulpit on Sunday. The joy that I experience from testifying to the words of God at the altar on Sunday while anointed by the Holy Spirit through adequate prayer, can not be described by words.

A Sermon and Church Revival

Testifying to the words of God without adequate prayer beforehand is a sermon that comes from the head and neck even if the content of the message is great. A sermon is not made up in the head, but it is conceived by prayer and born in the pulpit. Likewise, when the words received by prayer are delivered by passionate prayer, the church can grow. The flame of church revival blazes up from the sermon heated by the preacher's prayer. A sermon armed with God's words and the Holy Spirit will bring a new history of creation to your church.

CHAPTER 5

Church Growth and Cell Groups

A Cell Group is the Basic Unit for the Church Growth

Typically, Korean mega-churches grow with the leadership of a pastor. However, in case the pastor passes away, transfers to another church, or stops the ministry due to personal reasons, the church will face an ordeal. Although the Yoido Full Gospel Church grew with me from the start, it is not a church of my own. A church belongs to Jesus Christ, and it can not belong to one person.

When a cell group is launched, it is easy to see that all practical matters of the ministry are carried out at the level of a cell. When I am overseas and call my wife, I was often disappointed in the beginning by my wife's remark, 'Every thing is going well even if you are away.' I now understand that she was saying the church was growing well even in my absence. As we can see, a cell group is an important matter for the church growth.

What Is a Cell Group?

In a cell group, the saints have fellowship, but it is not a social meeting. The cell meets in a saint's home, but it is not a home church or home meeting. A cell shares the love, but it is not a center for charity. A cell prays overnight sometimes, but it is not an overnight prayer meeting. A cell has a sermon, prayer and praise, but it is not another style of church worship. Then, what is a cell group?

A cell group is the basic unit of a church. A cell group seldom has more than 12 families. Here is a clear plan and purpose. In addition, the cell has a definite leadership structure through training. The cell is composed of members with a similar background and style. Our cell groups continued to develop progressively for a long time, going through a difficult process. If a pastor wants his/her church to develop beyond his/her power and ministerial ability, he/she will realize that cell groups should be an important program of the church. However, in order for a cell to be successful, the cell groups should not remain as a program. First of all, when cell groups are believed firmly to be a will of God for the church, it will continue with a full devotion, that does not spare necessary materials and time.

The Purpose of a Cell Group

The cell group has a clear purpose. Thus, the cell leader should know this purpose clearly and lead its group. The following four clear purposes of a cell can be listed.

Firstly, It is to Worship God.

We were created to worship God. Thus, our daily life should be filled with the time to worship God always. So, the first purpose of the cell meeting is to worship God. God does not approve of a cell meeting, which lacks in worship.

Secondly, It is to Share the Words of God.

God's words is food for our soul. Thus, the cell leader should learn the words of God to feed all cell members faithfully. Then, the cell members will grow, and the cell leader also grows. The spiritual food of a cell meeting should be words of God.

Thirdly, It is to Share the Fellowship.

A fellowship means for the saints to share their testimonies and useful conversation in faith. It can fall into formality if it has a simple worship service, shares a few words of God and breaks up. It has to have a time for fellowship to greet and meet new members, to share graceful testimonies and a conversation of mutual friendly concern. Even so, having misconstrued the meaning of a fellowship, it will lose the true meaning of a cell meeting if members are more interested in a full course buffet after every cell meeting.

Fourthly, It is to Evangelize.

The cell meeting should be a front line depot for evangelism. Thus, it requires the atmosphere to lead a new member and worship together. The neighbors often are reluctant to come to a church, but they are more willing to come to a cell meeting upon sincere invitation. So, we should have this opportunity to evangelize by inviting the neighbors to a cell meeting.

The Goal of a Cell Group

Cell groups are the main driving force to make a church grow. One of the concerns, that occurs when people meet regularly together, is the group grows only within.

Like other countries, the minimum unit of identity is a family in Korea. The family relationship is very important to us. If a person becomes a member of a cell, he/she has a sense of belonging like a family with other members. People like to associate with the family members. So, when a visitor comes into our home, we are uncomfortable by the visitors. For this reason, it is often difficult for an outsider to associate with our family.

It is the same for a cell group. If we leave the cell on its own, it does not welcome new visitors, having grown to an adequate size. If a person comes from the outside, people, who have been freshly trained in a cell group, have an opportunity to teach somebody. All people should learn through their behaviors. If you teach a person with the words of God, he/she will apply the words in his/her life to experience the meaning of the words.

In a cell group, a new member receives a systematic training for the salvation of his/her soul. However, if the newly trained member does not have the opportunity to teach what he/she learned, he/she can not fully show his/her potential and passion. When a new member comes into a cell, it is more important to make a former member a new leader and provide him/her an opportunity to teach the newcomer than being satisfied with an increase in the cell size with this newcomer.

The Structural Principle of a Cell Group

Our church has many kinds of cell groups. There is one basic principle in structuring a cell. It is the principle of consubstantiality. My good friend and an authority in church growth studies, Dr. Peter Wagner, states in his book, 'Our Kind of People', that our church will grow if the congregation members of a church are of similar backgrounds.

Professionals like physicians and lawyers prefer to be with professionals in the same field than professionals in other fields. A homemaker will feel more comfortable with homemakers than with women teachers or professional career women. It is because their main concern and interests are similar.

We come to a realization that a cell is more successful if it is divided by similarity among the members of the group than by locality. When a cell is determined by the locality, the newly formed group often lacks in commonality. So, it requires to spend a good deal of time and effort to find the common ground. From the perspective of shepherding a lost sheep to find and nurture, it is no longer effective.

If a banker is the leader of a cell, the cell will be filled mainly with people in the financial field. A cell meeting that lasts an hour will usually be held over a lunch break in a restaurant. They have a specific goal. It is to save two souls in a year. If two heads of a household accept Jesus Christ as their savior, then their two families will also become the children of God. They will share their experience of how God worked in their lives and have the time for prayer over a specific topic. And before the end of the meeting, they will discuss how to evangelize the next person . Perhaps, he would be a troubled financier. If the person is evangelized and accepts the gospel, the gospel of Jesus Christ will be more helpful for him/her than any other religions that he/she or his/her family members follow.

There are two things to keep in mind when inviting a prospective convert to be evangelized to a cell meeting. Firstly, it should be a place that does not burden him/her. If we invite him/her to a church directly, the chances are that he/she would not accept the invitation. However, if we invite him/her to a restaurant, it does not cause any doubt or discomfort. Secondly, the new prospect should be invited by the cell member, who knows him/her. We can feel discomfort and displeasure if we are invited to an unfamiliar meeting. At the least there should be a person, whom the new prospect knows over a meal. And when the new convert realizes that they have a certain common ground with him/her, the atmosphere of the meeting will be promising.

Other members in the meeting will want to help the visitor. Even if he/she does not receive the gospel on the spot, they will feel the love and concern in the meeting. This is to put the gospel into action. Not only the cell leader but other members of the cell will help the new comer. Soon enough by the gospel of Jesus Christ, the gate to his heart will open. He and his family will soon attend the church, and his wife will also join another cell group composed of wives of the cell group. Then there is a home cell meeting for the families of the cell. After a few years, a close friendship will form among them. The new convert will be a member of the cell and pray for the next person to be invited.

As we have seen, the principle of consubstantiality is an effective principle to develop a cell group. However, we have to remember that this principle should be used only for the development of a cell group and not for the development of the entire church. In a church, we can not make any discrimination based on the wealth, status, education level, etc. It is because we are one in the body of Jesus Christ.

The Operational System of a Cell Group

There is no specific method to form a cell group. This cell meeting can be held in a classroom, hotel, store, and high-rise building, etc. However, each meeting has its leader. This leader should complete an education program. He/she should designate someone else as the leader of another group. When the size of the group grows big enough to be divided, a person, who is trained to assume the next leadership, is needed. The cell group also requires some sort of accounting. In the past, a close relationship like a family was established among the members of a cell, and a problem in the group broke out.

The cell leader began to borrow money from other cell members with no interest. When this problem surfaced, we appointed a treasurer for each cell in order to prevent this mishap occurring again. The treasurer accounted for all the money received from the cell and how the money was spent. All financial matters were recorded, and this record was made open for all the members to see. It is the only way to be rid of any doubt.

The cell group is not a social association. Thus, we limited the socialization of the cell. At first, the cell members invite each other over a pleasant dinner at their home. Then, the next home to host will try to serve better meal than previous home. Naturally, a poor home will be concerned about treating the other cell members because they can not match the abundant dinner of a wealthy home. If we did not control such a source of trouble, the entire cell group will be weakened and divided through doubt and mistrust. Nowadays, the food offered in a cell meeting at a home is limited to refreshments and a few snacks.

The cell meeting also requires a time control. At first, people wanted to have a long meeting. Whenever a person brings an important matter on the table, other members also request prayer for their personal problems. If there is no time control, the meeting will last long without a limit, and people, who have to work the next day, will feel a burden to attend the next meeting. It is a good idea to finish up the meeting when people feel like needing a little more time.

Vitalization of a Cell Group

'How can I have the members to attend the cell meeting with zeal?' There is no one, who has not encountered this problem as a cell leader. If this problem is resolved, the growth of a cell group happens naturally. The answer to this problem is to instill the sense of a mission from God and anticipation for God's blessing. What are practical ways, then?

Firstly, Appointment of Team Leaders in a Cell

For all the cells grown in faith, the cell should be divided into several teams, and several team leaders should be appointed to feel the sense of a mission. The team leader will feel his/her mission when the team leader encourages and prays for his/her team members.

Secondly, Effective Allocation of a Worship Time

The worship time should be finished in as short time as possible. An eloquent and long prayer and a long and boring sermon make the cell members wearisome. The time allocation for a cell meeting should be structured like the following; a short but clear prayer within 2 minutes, a Bible study within 20 minutes, and then prayer time for each member's personal problems.

Thirdly, Prayer Time for Solving Personal Problems

Have each cell member to write down their personal problem before the cell meeting and bring the note. There is no one in this world without a problem. So, have a time for praying in unison for each personal problem, and then afterwards, share the testimony of people, whose problem has been answered. Doing so, people will have more interest in the cell meeting. As the result, the cell meeting will be more productive and full of good anticipation.

Fourthly, Target Prayer for a Potential Member

If the cell members are eight in number, each of the eight people should pray for one non-believer in the neighborhood everyday. And in a cell meeting, discuss the best way to evangelize each target person. Above all, if we pray in the name of Jesus everyday, the force of the non-believing will fall like the city of Jericho. The walls of Jericho did not collapse on a single attempt. It took seven days and a loud shout. Likewise, when we pray, the non-believing mind will collapse. When the target prayer is answered, the cell members will attend the cell meeting with zeal and joy.

Division of a Cell Group and Its Reproduction

We often see a cell group, which started out with a few and then grew too big and inefficient. Then, the cell should be divided. However, dividing a group is not an easy matter. Since the cell group did not only grow in size but also in spiritual maturity, many members will think of the group as a family structure. In this case, the successful method for dividing the group is to leave a known leader in the group. As aforementioned, if a senior cell leader let all the group members know that a junior cell leader is being trained in preparation for a future cell division, the new cell leader is not a stranger. If the purpose to divide a cell is accepted as it was intended to follow the will of God, the group can be divided without much pain. The cell group has a meaning for its existence only when it leads a sinner to Jesus Christ effectively. If the group is too big, people can not learn about Jesus effectively. If the group members realize this point, then they will understand and participate fully in the cell division.

Once the cell is divided into two cells, the cell leaders of the two cells should meet regularly to check on how each other is doing. The cell leaders should continue to keep personal contacts with each members. If a member is hospitalized, the cell leader should visit the sick. If a member is troubled, the cell leader should share the pain and devise a plan to resolve the problem together. If these things are upheld, no matter how many the group members are, the cell leader can continue a more close and personal ministry.

After a Sunday morning worship was over, I saw many people were boarding several buses. I asked the guide. 'Where have you come from?'

'Pastor, we are cell members of a pastor from a Full Gospel church nearby Seoul.' The guide proudly explained to me. The young man started out a cell and gathered so many people to charter several buses to take them to a Sunday worship service. I can not take care of all Christian community over 50km away. However, our cell groups there were fulfilling their needs effectively.

I draw a triangle at a blackboard at the start of a seminar in a Church Growth Conference. If you draw a reverse triangle and place the pastor at the bottom of the triangle, it is to prove a mundane method. Because of this routine and outdated method, many pastors are disappointed and thinking about leaving the ministry. They had the calling to worship God, and they were not called to be burnt out with all kinds of responsibilities. However, the church can grow dynamically by developing its cell groups. I can show this fact by rotating the reverse triangle clockwise. Now, the pastor is at the top of the triangle. The size of the church is no longer a burden to this pastor. Pastors now realize that it is their duty to give a motive for the participation of lay Christians and to train them for this purpose.

Misconceptions about a Cell Group

'Reverend Cho, our church tried out the cell groups of Yoido Full Gospel Church but has failed. What do you think is the problem?' An American pastor recently asked me. Upon analyzing his church, I found many problem areas.

Firstly, although the pastor has heard about cell groups many times, he never participated in a cell meeting. This is a critical mistake. Only making a program does not guarantee a continued development and success. You have to give a motive and a sense of accomplishment to each member of the cell.

Secondly, he did not wait long enough for the cell groups to be an important part of the church ministry. If you try out a new thing, you have to progressively change the misconceptions of the congregation members in order for them to be receptive to accept the new method. It takes several months and years to change misconceptions that are deeply rooted in your church.

Thirdly, many a church folds out a map simply to make a cell based on the living area alone and then designate cell leaders to ask them, 'now have a meeting in your home.' Although the cell leader obeys the will and plan of the pastor and starts out a meeting in his/her home, the meeting will be only a reduced version of a church worship service. The saints have to feel a sense of belonging, especially, if they attend a mega-church.

The Requirements for a Cell Leader

Even if the cell group is wonderfully structured, the cell group can not fulfill its intended mission, if the leader is not prepared. A cell group should have a wonderful leader. If an incompetent leader leads a cell group, the group will soon be diseased. The cell leader is a leader, whom the Holy Spirit called through the servants of God. Because of it, the position of a cell leader is very important.

There are several requirements for a cell leader to lead his/her flock of sheep dutifully.

Firstly, They Have to Understand the Words of God Well

If a cell leader does not know the fundamental meaning of the words of God, he/she does not deserve to teach other people. The words of God make people born again and live fully according to God's will. Besides the words of God, any words of worldly advice, stories of world politics, history and stories on arts, etc. do not give salvation to people. The words to make people have a life can only be found in the Bible. Since a cell leader should know these words well enough to teach others, the cell leader should study the Bible systematically.

Secondly, They Have to Have a Zeal to Grow the Church

For any work in the world, one has to do his/her best to make the work successful. Moreover, teaching others to lead others is impossible without the zeal to make it happen. There is no one more expendable than a cell leader without the zeal. Although the cell leader may lack in education or knowledge, if he/she has the passion that is inflamed by the Holy Spirit, God will raise up the person to use him/her for His purpose and make him/her worthy of respect. Peter was definitely not an educated man and had a fiery temper. The Apostle Paul was educated, but his devotion for God's work was also as zealous as Peter's. The two pillars of Jesus Christ Church, the Apostle John and James possessed also fiery tempers to be nicknamed 'son of a thunder.' Likewise, the cell leaders should never lose the passionate heart for God above all else.

Thirdly, They Should Be Filled with the Holy Spirit

One can not teach nor move anyone without the power of the Holy Spirit. Thus, the cell leader should always make an effort to be filled with the Holy Spirit and lead all members to be filled with the Holy Spirit.

Fourthly, They Should Have a Vision for the Cell Group

Such thinking as today is OK, tomorrow will be OK no matter what is not permissible. The cell leaders should contemplate and ask God in prayer, 'How can I be used to have my cell members receive bigger grace and blessing?' 'What new program should be made to lead the cell well?' 'What should I do to lead more non-believing families and neighbors to the Lord?' The cell leader should have specific visions and dreams on the success of the cell.

Fifthly, the Cell Leader Should Have a Firm Faith

You should be a cell leader, who rely on God, never despair easily, and pray to God with a lasting patience. A firm faith is easily transferred to a neighbor and has the power to transform the entire group into a people of faith.

Sixthly, They Should Never Hesitate Leading the Group Members by Being the Role Model

If the leader does not practice what he/she preaches, his/her words do not manifest any power or results. If a cell leader has the above qualities, he/she can build a group on a sand beach, and it will soon develop and grow. It is because the most important element in God's work is not any system but people.

The Function of a Cell Leader

There are many people, who were once Christian but not living the life of faith, in our society. It is the trend that, whatever the reasons, more people are dropping out of Christian life. These drop-outs have almost the same story. They believe in God still. However, they are disappointed with church. Some of them may have been involved in the breakup of a church, or some of them may have felt a bitter disillusionment against a pastor or a church leader.

Some people may feel ashamed about returning to church because they have fallen into a life of sins. Some may feel deserted because the pastor never has visited their home. Whatever the reasons, there are many lost sheep. We need to visit them or help the Lord to heal them.

The cell leader is a trained fisherman, who catches souls. He/she knows his/her mission and believes his/her anointing by God as a cell leader. In addition, the cell leader has been trained to counsel the cell members. A counseling is very important for drop-outs, who have heard the gospel before. Hear their stories of why they left a church. What caused their pain? Then, afterwards, show them that God's grace will be upon anyone who looks forward to God.

A cell leader will connect the hurt Christian with someone, who can show a genuine interest in their coming back as Christian. Once the hurt Christian feels the love in the church, he/she is ready to return.

A cell group can approach a Christian personally, who does not come to church any more but is in need of help. If the group invites them to a church right away, perhaps they will be reluctant to start over again. However, in a comfortable atmosphere such as a home or a restaurant, they will talk about their stories freely upon an invitation. Some of the stories can be sad, but all these stories can end happily.

Each cell leader knows that nothing is impossible for God. God heals and forgives everyone, who comes to Him with a sincere heart. The ministry of reconciliation can be undertaken better by a lay Christian than by a pastor. The cell leader is not subject to a prejudice that the hurt Christian may have towards a pastor. Because all hurt Christians may feel that all pastors are the same, a lay Christian can be in a better position to approach them. The cell group does not only work for salvation. It is an effective ministry of a cell to invite a hurt Christian to a home to heal his/her soul rather than to an intimidating and sometimes detested church.

The Use of Female Leadership

When cell groups were started out first, we wanted to have a cell meeting in a man's home. However, this was often not feasible. The reason was many men were busy with their work and they often came home late. In addition, they often did not have any time to be in charge of a new task. Also, since men are very pragmatic and logical, they also thought to experiment a new task in a smaller system.

God had me realize that it is more effective to have a female cell leader. This was a revolutionary idea to me as not only a believing Christian but also a Korean. The function of a leader belongs to a man in Korea. Traditionally, the function of women was supposed to live a happy life of getting married, having children and making a happy home. Although there are many changes occurring in Korea, our culture is basically male-oriented. Thus, it was more revolutionary to have women take the position of responsibility and leadership than establishing cell groups.

The first concern that surfaced in using female leaders was of theological nature. The Apostle Paul scribes in 1 Corinthians 14:34, 'women should remain silent in the churches.' The same message is found in a letter of the Apostle Paul to Timothy, ' woman should learn in quietness and full submission. I do not permit a woman to teach or to have authority over a man; she must be silent.' (1 Timothy 2:11,12) However, Peter made the following speech on the Pentecost,

> No, this is what was spoken by the prophet Joel: 'In the last days, God says, I will pour out my Spirit on all people. Your sons and daughters will prophesy, your young men will see visions, your old men will dream dreams. Even on my servants, both men and women, I will pour out my Spirit in those days, and they will prophesy.' (Acts 2:16-18)

The promise of the Holy Spirit to give the power of prophesy was given not only to men but to women as well. I began to realize women were often more diligent, loyal and sincere in God's work. Jesus first appeared to Mary Magdalene to spread the good news of His resurrection to His disciples.

At last, I made the decisive conclusion that women can help the pastoral ministry as long as they are under the authority of the church. Only with one condition that women can not teach their own dogmas or creeds; they can, however, work and testify to the gospel in accordance with what they have been taught. So, I have decided to appoint women as cell leaders of my church. When women began to move actively, all the obstacles were overcome, and men became more cooperative in church affairs. During teaching about a cell group, I found that women were more loyal and trustworthy. Do not be afraid to use female cell leaders.

Church Revival Through a Cell Group

A trained cell leader is absolutely necessary for a church to revive and grow through cell groups. The cell leaders of our church are trained through the process of learning. They are also given the motive of using all their potentials for the work of God. Their activities can be promoted and enhanced by a good perception for their service, award system and a certificate of achievement for accomplishing an aim of the cell. It can not be overemphasized how important it is to explain a clear plan and goal to each leader. I hold an annual meeting with all cell leaders. Gathering at this time, I explain in detail the goals for each cell group as told by the Holy Spirit. Then, each cell group will be armed with a new spirit and act on the specific goal after praying for the goal. Recently, our church is doing its utmost to grow cell groups for the second leap of our church. This is because it is the vision for our church in the 21st century, that was given by God, and it is ultimately a will of God. A cell group is a systematic device for the revival of a church.

When all cell leaders are armed with the dream of God and devote themselves, the church will continue to revive and grow.

CHAPTER 6

Church Growth and the Mass-Media

Mass-media is an Effective Means for Church Growth

The world of today is often called the age of people, who control the mass-communication; those who control the mass-communication, control the world. Now, the mass-communication can not be separated from the public. Since our country published Hansung Soon Bo, a newspaper, in 1883, we have encountered radio and TV, etc. Nowadays, such electronic media as recorders, video tape players/recorders, computers, and even internet, have been poured on us. This mass-communication has an amazing effect and power.

When I first started a church in Bool Gwang-Dong, people were led to believe the eggs of a common quail were excellent for health. Farmers, who sold those eggs, became rich in a couple of years. Then several years after, newspapers reported that experts concluded those eggs were not any different from the eggs of a hen. And then, soon enough, farmers, who were still in the business to sell the eggs of a common quail, became bankrupt in an amazingly short time.

So, the mass-communication has a huge influence over people nowadays. A preacher can gather so many people, perhaps even thousands of thousands. However, the mass-communication can deliver words of God to several million people instantly. Since the gospel can reach the homes of unbelievers whether they want or not, radio, TV, recorders and videos are useful instruments of testifying to the gospel today. In the future, church growth depends on how well we use the mass-communication. In this situation, mass-media is an effective instrument for evangelism. Our church uses a good deal of our budget in using the TV to preach the gospel. And almost everyday, we are spreading the gospel of Jesus Christ in Korea and the world at the same time.

The Usefulness of Mass-Media

I realized, while traveling around the world, that not many countries have had the opportunity to spread the gospel through air and broadcasting. Many pastors in Europe request me to pray so that the government policy will change to be able to spread the gospel through mass-media. Since Korea and the United States can freely spread the gospel, I think the church has the need for mass-media to spread the gospel effectively.

Social scholars and psychologists say that mass-media is today's effective means for communication. Teachers know that seeing influences our memory more than hearing. There is a research data that reports over 70% of what we know has been obtained through seeing. Our old adage that seeing a picture is worth more than a thousand words may be remembered. An analysis of media effect to recognize a reality revealed the same result as the old adage aforementioned.

I think that, if Jesus was to spread the gospel, He would use TV and radio. Jesus used the best method to have God's words heard by as many people as possible. When the masses gathered around Him to hear His words, Jesus climbed to the top of a hill so that more people could listen to Him. On the sea shore, Jesus boarded a boat and had the boat floating on the Galilee Lake to amplify His voice by the reflective power of the water surface.

Jesus could spread the news of the Kingdom of God secretly. He could tell the disciples and have them to spread the message to others. However, His teaching was for everyone, who was anxious and thirsty to hear the words of life. Since Jesus knew how to make numerous people hear, so many people could hear the words of Jesus live and loud without an amplifier.

The Reason for Mass-Media Ministry

The reason, that modern mass-media exists whether it is radio or TV, is to spread the gospel of Jesus Christ. If you want church growth, you would definitely desire the spread of the gospel. You will want more people to become Christian and become part of a church by having the lost souls saved.

Thus, a pastor should use mass-media. The bandwidth is full of evangelists, who spread the gospel at this time. Likewise, I think the evangelists should work not only inside and outside his/her church but also work on the broadcasting ministry. I believe in the usefulness of mass-media, and I think the pastors more than anyone should use the media more widely. The pastor no longer has to carry a heavy burden to revive his/her church.

TV Broadcasting Ministry

This is a story that happened when I was in Washington, D. C. to deliver a congratulatory sermon on the occasion of the inauguration of the former 40th president of the United Sates, Donald W. Reagan. Doctor Cha, Il-Seok, the former assistant mayor of Seoul, let me know that God had told him to start a TV broadcasting ministry in the United States.

At first, I disagreed with his idea. 'How can my TV broadcasting ministry succeed in a country that is the most advanced and full of TV broadcasting ministries? Doesn't America have so many famous and talented TV evangelists already? Americans will never accept the teaching of an Asian in English.' With these rational reasons, I could not hear the voice of the Holy Spirit that was saying inside my mind that the remarks of Dr. Cha were to come true.

I told him, 'Dr. Cha, if you would first volunteer in this ministry, I would partake in it.' I thought that, due to his high social status, he would not give up his successful business and jump into a TV ministry in America without pay. However, I was surprised once again by his answer. 'Reverend, I believe the Holy Spirit told me to sacrifice my business for His work. I will do it.' I could not even guess that Dr. Cha would decide to sacrifice himself for this risky adventure. Now, I firmly believe that God has led me to a TV broadcasting ministry in America. Based on these experiences, I would like to share with you 10 steps required for a successful and effective TV broadcasting ministry.

Step 1, Know the Leading of God

To use a broadcasting media for spreading the gospel requires expansive efforts and time. If I had known these difficulties beforehand, I may not have been able to obey the Holy Spirit. A broadcasting ministry has many problem areas embedded in it. It requires a thorough preparation because any mistakes are not allowed while on air. And it has an inherent problem of hiring special experts and obtaining special resources.

Likewise, one thing that sustained me amidst of all kinds of difficulties was the faith that the Holy Spirit had spoken to do such ministry.

Step 2, Decide on the Target Audiences

Nothing can succeed without a clear purpose. Thus, when structuring a TV broadcasting ministry, you have to know whom to approach. Typically, the TV and radio broadcasting ministry is to approach a lost soul with the gospel message of Jesus Christ. However, the Holy Spirit led me to approach churches in the United States with the message of church growth. American churches have been blessed because of their passion to spread the gospel of Jesus Christ all over the world. Nevertheless, God needed someone to encourage, hope and pray for church growth among American churches.

Step 3, Develop a Ministry that Suits Your Style

The pastors should carry out the ministry that suits him/her. They can not just mimic others. At the beginning of my ministry, I tried to preach like Reverend Billy Graham. I stood up like him with a Bible raised high up in the air and spoke in such a high tone that it hurt my vocal cord. However, I became weary after trying to emulate Reverend Graham after a few minutes. Reverend Billy Graham eats steak, but I realized I eat rice and Kimchi. Now, I preach in my most natural style.

I raise my voice only when I want to emphasize the main point. And in most cases, I speak in my natural tone as it resonates from my heart.

Since I often go overseas to deliver a sermon in international conferences on church growth, and the TV broadcasting ministry developed naturally as my circuit project. Because my ministry not only gives a spiritual sense but also contains some educational materials, it developed into a program to provide information. Most people, who write letters to me after the broadcasting ministry, are pastors or church leaders. I received many letters that told me about how they received a prayer answer from God through my broadcasting ministry. A pastor in Southern California wrote;

> When the church that I served was on the verge of being broken up, I saw your message of receiving a new vision from the Holy Spirit by spending so many hours in prayer through your broadcasting program. Now my ministry has been anointed anew. The church did not split up. On the contrary, it began to grow for the first time in several years. I thank God for Reverend Cho's TV broadcasting ministry. I can not make it to the international conference on church growth, but I am meeting you every week through channel 9 of a TV station in LA.

Step 4, Learn How to Speak to One Person

The problem that most preacher have in TV broadcasting ministry is that they do not understand the media. TV is basically a personal media. TV does not approach people in a theater but goes to a person's home.

When you are relaxing by sitting on a cozy sofa, you are not ready to hear someone shouting. How would you react if someone knocks on your door and sits in your livingroom to shout out all of a sudden? This is the scene of many preachers evangelizing on TV. Looking directly to the lens of a TV camera, I think of only one person. I tell him with all my sincerity. It is as if I am in a heart to heart conversation in a living room.

Step 5, Be Honest Always

The TV has a new power. It shows all your behavior as well as revealing your state of mind. It points out all your blemishes of unconcern and oversensitivity. If you open your heart and sincerely share what God has taught you, people will intuitively recognize it. Stay away from any ostentatious and belying expressions, and spread only truthful and honest facts.

Step 6, Delegate Responsibilities

A PD (Production Director), who is in charge of the TV broadcasting ministry, should be a person of spiritual disposition. Since he knows how I feel, he leads the program toward reflecting my genuine concern. He may be a specialist in broadcasting field, but I am a professional preacher. I have learned to heed to his direction and cooperation. Now and then, there were times when it was hard to continue the broadcasting program. Then, he would say this to me, 'Excuse me, Reverend Cho, we have to redo this part. I think there is a problem with the tape, and I am afraid it will not come out alright.'

No matter how hard the process was, after following his directions and seeing the finished product, I feel a great satisfaction. Because many pastors do not heed to others' saying, problems creep up. They think they know all the answers. I have learned personally to delegate not only the responsibility but the authority as a key to successful ministry.

Step 7, Secure Adequate Budget

A TV broadcasting ministry can cause financial bankruptcy. Not only the equipments are very expensive but the cost to broadcast is not easy to deal with. If more cost than you have expected and calculated is incurred in a TV broadcasting ministry, it will become a great burden on your ministry. First of all, you have to take the attitude of developing step by step within the range of your church budget. If you spend without a consideration for the church budget, it can cause bad consequences for your ministry and your entire church. To calculate the cost of a task beforehand is the only way to avoid trouble in the future.

Step 8, Do Not Make It Too Monotone and Boring

There is nothing more boring than watching the same scene on the TV. One of the ways to find out if the preaching is wonderful or not is to turn down the sound volume and watch the moving pictures only. When we preach as ministers, we prepare a verbal means of communication. We believe that the words of God have been communicated to the authors by the inspiration of the voice of God. A ministry is generally not concerned with any non-verbal means of communication.

The most important purpose of communication before anything else is to transmit your thoughts to others.

In this respect, the transmission of thought should be understood. Preaching at a church, you are not communicating to a person but to audiences. As they respond and react to you, you also respond and react to them. At the pulpit, you can meet the eyes of as many people as possible. A person can sit for an hour at a church, but he/she would not sit still for an hour if the same sermon is being delivered at his/her living room through a TV broadcasting. The dynamic reactions that are exhibited in a meeting of the saints are hard to observe in a TV broadcasting at home. And the person will react to every desultory things happening around him/her.

Thus, you not only have to speak in an interesting manner but have to recognize the necessity of entertaining the viewers without obstructing the message for an effective transmission of the message. It helps to see your preaching scenes repeatedly and to apply what you felt in the next broadcasting for the transmission of not only the audio but also visual images.

Step 9, Be Aware of Offering Drive

The matter of materials is one of important debate issues of a TV broadcasting ministry in America. If you started out a TV broadcasting ministry to save a lost soul but lost their trust afterwards because of an offering, then what would you have gained? One of the questions that I have while seeing such enormous offerings are being collected through American Christian broadcasting programs is how the non-believers would think about it. In Korea, this type of collecting offerings is just not allowed. Thus, this is a problem in America.

I know the cost of broadcasting is very high. In New York, our program is on the air every Sunday morning.

The cost that we pay to this broadcasting station is huge. However, this broadcasting station will only feed the preaching scenes to 3,400 local cable companies in the Unites States. We requested earnestly to attend the international conference on church growth in order to continue the broadcasting. Viewers, who received the grace of God through our broadcasting ministry, have done so. However, we never received any vocal reply that suggested a contribution to a fund raise. Above all, I do not know how to ask for money due to my character. I would quit broadcasting before asking for money to continue the broadcasting. I believe the viewers will participate and contribute financially if the American viewers see what God is doing through the ministry of international conference on church growth.

Step 10, Do Not Be Afraid To Repeat

Pastors think that the viewers understand first time what they said and retain the memory for a long time. However, most people do not remember what they learned for a long time. There are times that I have to repeat several times for most people to understand what I am saying. How many times did Jesus repeat? He taught the same principle although He used different parables at different circumstances with different audiences. As a matter of fact, the disciples did not understand Jesus' teaching on the resurrection until after Jesus died and resurrected.

If the content being broadcasted is important, it can be repeated. I have taught the truth about vision and dream to numerous people for the last several years. I feel frustrated because few people understand what I have been saying.

Even though I repeatedly emphasize the importance of continuous prayer to receive a clear blue print, a vision, from God, many people still do not understand me. I remember what the Holy Spirit taught me about the lesson when He gave me a bicycle, chair and Mahogany desk. People just say they received a grace of God after hearing the story. However, I realize they do not understand the point of this story when I ask them about it. In fact, this principle is important not only for a TV broadcasting ministry but also for preaching ministry at a church.

The Fruit of a TV Broadcasting Ministry

Many pastors make appearances in TV broadcasting with the programs about their church for the public relation and promotion of their church. Other pastors think they can invite new comers to their church through a TV broadcasting ministry. Still some pastors feel that a local TV broadcasting ministry will contribute to earning trust for church. All these thoughts are rational and reasonable. However, there are some invisible results when the pastor pours his/her precious time, effort and resources on a TV broadcasting ministry.

A lady wrote me a letter and sent it to my office of broadcasting ministry in New York. She was bed-ridden for a long time due to an illness. However, she received so much grace through the TV broadcasting ministry that she finally wrote me a letter. She saw how passionately our saints climb up the prayer mountain and pray through our broadcasting. Usually, between 5,000 and 10,000 people are praying for their personal prayer issues, evangelisation of the country and world, and prayer request sent to me from all around the world including America and Japan day and night in the prayer mountain.

When the TV broadcasting program in the United States is about to end, there are scenes showing people, who are crying out to God for the prayer request of Americans. This is not a made-up scene, it is a real scene happening right there at the moment.

Ms. Sally Porter, who wrote me a letter some time ago, asked me how she can work for God by being touched by the Holy Spirit.

> Father, you know I am old and sick. I don't have a family and money. Jesus, I have waited only to die up until this time. I earnestly asked the Lord to take me. However, I would like to live now. I can do the same if Christians in Korea are working for the Lord by praying.

Her letter was so emotional. I immediately sent her a letter. Through the letter, I encouraged her to read the Bible whenever and wherever praying. She still did not have a family and money. However, she now has a holy purpose to live. She rides her wheelchair to visit other patients and distribute a small piece of paper to ask them to write their prayer requests on it. Afterwards, she comes back to her room and pray all day with the prayer requests. She is now very happy to be in a hospital. She is reaping the fruit of prayer now. Other patients come to see her regularly now. And even the hospital staffs come to her for her prayer. She thinks now she has a new family. This incident happened through a regular TV broadcasting ministry in the area.

She would not be able to come to our church and can not give a financial contributor for the broadcasting ministry. However, she heard the words of God through the broadcasting, changed for a positive life in a hospital in California, and earned a new strength to live.

Your church may also explore the possibility of changing your area for the better through a TV broadcasting ministry. This will eventually help your church growth. Nevertheless, there will be people, who do not respond to your appeal and insist on not attending your church, although they can receive God's grace through your broadcasting ministry. Do not jump into a TV broadcasting ministry only with the thought to get something. Start your ministry with the mind-set that you want to give something to be blessed to your city. Then, you will never be disappointed no matter what.

Radio Broadcasting Ministry

Radio is on the way to decline unlike TV as a mass-media. However, many parts of the world still do not enjoy the benefit of a TV. Especially, the best way to approach the third world is to use this radio media.

We are currently operating a radio program throughout Korea. In addition, we are carrying out a radio ministry program in a standard Chinese language every Sunday. I can write everything that God is doing for China. Nevertheless, I can say that the churches in China are doing much more than before. We have a report from local missionaries of what the Holy Spirit is doing for them every week. So many people in China are being saved and gather in a home church.

I believe that there are at the least 30 million Christians in China now.

The method of growth for a Chinese church is through a home church. I can not say exactly where and how these churches are growing, but a general report can be made. The reason, I am so careful publicly with this information regarding a church in China, is because the Chinese government soon dissolve the meeting.

The cell organization in certain areas in China operates too rapidly that the local government do not have a desire to stop the work of the Holy Spirit. China is in the center of a new reform and modernization. In order for China to grow and escape from current economic difficulties, they need newly trained people devoted to the development of their country's economy.

The church in Korea could grow because the patriotism of

Christians at the time of the introduction of the gospel. In other words, a good Christian meant a good, patriotic Korean. When Japan colonized our country, the pioneers to fight for the independence of the nation were Christians. The leaders of the church had to endure extreme hardship and persecution. In fact, the most important reason for our success is the blood of these martyrs, who cried out justice. They paid the price to establish the trust for Christianity in our country.

It is the same in China. These Christians are not connected with any other society overseas. They all are devoted Christians. They don't know the meaning of liberalism and evangelism. However, they believed every thing in the Bible is true and believe so today. They believe in the miraculous power of God.

They see miracles happening like any body else. However, the more important thing is they work and make efforts to do more than their non-believing counterparts. They are diligent people.

For these reasons, the local governments do not dare to get in the way for the large-scale conversion taking place in their area. Preventing the local evangelism means the downfall of their productivity. Thus, they figure it is in their best interest to help the church to grow. The best way for the Christians in China to encounter the news of gospel is the regular radio broadcasting. Since this broadcasting is not coming from far away Western countries but from a neighboring country, they are very receptive to our radio broadcasting ministry.

The Characteristics of Radio Broadcasting Ministry

The radio broadcasting has only verbal means of communication. Thus, you have to draw the picture with the words being broadcasted. When quoting an illustration, you have to explain in more detail than you would in a TV broadcasting. You have to give a visual stimulation for the people to listen and remember what you are saying. Thus, you have to think in many ways before the radio broadcasting.

Usually, I speak succinctly and clearly to the point in a broadcasting. I have learned that I can do more work at the same cost by speaking briefly and repeatedly what I have to say. Since a radio broadcasting ministry is much more inexpensive than a TV broadcasting ministry, it will be a preferred ministry for many evangelists.

In a radio broadcasting, you have to set the goal for the audiences. Depending on the style of your broadcasting ministry, the audiences will increase. If you are very much involved in teaching

Christians, you will know the long hours required to prepare the message to teach. If your main audiences have not received the salvation yet, then you will be introducing basic evangelical programs.

In addition, we have to remember radio broadcasting is a multipurpose transmission media. People listen to the radio whether they are driving, relaxing outside or work at home. Since a radio broadcasting does not require so much concentrated attention like the TV broadcasting, people tend to turn on the radio all the time. This is the reason why one requires more preparation to testify to the gospel through the radio. I have learned to describe vividly during the sermon. I share many of my personal experiences as a pastor in the radio broadcasting. The story of how people are living raises the interest of the audiences way up.

The Influence of Mass-Media Ministry

Our church is currently broadcasting all around Japan including the areas of Tokyo, Osaka, Nagoya, Kobe, Hyogo, Oyama, etc. through the media ministry of TV, radio, and internet, etc. After we tape-record our church program, it is dubbed in Japanese. We use the same format as my TV broadcasting ministry in America. However, since each country has a different culture and different target audiences for evangelizing, each program is modified. The result was a success, and the focus of media ministry in Japan is mainly on evangelism.

Christians number 0.5% of the population of Japan. A lot of energy is spent in gospel evangelism ministry in Japan. In contrast, the fruits of this ministry are minimal. Especially, it is hard to find the appropriate way to name God in Japanese. There are many gods in Japan. Thus, it is very difficult to speak of the one and living God in Japanese. The Japanese people ask me, 'Which god are you referring to? god of Israel or America? or god of Hindus? What do you mean by God?' It is most important to understand their culture and to have the ability to preach fluently in Japanese to spread the gospel of Jesus Christ to 120 million lost souls in Japan.

A Japanese traveller showed me a few pictures. His family received Christ while watching our broadcasting ministry program and sent a letter to a broadcasting office in Osaka. One of our staff visited his home to begin the Bible study. They were baptized and registered to our church as regular church members. Since the words of God began to take deep root in his mind, he had a guilty feeling on account of the idols they were worshipping at home. What did they do with these idols? Did they sell them? How did the other family members react? This family decided to burn these idols publicly after much prayer. They wrote a letter and sent me these pictures of burning idols. Now this family are tasting true freedom and peace. Other relatives began to understand them soon enough. The broadcasting ministry bears unexpected fruits of salvation.

Mass-Media and Church Growth

It is our duty to spread the gospel. Leading people to salvation is the work of God the Holy Spirit. Today's churches have to spread the gospel in harmony with modern culture. Since today's mass-media has so much influence, it has to be used as an effective instrument for spreading the gospel. Evangelism and church growth requires effective strategies, and mass-media is one of the most useful strategies among them. I pray that your church experiences a revival and growth also through creative mission strategies continuously.

CHAPTER 7

Church Growth and the Kingdom of God

There was a beautiful old lady, who preached the Kingdom of God all her life. She was captured by North Korean soldiers during the Korean War and faced the danger of execution. However, she was repeatedly saved amidst hopeless situations. Fear and anxiety attacked her when she was captured. She faced the impending death with the peace and joy of God and with dignity and courage.

She sang the praise for the last time while being taken to an execution site and prayed for the young North Korean soldier, who was taking her. Thereupon, the soldier was touched deeply by her earnest prayer and joyful praise, and he let her free. Afterwards, she held the first presidential breakfast prayer meeting and testified to the kingdom of God until her last breath.

Once, she invited me to her house for dinner and said, 'Pastor Cho, I would like to share with you a fact that you should never forget. Pastor, preach the kingdom of God. Preach all the gospel of the kingdom of God. I say again. Preach the kingdom of God!' I have never forgotten her words even once. Thus, I would like to speak about the reason for preaching the kingdom of God and actually experiencing the power of the kingdom of God.

Understanding the Kingdom of God

Before we delve into the gospel of the kingdom of God that Jesus preached, we have to understand what the kingdom of God is. The kingdom of God can be explained by two images. The futuristic image and current realistic images. First of all, we know the futuristic image of the kingdom of God through the prophesy of the prophets in the Old Testament. They prophesy that there will be no war in the future. Isaiah foretold spears will turn to hoes, and nations will not raise arms against each other. In fact, he used the analogy of wolves and sheep, leopards and children, and young lions and calves to let us know the dramatic change that will occur in the world in the future.

One of the messages that Jesus preached was 'Repent, for the kingdom of heaven is near.' (Matthew 4:17) His teachings, parables and metaphors were mainly about the kingdom of God. As a matter of fact, the prayer that the Lord taught His disciples was, your kingdom come, your will be done on earth as it is in heaven.' (Matthew 6:10) Until the last moment, Jesus continuously emphasized the kingdom of God to His disciples. Likewise, although it is clear that Jesus' main emphasis was the kingdom of God, I find many differences in people's conceptions on what is the kingdom of God or what is the message of the gospel of the kingdom of God.

Saint Augustine understood the church and the kingdom of God to be synominous. The Reformist Movement exerted so much effort in reestablishing the meaning of the kingdom of God. Calvin agreed with St. Augustine in principal. However, he disagreed with him on the point that the church represents the kingdom of God.

He thought that the true church hidden inside the visual church is the manifestation of the kingdom of God on this earth. The church has the responsibility to change all countries in the world for all its people to recognize the fact that Jesus Christ is the Lord. A church can be likened to yeast or leaven that spreads in the dough, called the world. At some point in the history of mankind, all the world will proclaim Jesus Christ as the Lord and the King. At this point, Jesus Christ will return to this world to rule and govern the kingdom that God the Father has prepared for Him.

There are some scholars, who try to understand the kingdom of God in the current social context. Harvey Cox regards the kingdom of God as a social order that is created by the church. Like other social problems, problems such as complaints, biases, etc. should be approached and dealt with by the church. Although I will deal with my point of view on the kingdom of God later, I believe a theological perspective on the kingdom of God has an inherent fault in it. I trust reasoning, but I do not trust errors of reasoning. Actually, there is a greater basis than reasoning for establishing what is the kingdom of God. It is the simple but profound words of God.

Biblical Principles on the Kingdom of God

Looking at several basic Biblical principles that help to understand what is the kingdom of God, it can be summarized in the following five points.

Firstly, the Kingdom of God Is Not only for the Future but for the Present

'For the kingdom of God is not a matter of eating and drinking, but of righteousness, peace and joy in the Holy Spirit'. (Romans 14:17)

The Apostle Paul says to us that the kingdom of God transcends the human natural existence and lets us to experience the fruit of the Holy Spirit here and now. If you are united with the Holy Spirit, you will have more interest in what God gave us than other necessary things such as eating and drinking.

Secondly, the Kingdom of God is the Place That We Can Enter As the Result of Gaining a New Life by the Holy Spirit

The Apostle Paul says, 'For he has rescued us from the dominion of darkness and brought us into the kingdom of the Son he loves,'. (Colossians 1:13) Here, the word, 'brought' has the literal meaning of 'changing the side'. While I was studying this word, I related it to a soccer game. Each team stands on the opposite side. If one team represents the kingdom of darkness, the other team represents the Kingdom of God. During the game, a main player of the kingdom of darkness team takes off his/her uniform and then goes to the bench of the other side to wear the uniform of the Kingdom of God team. Then, he/she reenters the game to fight against the kingdom of darkness players. He/she simply changed the side. This is what happened to us. We have changed the side from the kingdom of darkness to the other kingdom, that is the Kingdom of God.

Thirdly, the Kingdom of God Represents the Hope for the Eternal Happiness in the Future

In 2 Peter 1:10 and 1:11, 'Therefore, my brothers, be all the more eager to make your calling and election sure. For if you do these things, you will never fall, and you will receive a rich welcome into the eternal kingdom of our Lord and Savior Jesus Christ.' Jesus says of the future in the book of Matthew, 'I say to you that many will come from the east and the west, and will take their places at the feast with Abraham, Isaac and Jacob in the kingdom of heaven.' (Matthew 8:11) Furthermore, in Matthew 13, Jesus used a metaphor to explain what is meant by the kingdom of heaven. And then the Lord says the righteous will shine like the sun in the kingdom of heaven.

Fourthly, Jesus Explains What the Kingdom of God Is Like

'The kingdom of God does not come with your careful observation, nor will people say, 'Here it is,' or 'There it is,' because the kingdom of God is within you.' (Luke 17:20-21) Here, 'you' is plural. Jesus was within them. The Pharisees were not really looking for the future signs of glory. The Kingdom of God was right in front of them. However, they were too ignorant spiritually, they could not see the presence of God without hearing the sound of the victorious trumpet.

Fifthly, the Paradox of the Kingdom of God Should Be Interpreted Based on a Balanced Understanding

Jeus said in John 18:36, 'My kingdom is not of this world.' However, in Luke 13:19, the Lord said the Kingdom of God would start out almost invisible as small as a mustard seed. However, this seed, which is almost negligible, would grow to influence all the world.

These descriptions in the Bible should not be viewed as contradictory, but as complementary. Thus, the Kingdom of God is in the future, but it is also in the present. Although it is not of this world, it will influence all the world. The Kingdom of God starts out right now, but it will be completed in the future. You can not see it with your eyes. However, the Kingdom of God exists everywhere Jesus Christ is present.

Basileia is a Greek word, meaning 'nation', and *malkuth* is a Hebrew word, meaning 'the position and authority of the king'. We are dealing with people, who are subject to the king's authority or under the king's authority. Therefore, the real nature of 'authority' can be better understood in the context of the Biblical concept of the 'nation'.

In Psalms 145:13, this thought is expressed in a poetic verse, 'Your kingdom is an everlasting kingdom, and your dominion endures through all generations.' In the ancient Hebrew poetry, the two parallel verses express the same meaning in different ways. Thus, the concept of the Kingdom of God meant the actual reign of God.

King Herod was definitely not a great king of Israel. Although he built the temple again, an awesome and beautiful building in Jerusalem, he did not possess a true kingdom. If his authority was detached from the Roman influence, it lacked a pure and justifiable basis. He did not have the legitimacy. Although he lived in the palace, wore the crown, and was called king Herod, his kingdom was not earned but bought.

A position can be bought in England. However, receiving a title from the queen is entirely different from this practice. Money can buy a position, but the title would not be legitimate.

If we analyze this thought further, we can understand the prayer that Jesus taught us. 'your kingdom come, your will be done on earth as it is in heaven.' (Matthew 6:10) These words show the Lord's longing for the authority of God to reign this world as in heaven rather than requesting God to rule over this rapidly changing world.

The Power of the Kingdom of God

I think the Kingdom of God is the true nature of the authority or the reign of God. The Kingdom of God is eternal. The reign of God is a thing of the present. However, it is also that of the future. God is the creator of all this world and all the universe. He is almighty. However, He allowed Himself to be limited on this land. Satan received the power to reign. He has the authority on the worldly organizations. Nevertheless, God did not allow satan to rule humans at will. God gave us a place to escape to from the realm of satan's authority. God gave us the last Adam, Jesus Christ.

The last Adam gave us, the believers, more than the first Adam lost. Satan lured Jesus Christ, but Christ won the fight. As soon as Jesus won the first fight over the authority to rule the world, He declared the power of the Kingdom of God.

Jesus healed the sick and drove out demons.

Jesus called the disciples. They were sent out upon receiving His power, but they were also tempted. Seventy people upon Jesus' resurrection were called to heal the sick and drive out the demons. The last fight of Christ and satan took place on the Cross. Satan used all his authority to make it advantageous. He tried to kill the Son of God and scatter the disciples. Jesus not only died for our sin but resurrected in three days from death and defeated satan and all his force. The Lord had the key to death and hell, and so He is the Lord of every creature. Jesus said this before He ascended into Heaven after His resurrection.

> All authority in heaven and on earth has been given to me. Therefore go and make disciples of all nations, baptizing them in the name of the Father and of the Son and of the Holy Spirit,' (Matthew 28:18,19)
>
> and
>
> And these signs will accompany those who believe: In my name they will drive out demons; they will speak in new tongues; they will pick up snakes with their hands; and when they drink deadly poison, it will not hurt them at all; they will place their hands on sick people, and they will get well. (Mark 16:17,18)

In the Gospel of Mark, Jesus said the signs of the Kingdom of Heaven are the power of God to heal the sick and drive out demons. Because Jesus defeated satan and won the final victory, the Lord gave us all believers the same power. The fact that Christ is reigning is revealed to the world through not only the sermon, that manifests the power of the Holy Spirit but also our power, that we pray and heal the sick, and the power, that has an authority over those living in the kingdom of satan.

The theme of divine healing can be a subject of debate today. However, it has never been an issue for me. It is because, if I myself was not healed, I would have been a dead Buddhist. I converted to Christianity when I was waiting for my death at the last stage of tuberculosis. However, I realized that divine healing can be a theological issue to many evangelical pastors. I have been very careful on this issue. In fact, some of my closest friends believe that divine healing was temporarily needed in the early churches. Although I do not agree with the theological point of view that, once the Bible was canonized, the divine healing was no longer needed and the miracle of divine healing has ended. I do not view them as loving Jesus less or as faulty pastors.

I experienced the divine healing in our church many times. I believe in God, who grants health to our saints. We believe that God will perform a miracle if we pray for the sick. I also believe in the ministry of using medicines. Many physicians attend our church. We see them asking the Lord to bless the use of the medical technology to heal the sick or for God to perform a miracle. Likewise, we see that God heals the sick through them. God uses both ways. I believe in God, who performs miracles in our church.

A demon is an entity that actually exists like Jesus. When we pray, we learned that we have to use the authority that Jesus gives us. Jesus said to Peter and other disciples, 'whatever you loose on earth will be loosed in heaven.' (Matthew 16:19 and 18:18) We learned we are not fighting blood and flesh. Our main concern is to bind the authority of satan that works on the earth. We can confront and defeat satan through prayer. Just like the Israelites had to keep the arms of Moses up to defeat the Amalekites (Exodus 17:11), the power of intercessory prayer is awesome. We have the power and authority that Christ gave us.

The saints of a growing and dynamic church know that the fight against the demons is for real and they have to be awake and coolheaded all the time. The authority of satan is only a temporary historical phenomenon. In Genesis 3:15, God said to the snake (satan), 'And I will put enmity between you and the woman, and between your offspring and hers; he will crush your head, and you will strike his heel.' In ancient battle, the fight was finished and the victory was ensured by crushing the head of the enemy.

Satan knew that a man will come to this world to limit the realm of his authority. He was not to be an angel but a person. This person was Jesus Christ. The prophecy of the Old Testament said He was of the tribe of Judah and an offspring of Jesse. Because of it, satan attacked the offspring of humans. Since the angelical beings became one flesh with the daughters of man, giants came to be everywhere. The family of Noah, however, was not defiled. Thus, God kept humans even through the Great Flood. However, satan continued to attack Israel, the chosen nation of God.

In many cases, they would have been destroyed if they were not protected by God. Satan devised every possible plans to prevent the prophecy of Genesis 3:15 from being realized.

The Apostle Paul says in Ephesians 1:21, the authority of God is 'far above all rule and authority, power and dominion, and every title that can be given, not only in the present age but also in the one to come.' Thus, the authority of Christ does not have an ending point. The questions about Jesus's successor are answered by His Apostle. The Apostle Paul says we became the successors with Christ. Thus, we will sit together with Christ in the kingdom of heaven, which has much better standards than the worldly standard. Thus, we possess all the authority to accomplish Jesus Christ's Great Commision to go and make disciples of all nations.

The Gospel of the Kingdom of God

The gospel means the 'good news'. People come to church and often listen to something other than the gospel. They hear about what satan is doing. They hear about what politicians are doing. They also hear about what's happening in the world. I often see that Christians come to church with anticipation and leave with worry and melancholy. They listen to bad news, and not the good news.

The thing that saints in the church need is the Good News. The Good News is that we belong to the winning side of God's reign. Matthew 13:16 says, 'But blessed are your eyes because they see, and your ears because they hear.' This verse makes us to realize how special we are. For a contextual understanding, we can read a few more verses and understand that Jesus blesses us for being able to see the overall picture.

While I am reading this verse, I associate this story with my experience of the picture puzzles I used to give to my sons. The children take out all the pieces and spread them out on the wooden floor. Some pieces of the puzzle are easy to see where they belong, but some pieces are hard to figure out where they belong until after the puzzle is almost finished. The prophets were the same. They prophesied only in parts. They only spoke the parts that the Holy Spirit anointed them to prophesy. However, we are blessed since Jesus

Christ completed the puzzle for us. When we look at the book of Isaiah, we can see what God meant when He gave the prophet Isaiah chapter 53.

However, the gospel of the kingdom of God falls on different soils. The words of God fall on four types of minds. The soil on the path is hardened from people walking on them. The seed that fell on this type of soil can not produce any good plant. These people do not allow the message of the gospel to root deeply in their minds. The rocky soils can be likened to people, who listen to the message but do not pay the price to change their lives. The thorny soils mean the minds of people, who are too interested in their present life to allow the message to take root in their minds. However, the fertile soil represents people, who listen to the message of the kingdom of God and are willing to pay any price to bear the fruits of the kingdom of God. Since they prioritize their works based on the need to bear the fruit of the kingdom of God, they end up bearing fruits according to their ability given by the Holy Spirit.

We have gone through two wars in the last 40 years. So, we have not slighted the promise of God. The early churches were persecuted by the Roman empire. They knew what dying for Christ meant. This is the reason why Christ sent the early Christians a letter through the Apostle John at Patmos Island. The Revelation of John makes many people, who do not understand the words, feel afraid. However, when we see the overall Revelation in this context, we realize that Christ is the Lord. Although there may be many obstacles awaiting for us, Jesus Christ is in control completely. And the final victory of Jesus Christ has already been accomplished. Because of the resurrected Christ, the early church could stand firm on a steadfast faith. And at last they won victory over their persecutors.

The early church overcame formidable foes. They defeated them not by swords and spears but with the gospel message of the kingdom of God. The great Roman empire yielded to the Christian world not by the sword but by peaceful conversion. The Roman empire accepted the fact that Jesus was the Lord at last, and Constantinus, the Roman emperor, knelt and bowed down in front of the great king, our Lord, Jesus Christ.

The Gospel of the Kingdom of God and Church Growth

The gospel of the kingdom of God should be preached from all pulpits of the world on Sunday worship service. Then, people will be excited by the Lord, whom we are serving, and love Him.

That's right. If the sinners in your local society realize that God, whom the church worships, is living and working on us, your church will grow truthfully. God is living and fills our needs. When people experience the life of God, they realize the working of God, and they devote themselves to Him. Among them, the kingdom of God comes. In addition, the changed saints will turn to be witnesses to the gospel of the kingdom of God in their society. The kingdom of God may not be visible, but it is working through the power of the Holy Spirit. The church should do all it can to proclaim the gospel of the kingdom of God till the last day of the world. A church growth should have its foundation on the gospel of the kingdom of God through Jesus Christ.

Bibliography

1. Cho, Yonggi, *Do You Truly Want your Church to Grow?*, Seoul, Seoul Logos Inc., 1995.
2. Cho, Yonggi, I *Pray this Way, I, II*, Seoul, Seoul Logos Inc., 1998.
3. Cho, Yonggi, *I Preach this Way*, Seoul, Seoul Logos Inc., 1999.
4. Cho, Yonggi, *Key to a Successful Church Growth*, Seoul, Seoul Logos Inc., 1990.
5. Cho, Yonggi, *Spiritual Leader for the 21st Century*, Seoul, Seoul Logos Inc., 1999.
6. Cho, Yonggi, *How Should I Pray?*, Seoul, Seoul Logos Inc., 1998.
7. Cho, Yonggi, *Fivefold Gospel Story for Modern People*, Seoul, Seoul Logos Inc., 1997.
8. Cho, Yonggi, *The Fourth Dimension*, Seoul, Seoul Logos., 1996.
9. Cho, Yonggi, *More than Numbers*, Seoul, Seoul Logos., 1993.
10. Cho, Yonggi, *Successful Home Cell Groups*, Plainfield, Logos International, 1981.

PART 3

ANALYSES OF THE REV. CHO'S CHURCH GROWTH

1. The Influence of Rev. Cho's Leadership on the Churches of Korea

   Dr. Myung, Sung-Hoon

2. Rev. Cho's Cell Groups and Dynamics of Church Growth

   Dr. Joel Comiskey

3. The Effect of Rev. Cho's Sermon Style for Church Growth on the Development of Theology

   Dr. Ma, Won-Suk

4. A Study of Rev. Cho and the Growth of Yoido Full Gospel Church

   Dr. Park, Myung-Soo

5. The Influence of Rev. Cho's Church Growth on Korean Society

   Dr. Hong, Young-Gi

CHAPTER 1

The Influence of Rev. Cho's Leadership on the Churches of Korea

DR. MYUNG, SUNG-HOON

Yoido Full Gospel Church is a world class symbol of Korean church growth. It is well known already that Yoido Full Gospel Church is the world's largest single church unit. The churches, that have been supported and branched off, number 900, and the number of pastors, who have been attending this church, is in several thousands. All reformed churches in the world, including churches in Korea, of course, have had a deep interest in the growth of Yoido Full Gospel Church whether in good days or bad days. And the church growth model of this church has had a powerful influence on the churches around the world.

Many opinions have been raised on the factors for the growth of Yoido Full Gospel Church. That is the church growth is not due to a couple of factors but due to a complex, interactive factors of spiritual, personal, societal, systematic, and environmental matters. The church growth studies have two premises. The first is that 'church growth is the will of God.' A church revival or growth is not made by human plan, but it is a gift of God. The main actor of the church growth is not the pastors nor the saints but God. Humans only sow and water, but it is the Holy Spirit, who makes it grow.[1] The second premise is that church growth is complex. A church growth is not the result of any one cause or factor. Besides objective and visible elements that humans can analyze, it has mystic elements embedded in it.

I have been attending Yoido Full Gospel Church for a long time. I have analyzed the dynamic spirituality, that influenced the church growth, into four factors: the Holy Spirit, prayer, sermon and leadership.[2] Reverend Lee, Young-Hoon has suggested six factors for

1 cf. 1 Corinthians 3:5-9.

2 cf. Myung, Sung-Hoon, *Spiritual Resources for Church Growth* (Seoul Logos Inc., 1992)

growth, prayer, experiencing the Holy Spirit, the leadership of the pastor, divine healing movement, the cell organization and evangelical movement through lay Christian leaders, etc..[3] The most important factor among these factors is, of course, the work of God, the Holy Spirit.

However, I can not help but say that the most important reason for the growth of Yoido Full Gospel Church is the leadership of a spiritual leader, Reverend Cho, Yonggi. This is based on the perspective that all other factors such as the work of the Holy Spirit, prayer, organization, and sermon can not exist without the personal leadership that can carry these on. In this context, this paper, argues that charismatic leadership is the key principle of church growth. In this paper, therefore, I look at the characteristics of Reverend Cho, Yonggi's personal leadership and answer the question of how the leadership of Reverend Cho has impacted the churches in Korea.

The Characteristics of Reverend Cho, Yonggi's Leadership

John Maxwell, who is one of the foremost authority in America on leadership, often uses the catch-phrase, 'leadership is everything.'[4] Whether it is home, business, or nation, the organization grows and develops if it has a strong and effective leadership. The church, which is a Godly entity of life and a human organization at the same time, is no exception. The church can grow if the leadership of the Holy Spirit and human leadership work together.

There is nothing more important than the leadership of a pastor. Dr. Peter Wagner says that pastoral leadership is the most important factor in the church growth:

> Reverend Cho of Korea will be remembered as one of the most influential spiritual leader for the churches around the world upon the later 20th century.[5]

The type of leadership represented by Reverend Cho is called church growth leadership. The church growth leadership of Reverend Cho is the result of inner personal leadership. What are the key characteristics of Reverend Cho, a strong pastoral leader? I answer this question with seven self-portraits of leadership.

---

3 Lee, Young-Hoon, 'Evangelism and Church Growth of Korean Churches', *Theological Thoughts* (1998. Spring) pp. 235-236.

4 John C. Maxwell, *Developing the Leader Within You* (Nashville: Nelson/Word Publisher, 1993), pp. 8-11.

5 C. Peter Wanger, *On the Crest of Wave* (Ventura: Regal Books, 1983), p. 29.

1. Spiritual Authority

The reason, that Reverend Cho is regarded as a model of strong pastoral leadership is because of his spiritual authority. The spiritual authority is not given by a certain position or qualification. It is a Godly authority that is allowed through the Holy Spirit. This spiritual authority makes the pastor instill a firm faith among saints that he is the spiritual authority, which God has entrusted and delegated. This spiritual authority makes the pastor believe he is speaking the words of God on behalf of Him. Regardless of any church, the church is bound to grow as much as the congregation members obey the leader's spiritual authority.

When there is a spiritual authority, that makes people want to have a contact with the supernatural world, people give undivided obedience and devotion to a church. One of the most powerful factors in Reverend Cho's leadership is that the saints expect to have a contact with the supernatural world and actually experience it. As the result, the saints following Reverend Cho have the faith that Reverend Cho is clearly the chosen servant of God. This leadership with spiritual authority is the result of being filled with the Holy Spirit. Being filled with the Holy Spirit is manifested through a couple of miracles, signs and experiences.

It is the crystal of countless prayer, fasting, tears and sweat. A consistent and persistent prayer is the passage to receive, preserve and develop the leadership of spiritual authority that God allowed. It is difficult to expect a voluntary obedience since we don't feel the spiritual authority from a leader, who does not pray. However, the spiritual authority, that flows from a praying leader, makes many people obey and devote themselves.

Thus, Robert Clinton, who is an expert in leadership development, has spoken the following regarding the relationship between the spiritual authority and prayer.

> The core of spiritual leadership is invariably in the communication between God and the leaders. Prayer becomes a factor, that teaches the meaning and importance of being in today's age of doing. There is no other important habit for a leader than prayer in communicating with God and having a vision for a mission. The leader, who makes time to fast and pray alone, will certainly reap the spiritual fruit.[6]

6 Robert Clinton, *The Making of a Leader* (Colorado Springs: Navigator Press, 1988), p. 116.

2. *Vision and Dream*

Reverend Cho is one of the pastors, who emphasize the importance of dream and vision for success and victory. He believes that the church growth starts in the mind of the pastor. The mind of the pastor can control his/her behavior. Dream and vision is a language of the Holy Spirit, the clothes of faith, and a blue-print of goal. The Lord promised that He will let you know of the future when the Holy Spirit comes. In other words, the dream and vision of the future will come to those, who are with the Holy Spirit. According to Reverend Cho, the true nature of the church growth leadership is the vision and the confidence that the vision will be realized.

> The biggest obstacle that hinders the growth of a church is the lack of vision among church leaders to satisfy the desire of God. The lack of vision brings the lack of growth. 'I can not do it no matter what. I can not do it here.' These words should disappear from our language. The leader should first use the language of the Holy Spirit and plant the mind of success in the hearts of all people.[7]

The dream and vision are not only the language of the Holy Spirit but the faith itself or the expression of the faith. Having faith means having the dream of God. Faith is to experience the future at the present time. God is of the eternal now. God sees from the beginning to the end. The faith that pleases God is the present faith.[8]

The vision and dream is also the act to set the goal. Reverend Cho and his church have experienced the great power of setting the goal from the beginning. He asserts that a clear goal and the faith, that the goal will be attained, are the real key to prayer answer.[9] When Reverend Cho started his church in a tent with 5 people in 1958, he immediately set the goal to grow his church to 150 people. That goal was achieved within the same year. Then, he achieved the goal of 600 congregation members within 3 years of his ministry. And again, he accomplished the goal of having 3,000 congregation members within the next 3 years. Likewise, he realized the formidable goal of having half a million congregation members in 1986. Although there were some complications that arose from a hard-pressed goal, the tenacity of Reverend Cho on achieving his goal eventually made the unbelievable growth of his church possible to build the world's largest church in the grace of God.

---

7 Paul Yonggi Cho, *More Than Numbers* (Waco: Word Books, 1984), p. 24.

8 Paul Yonggi Cho, *Key to Revival* (Waco: Word Books, 1984), p. 150.

9 Paul Yonggi Cho. *Successful Home Cell Groups* (Plainfield: Logos International, 1981), p. 2.

3. Brokenness and Surrender

The third characteristics of Reverend Cho's leadership is brokenness and surrender.

The stronger the leader is, the more tendency for him/her to be self-conceited and a slave of blind ambition. These erroneous attitudes justify the means to achieve the purpose. The experience of being totally broken in front of God is very much needed to cure these pastoral diseases. Reverend Cho had to experience so many excruciatingly painful encounters as an expert on church growth. Many troubles such as disease and weakness, financial and interpersonal conflicts, and heresy criticism and absolute loneliness, etc. made him to kneel and surrender to God.

According to Reverend Cho, the more willing the pastor is to grow his church, the more painful surrender he/she has to make to God. A success is not attained through learning the formula for success. When you are broken in the eyes of God and receive the mercy and grace of God, you can succeed finally. The reason, God is constantly breaking us, is to give us an endless blessing.[10]

The best blessing, that we can receive on the verge of complete brokenness, is being filled with the Holy Spirit. Thus, the mission of a leader is to break himself/herself completely so that the Holy Spirit can occupy him/her. (Colossians 1:24) Brokenness and surrender is not for the sake of itself. It is just an effective means to be held in the hands of God to be used in the revival and growth of the church. In this respect, the church growth leadership is not the practice of asceticism or stoicism. It should be a self-surrender by charismatic regeneration to focus not on himself/herself but on God. It should be the ultimate focus not that how holy I become but that how much I obey and follow the Holiness of God.

4. Excellent Communication

The fourth characteristics of Reverend Cho's leadership is excellent communication skills. Most leaders are excellent communicators. The leader is the one, who persuades people to lead them to a better direction for life. So to speak, they are the ones, who received the gift of words. The gift of words includes the charisma of knowledge, wisdom, prophecy, education, advice, speaking in tongues, and interpretation, etc.[11] Reverend Cho not only received these gifts

10 Paul Yonggi Cho, *Praying with Jesus* (Altamonte Springs: Creation House, 1987). p. 39.

11 Clinton, *The Making of a Leader*, p. 143.

of words but showed how to be a role model for leaders, who tried his utmost to receive and enhance these gifts. The efforts, that Reverend Cho made, are prayer and reading in order to be an excellent communicator. He made it a part of his life to pray for a long time before a sermon or lecture. He is well known to be a minister, who not only prays a lot but also has a strong drive to learn. We can never overemphasize the importance of reading habit for self-improvement. The more the leader is used by God, the more he/she reads in a wide variety of area. And they are known to apply what they read on their life, especially communicating.[12]

In communication, the character development is as important as charisma and skill development. It does not need to mention that the leader's morality and ethics should be a role model for others in communicating the truth. Especially, it is more important for senior pastors, who face the same audiences for a long time. Because the leader is also a human, he/she can commit some acts of flesh. The act of flesh means the leader is making a hasty decision to react based on his/her emotion without asking and not sensing the will of God. In this case, Reverend Cho used to resolve the issue by confessing to God and people honestly, and this practice is also an essence of an effective communication.

Although a public confession is very hard to do, because it makes the confessor hurt his/her pride and shameful, it is wiser to deal with an issue honestly to gain more people to Christ. Reverend Cho speaks the following on this issue.

> Living by the Holy Spirit is to live honestly. Of course, losing a face is not a pleasant thing. However, the Holy Spirit makes us overcome hurt pride. I detest confessing my shameful mistakes in public. However, an honest confession brings an unexpected result of gaining a renewed trust in the relationship with the saints.[13]

5. Delegation

The fifth characteristic of Reverend Cho's leadership is appropriate delegation. To lead is to delegate.[14] In 1964, Reverend Cho fainted due to a burn-out from ministering over 2,000 congregation members. While he was recuperating, he felt the need for delegation. From that point on, he delegated the task of ministry to assistant

12 Clinton, *The Making of a Leader*, p. 141.

13 Cho, *Prayer: Key to Revival*, p. 31.

14 Oswald Sanders, *Spiritual Leadership* (Chicago: Moody Press, 1980), p. 202.

pastors, cell leaders and other lay Christian leaders. As the result, even when he was on overseas mission for over a half of the year, the church continued to grow and became to be known for having the most staffs.

The real purpose for delegation is to develop and arm the people. A church is a participatory body in its nature. Thus, a proper system has to be set up to teach the body, Christians, the gifts of the Holy Spirit and to lead them into using their talents. Parish system and cell system is the successful result of this system.[15] Likewise, the delegation brings the effect of growing the saints before growing the church in terms of the number of congregation members.

In this respect, the church growth leader should not only be the leader but also an equipper. It is the true nature of delegation to grow people more so than using people.

Reverend Cho, Yonggi of Yoido Full Gospel Church not only delegates tasks without reservation but keeps training and supervising constantly. The purpose of delegation can only be achieved if training and supervision follow. He emphasizes the importance of want-to-motivation over ought-to-motivation to his fellow partners in ministry. From the beginning, he asked his assistant pastors to work diligently and even instilled a competitiveness in good will among them, although he changed in the 90's. Of course, there were some conflicts of pastoral ethics among these fellow assistant partners, most of them maintained the obeying attitude completely to the directions and operating policy of their fellow senior minister. This loyalty and devotion for the organization is one of the most powerful inner factor to make it possible for the Yoido Full Gospel Church to be the world's largest church.

6. Situational Leadership

The sixth characteristics of Reverend Cho is situational leadership. An effective leadership changes the style of the leadership in dealing with a variety of situations. In other words, it is not a dictatorial style of leadership, in which the followers change to the leader, but a free style of leadership, in which the leader varies the leading strength and forms in accordance with the maturity of the followers. In situational leadership, there are types of directing, selling,

15 Yoido Full Gospel Church is currently operating a mega-size church ministry as of January 2003, including 560 pastors, 350 full time staffs (excluding employees at Kookmin Daily News, Elim Welfare Town, and Hansei University) as well as about 8,000 cell leaders.

persuading, and delegating. Reverend Cho is a model leader, who has applied this theory of situational leadership in the ministry field.

He does not ignore the principles and reasonableness, and yet he does not hesitate to change his alternative methods for an effective result. This attitude is in congruence with the church growth leadership as suggested by Carl George.

A growing church has a clear picture of what God wants from it. They do not insist on their own program for the very cause of achieving God's purpose. We have to align ourselves to the purpose and move forward rather than aligning the purpose to us. The purpose does not move or change. We have to change our methods or means. Thus we have to be rid of things that do not edify the church and reorganize in accordance with the situation for the ministry to be effective.[16]

This situational leadership has the advantage of making the relationship between the organization and the dynamic and interactive task. It regards the contents to be more important than the format. We can change our format without any hesitation for the purpose of God. We have to take the ministry-first-approach rather than structure-first-approach.[17] We can change the organization, custom, and structure any way, the Holy Spirit makes us realize, in accordance with various situational needs, if it is better for the church growth and the senior pastor is willing. Behind the remarkable growth of Yoido Full Gospel Church, there is this flexibility and adaptability that interacts with the needs of people unlike many other megachurches.

7. Servant Leadership

The seventh characteristic of Reverend Cho's leadership is the servant leadership. In a healthy church, a servanthood goes with the authority.

A leadership, which is strong but has the servanthood mind, is necessary for true Christian ministry.[18] Reverend Cho makes an effort to understand this seemingly contrasting aspects of church ministry in a framework of pastoral philosophy.

---

16 Carl George & Robert Rogan, *Leading and Managing Your Church* (Old Tappen: Fleming H. Revell Company, 1987), p. 56.

17 Flank R. Tillapaugh, *Unleashing the Church: Getting People Out of the Fortress and Into Ministry* (Ventura: Regal Books, 1982). p.73.

18 C. Peter Wagner, *Leading Your Church to Growth: A Guidebook for Clergy and Laity* (Glendale: Regal Books, 1984), pp. 80-87.

> What is most urgent for us is the recovery of ministry. A pastor is not the one, who rules, but the one, who serves others. Our authority is not compulsory but voluntary in nature.[19]
>
> ... Our church allows authority with love. If a pastor loves the saints truly, they will fully accept the authority of a pastor. However, if a pastor abuses his title and use a force to influence his/her authority, the saints will resist and the pastor will be trapped in the problem issue.[20]

As mentioned before, Reverend Cho confesses his unintentional mistake and asks for the forgiveness and prayer of the saints. In this manner, when a pastor honestly confesses his mistake and asks for a forgiveness, the saints will respect the pastor and follow him/her more in most cases. It is because all the authority comes from love. Reverend Cho has conceived of 'seven principles of servant leadership' for himself and other fellow ministers and tries to make every efforts to reflect them on himself.

1. Our attitude should be not arrogance but humility.
2. Our motive should have no room for doubt.
3. Our ministry should not be self-centered.
4. Our resources should not be used for our advantage or popularity.
5. Our time should not be invested in anything other than that which benefits the church.
6. Our prayer should continue to receive the direction of the Lord incessantly.
7. Our bodily desires should be purified and concentrated on the kingdom of God.[21]

The Influence of Reverend Cho, Yonggi's Leadership

Up to now, I have analyzed the characteristics of the leadership of Reverend Cho, Yonggi of Yoido Full Gospel Church. Those are spiritual authority, vision and dream, brokenness and surrender, communication, delegation, situational leadership, and servanthood. These leadership characteristics have influenced numerous would-be-pastors and theological students in a variety of way. It is a fact that these characteristics influence those ministers, who want to be

---

19 Cho, *More Than Numbers*, p. 140.
20 Cho, *Successful Home Cell Groups*, p. 94.
21 Cho, *More Than Numbers*, p. 140.

like Reverend Cho, Yonggi and want to grow their church like Yoido Full Gospel Church, especially more.

Professor Park, Eun-Gyu of Mokwon University has classified the ministerial types of Korean churches into 10 types – sermon-centered ministry, nurturing ministry, church growth ministry, healing ministry, prophetic ministry, team ministry, evangelizing and overseas mission-centered ministry, lay Christian training-centered ministry, koinonia centered ministry, and special-mission ministry, etc.[22] All these 10 ministerial types can be found in the ministry field of Reverend Cho, Yonggi's Yoido Full Gospel Church. That is to support the saying that the 40 years of ministry at Yoido Full Gospel Church have influenced the ministerial style of Korean churches in a variety of ways.

Which areas of Korean church does the influence of Yoido Full Gospel Church, especially Reverend Cho's leadership and ministry, manifest itself? I explore that it has influenced the churches in Korea in five areas – church growth area, the Holy Spirit movement area, preaching ministry area, world mission area, and ecumenism and Christian cultural area, etc.

1. The Leadership Influence on Church Growth

Yoido Full Gospel Church and Reverend Cho, Yonggi as the synonym for church growth began with an 'explosion rather than growth'.[23] This church revival at Yoido increased the number of members in the new main sanctuary to 10,000, after moving from SeoDaeMoon in the 1970's.

After Yoido Full Gospel Church surpassed 10,000 congregation members, several mega-churches with over 10,000 congregation members began to emerge not only in Korea but around the world. When this Yoido Full Gospel Church again broke the common conception that believed having a mega-church with over 100,000 congregation members was impossible for the first time in the church history, some churches with over 100,000 congregation members began to surface in Latin America and Africa.

The biggest contribution of Reverend Cho, Yonggi of Yoido Full Gospel Church to church growth area is that he showed the vision and system. That is, he undertook the function of a visionary to

---

22 Park, Eun-Gyu, 'Analysis of Korean Ministry Style', *Christian Thoughts* (November, 1996), pp. 10-20.

23 Kang, Yoo-Il, 'Shinang-Gye Invitation: Reverend Cho, Yonggi of Yoido Full Gospel Church', *Shinang-Gye* (May, 1985).

show a church growth thinking. The church growth thinking is the belief, that church growth is possible in any circumstances, if there is a firm faith that the church growth is the will of God. In church growth, vision, thinking, and spirituality are more important than the skills and techniques.[24] In other words, Reverend Cho, Yonggi charged forward ahead of anyone to promote the faith that a church can grow by the help of the Holy Spirit no matter how the circumstances are stacked up against it if one has the positive attitude of 'I can do it, It will be done, Let's do it.'

The leadership of Reverend Cho is highly evaluated because of his vision of church growth and his contribution to develop and propagate the church growth system, which remakes the dynamic interactivity of church growth and the style of ministry. Reverend Cho has successfully carried out the remake of church growth through his disciples. Of course, not all his disciples succeeded in their church growth. However, almost all his disciples or pastors, who learned from the example of Reverend Cho's ministerial philosophy, strategy, and method, showed an excellent growth of their church without exception.

With repsect to this point, Reverend Oh, Jeong-Hyun of Church of Love, who grafted and succeeded the ministerial system of the Church of Love in America, made the following evaluation.

> About 2 years ago, Reverend Lee, Joong-Pyo of Hanshin Church, said in a Korean Mega-Church Pastors Seminar that the reformed churches in Korea have been influenced deeply since the 1970's by two ministerial flows. He said One was the Holy Spirit movement through Reverend Cho, Yonggi of Yoido Full Gospel Church, and the other was the ministry of disciples training centered on Reverend Oak, Han-hum of the Church of Love. Easily speaking, the two giants, that influenced Korean reformed churches for the past 20-30 years, were the two churches aforementioned. I would like to agree with this opinion from my perspective of studying network ministry. The reason is because many ministries were remade by grafting the system of Yoido Full Gospel Church or the system of the Church of Love. Full Gospel Churches, which have the same system as Yoido Full Gospel Church, often have their senior pastors trained and takes the same position on the Holy Spirit movement of Full Gospel Church, and these churches – Inchon Full Gospel Church, Kwangju Full Gospel Church, Busan Geumjeong Full Gospel Church, Daejeon Full Gospel Church, Jeonju Full Gospel Church, etc. – are booming with thousands and

---

24 Myung-Sung-Hoon, *Principles and Strategies for Surpassing 300 Adult Congregation Members* (Kookmin Daily News, 1998), p. 24.

tens of thousands congregation members. In the cities overseas such as Sydney or New York, these Full Gospel Churches have been remade (of Yoido Full Gospel Church) to be the largest church in the area.[25]

Reverend Cho, Yonggi was not done at the point of making Yoido Full Gospel Church an example of church growth. He showed his charismatic leadership to open his know-hows of church growth to the public and to propagate it to other ministers. He has held a church growth seminar for all domestic and international ministers from a long time ago. Especially, he established Church Growth International for churches in the overseas and Institute for Church Growth for domestic churches as his heartily effort to spread and propagate the church growth movement.

2. The Leadership Influence on the Holy Spirit Movement

The Holy Spirit movement of Korean churches stems from the revival movement of early 20th century at Pyungyang. Ever since Reverend Lee, Yong-Do's mystic Holy Spirit movement in the 1930's that continues to flow till the great revival of Korean churches in the 1960's, the Holy Spirit movement of Korean churches are evaluated to culminate in the Pentecostal Holy Spirit movement of Reverend Cho, Yonggi.[26] The Assemblies of God, the largest denomination among Pentecostal Christianity, came to Korea for mission only during the 1950's, it is no doubt that the main power base of Reverend Cho's Yoido Full Gospel Church enabled for this denomination to exert a great influence on Korean churches as the forerunner of the Holy Spirit movement.

Reverend Cho, Yonggi has served as the president of the World Assemblies of God with a membership of 30 million people for the past several years to lead the Holy Spirit movement of the world. The Holy Spirit movement of Reverend Cho can be summarized by prayer movement, charisma movement, and evangelical movement. So called Korean style prayer, that is early morning prayer, all

---

25 Oh, Jeong-Hyun, 'You should have a dynamic network', *Monthly Ministry* (April, 1998) p. 98.

26 The first, evident researches on the Holy Spirit movement of Korean churches are published in *The phenomenon and structure of the Holy Spirit movement of Korean churches* (Christian Academy, 1982), Kang-Won-Yong, ed., and in this book, professor Yoo, Dong-shik analyzed and introduced the Holy Spirit movement of Yoido Full Gospel Church led by Reverend Cho, Yonggi as an exmaple of 'motherly Holy Spirit movement'.

night prayer, fasting prayer, and all-crying-out prayer are important style of prayer ministry of Yoido Full Gospel Church. The prayer movement of Yoido Full Gospel Church starts its dynamic power from Reverend Cho's leadership on prayer. Reverend Cho, himself, prays over three hours a day and made praying his habit for life to set the example for all saints.

Especially, the passage for the Yoido Full Gospel Church to show its leadership on the Holy Spirit movement through the prayer of Korean churches is Choi, Ja-sil Memorial International Fasting Prayer Hall located at Osan-Ri. To the degree that almost all pastors or saints, who have an interest in prayer answer have visited Osan-Ri Fasting Prayer Hall, the prayer hall or house exerted a great influence on the spirituality of Korean churches. Several millions of saints have visited Osan-Ri Prayer Hall ever since 1973, and even now at the least several hundreds of people are fasting and praying on any given day. According to the statistics of 1995, 82 percent of the people, who visited there to pray, stated that they came to experience the full filling of their spirituality with the Holy Spirit.

This is a simple barometer of how much Osan-Ri Prayer Hall is influencing the Holy Spirit movement, straightforwardly speaking.[27]

The charisma movement of Yoido Full Gospel Church, well known for its speaking in tongues and divine healing, is well noticed by the outside manifestation of the Holy Spirit movement. It values more the experience of the Holy Spirit and the dynamic interactivity of the worship service than that of speaking in tongues or divine healing.[28] However, the Holy Spirit movement of Reverend Cho is often mistakenly regarded to emphasize speaking in tongues or divine healing more form the outside perspective. For a while, there was a friction with other denominations because of the issue of emphasizing speaking in tongues from the outside perspective. However, Reverend Cho does not insist on speaking in tongues as the only sign of being filled with the Holy Spirit or the baptism by the Holy Spirit. He regards the true peace of mind or life habit of evangelism along with speaking in tongues as the sign of being filled with the Holy Spirit or the baptism by the Holy Spirit.[29] He also accepts naturally divine healing and benediction as the

27 Kim, Shin-kook, 'Pastor Studies: Reverend Cho, Yonggi of Yoido Full Gospel Church', *Monthly Ministry* (June, 1996), pp. 117-118.

28 Myung, Sung-Hoon, *Church Growth and the Holy Spirit* (Seoul Logos Inc.. 1992). pp. 49-75.

29 Cho, Yonggi, *Fivefold Gospel and threefold blessing* (Seoul Logos Inc., 1997), pp. 100-101.

nature of ministry of Jesus and a natural phenomenon manifested when the Holy Spirit is upon us.

The most strong nature of the Holy Spirit along with prayer and charisma is evangelical movement. The reason for the Advent of the Holy Spirit is the spreading of the gospel of Jesus Christ. As Jesus evangelized through the power of the Holy Spirit, the church can become an evangelizing church and saint upon the power of the Holy Spirit. After all, the Holy Spirit movement is a movement to live and evangelize like Jesus. A healthy church or a church filled with the Holy Spirit should be able to replay Jesus ministry as Jesus taught, evangelized, healed, and prayed.

This Pentecostal Holy Spirit movement exerts its influence on Korean churches as a generally accepted ministry style. Beyond the Pentecostal denomination, every church, that oriented to the Pentecostal faith style of emphasizing the importance of being filled with the Holy Spirit, ardent prayer, dynamic worship and strong spiritual experience as the basis of their ministry, are now experiencing a remarkable growth.

Now, which denomination is not the issue, but which pastor has what kind of spiritual charisma is the issue. It is the age in which the aforementioned conditions determine the orientation and character of a church. In other words, if a pastor is Pentecostal, his church will be a Pentecostal church, although the pastor is not Pentecostal by the denomination. Also, it is a general observation that the growth rate of such Pentecostal church surpasses that of counterpart churches. Reverend Kim, Myung-Hyuk, known as a Reformist theologian, analyzed it as follows.

> The Pentecostal Holy Spirit movement centered on Full Gospel Churches exerted a great influence on not only Pentecostal churches but entire churches in Korea. This influence made its impact on conservative denominations, especially to those pastors and theologians of conservative denominations, who were losing their spiritual vitality. After all, there arose pastors and theologians, who became to have a more goodwill to the Pentecost although they did not imitate and still pointed out problematic issues of the Pentecost.[30]

3. *The Leadership Influence on Preaching Ministry*

The Pentecost emphasizes the Holy Spirit, but it concentrates on the work of the Holy Spirit through sermon and words of God. It is for

30 Kim, Myung-Hyuk, 'Korean churches and the Holy Spirit', *Tyrannus Ministerial Resources Big Encyclopedia* (vol. 8, 1996), p. 72.

this reason that almost all Pentecostalists are excellent preachers. Pentecostal preachers make the saints experience living words (Jesus Christ) from the recorded words (the Bible) through the channel of proclaimed words (sermon). Here is the very reason that the message of Reverend Cho, Yonggi changes so many people. The preaching ministry that is not the said word in the past but the saying word of living God through the preacher has become the main driving force to make Yoido Full Gospel Church the largest church in the world.

Even if how hard the Yoido Full Gospel Church worked on the Holy Spirit movement, if the preaching ministry of Reverend Cho was not superb, it would have been impossible for Yoido Full Gospel Church to be as it is today.

The reason that the preaching ministry of Reverend Cho creates so much responsiveness is because it applies the eternal Biblical truth (Gospel) to a practical power that fills the needs of today's life. His so called 'fivefold gospels and threefold blessings' simplifies the gospel of the Cross of Jesus Christ to apply it in today's life. The 'fivefold gospels' stresses the Holy Spirit (the Gospel of the Fullness of the Holy Spirit) instead of Holiness and added the dogma of blessing to fourfold gospel of Pentecostal holiness churches (regerneration, holiness, divine healing, and the Advent).[31]

The dogma of blessing is a holistic salvation of spiritual blessing, blessing for daily life, and blessing of the health. Above all, the message of Reverend Cho is ministerial concern itself, that fills the needs of people with the gospel of Christ. In this manner, the positive and aggressive message of fulfilling the needs of people, solving the problems, and healing the wounds exerted an unforgettable influence on so many pastors and other churches in the form of 'church growth style sermon'.

Of course, it is true that the message of emphasizing the blessing has been criticized as materialistic faith. The Church has expanded quantitatively, but it is the common criticism that it has failed in creating unselfish community life of mature spiritual, ethical self-devotion that change people's lives and society.[32] However, a fact that no one can deny is that the Reverend Cho's message of hope

31 Vinson Synan, *Current address of 20th century Holy Spirit movement* (Yeiin, 1995). p. 246.

32 Reverend Oak, Han-hum, the forerunner of disciples training, criticizes the false image of Korean churches, 'Korean churches are successful in getting people to follow Jesus to receive bread and health, but they are failing in making them disciples of Jesus.' Oak, Han-hum, 'Church is obstructing the church revival.' *Monthly Ministry* (April, 1998), p. 52.

and healing has approached the life of many people (Minjung) more friendly than Minjung theology to have more desperate people come to a church.[33] Regarding this point, we should not down-value the Reverend Cho's Full Gospel movement as materialistic, but we need to accept it as a meaningful event to manifest the kingdom of God today by adapting the Pentecostal theology to the religious minds of Koreans.

The preaching ministry of Reverend Cho, Yonggi instilled faith in people's minds to overcome the borderline of desperate lives by giving them a hope and consolation and by having them meet the living God. As the result, it is an undeniable fact that it has influenced the churches in Korea greatly from the perspective of church growth studies by having people experience the church as the kingdom of God and by having them devote themselves for the church. Many cases of creating huge church revival by applying the Reverend Cho's preaching philosophy and approach have testified for that fact.

4. *The Leadership Influence on the World Mission*

Yoido Full Gospel Church walked on the path to the world early. Reverend Cho started on a mission tour in 1964 by the invitation of the Department of State six years after he began his ministry. His age was 28 at that time, and his congregation members were 2,000. Afterwards, while he was on several overseas assemblies, he felt the need for a church for overseas Koreans and began to build a branch church overseas centered on America by sending out overseas missionaries for them since the early 1970's. In 1975, he established Full Gospel World Mission Center. And numerous missionaries have been sent out overseas since then. In addition, these missionaries are invited once a year to the mother church, Yoido Full Gospel Church, for a grand-scale missionary meeting to stimulate the saints' desire for mission. Since the beginning of 1990's, the church has changed its mission policy from overseas Korean missionary to native missionary, and it has sent 114 native missionaries in 40 countries as well as supporting and managing the follow-ups for them up to now.

The influence that Yoido Full Gospel Church and Reverend Cho, Yonggi on the world mission is more than sending out missionaries. Rather, it should be viewed that Reverend Cho's overseas ministry

33 Myung-Sung-Hoon, *Church growth and sermon* (Seoul: Seoul Logos Inc., 1992), p. 71.

and the ministry of Church Growth International seminars contributed more to the world mission.

We fall into a simple computational logic of how many missionaries have been sent when we evaluate the 'world mission'. However, it is current situation that sending out many missionaries do not guarantee their success in the mission field. On the contrary, it is more effective and efficient to train the leaders of target mission countries and help them to evangelize their country.

Reverend Cho's influence on the world mission can be attributed to his circuit mission ministry. Reverend Cho started overseas assembly for foreigners openly since 1978, and he held on the annual average of 30 large-scale assembly for the last 20 years. All together, he led more than 780 overseas assembly. His flight distance is calculated to go round the Equator 60 times.[34] Reverend Cho not only led the assembly but spread the gospel to every possible corners in the world by TV broadcasting ministry. He also have trained over 7 million pastors and church leaders in the world through 250 seminars and workshops of Church Growth International (established in 1976) in 50 countries.[35] This dynamic ministry has instilled the churches around the world a reverence for churches in Korea and functuioned as a stimulant for Korean pastors to go out to the world.

5. The Leadership Influence on Ecumenism and Christian Culture

It is true that, among the leadership realms of Reverend Cho, his weight in domestic churches was comparatively lighter based on his church size or world-class mission activities. Usually, people have spoken of Reverend Cho as a pastor better known overseas than in Korea. That is perhaps because the biggest mission given to Reverend Cho by God is to serve churches around the world as Reverend Cho confesses himself.

However, it could also be because of the reverse interpersonal relationship that can happen during the process of a church of a small denomination becoming the world's largest church in a short time.

---

34 Special article, 'Overseas mission ministry of Reverend Cho, Yonggi', *Full Gospel Family News* (May 3, 1998), p. 8.

35 CGI.(Church Growth International) is a world organization with its board of directors composed of 67 mega-church ministers and theologians in 22 countries. It holds international seminars and publishes books on church growth in English. Its magazine written in English, Church Growth, is delivered to subscribing, registered members of 17,000 in 150 countries (non-official members total 6.8 million people)

However, the situation changed a lot since the late 1980's. The relationship between different denominations changed for the better, and above all the societal ministry began to have a great impact. A turning point may be said of Kookmin Daily News established in 1988. As a platform of Korean churches for speaking to the society and a literary mission to spread Christian gospel and culture, the establishment of Kookmin Daily News set a landmark for directing the leadership of Reverend Cho from reformed churches to all the churches in Korea and Korean society. Although it is still not self supporting, I believe the Kookmin Dialy News is exerting its spreading effect in many areas as the only Christian daily newspaper throughout Korea.

Besides Kookmin Daily News, there are many cultural tasks that Yoido Full Gospel Church showed its leadership to churches in Korea. It opened a chapter in Christian social welfare task through Elim Welfare Town and prepared for the beginning of Christian newspaper through literature and publishing.[36] It started the first video worship service in Korea for the first time through its TV broadcasting station, and it is remembered as one of the first churches to start Gospel Songs movement. In addition, it has been in the front line to lead and set the example for service ministries such as heart troubled children saving movement, the bread of love movement, and blood of love donation drive, etc., throughout a wide variety of society by using the supportiveness of the entire church.

Toward the Leadership That Suggests A Vision

Up to now, the leadership of Reverend Cho, Yonggi and Yoido Full Gospel Church, that has grown to be the world's largest church, have been examined. How Reverend Cho's leadership has influenced the Korean churches was also explored in many areas.

As a conclusion, the ministerial leadership of Reverend Cho, Yonggi showed a strong pastoral leadership for church growth and influenced the Korean churches gravely. Especially, Yoido Full

---

36 The church newspaper, 'Full Gospel Family News', was established in 1978. As of May 8, 1998, it has published 1,000 editions. This is the first church newsletter in the history of Korean churches. It is 16 pages tabloid, and the publication volume numbers 896.8 million. This is the volume to reach 63 floor building 600 times. Special project 'Commemorating 1000th publication of Full Gospel Family News', *Full Gospel Family News* (May 8, 1998), p. 7.

Gospel Church showed a great church growth leadership to many churches, that followed its example of remarkable growth pattern during 1970's and 1980's when rapid economic development was on the way and authoritarian military government was ruling the country.

The strength of Reverend Cho's church growth leadership is that he suggested a dream and hope in faith to people. Today, the Korean society is changing rapidly. Even if time passes by, people will still live with pain and suffering. The lesson of Reverend Cho's leadership is that people follow the person, who suggests a vision. The church growth leader should instill a faith in people so that they will look forward God under any circumstances and get strength from God. The new age will require a new leadership. No matter how the situation changes, people will be attracted to a leadership that suggests a vision. The influence of Reverend Cho, Yonggi on the churches of Korea will be evaluated continually with the time. In the future, many people will talk continuously about the Reverend Cho's leadership of hope. I hope and would like to believe that many korean church leaders in the future will proclaim the hope in God to people, following the example of Reverend Cho, Yonggi.

CHAPTER 2

Rev. Cho's Cell Groups and Dynamics of Church Growth

DR. JOEL COMISKEY

Yoido Full Gospel Church is located in Seoul, Korea. Yoido Full Gospel Church has beautiful buildings built with dark orange bricks. A beautiful and magnificent Cross, hanging on two concrete pillars, is located in the front of the entrance to the main sanctuary and long stairs lead to the main sanctuary. I could not help being amazed at the Lord's sovereign plan to build the world's largest church just on the right side of the Korean National Assembly building. Yoido Full Gospel Church experienced not a growth but more appropriately explosion in leading the saints to the Lord. This church became the originator of all cell churches. We have to acknowledge that modern cell movement started from Yoido Full Gospel Church. There are many factors to make it grow to be the world's largest church, but I think the cell groups of Yoido Full Gospel Church is the essential factor. In this paper, I would like to find out the strengths of Yoido Full Gospel Church and especially the cell groups among them in order to examine the influence of Reverend Cho, Yonggi's cell ministry on the cell churches around the world.

Areas of Strength in the Church

There are so many areas of strength in this church. It seems that there is something for everyone in this church. Those, who emphasise spiritual warfare, discover a kindred spirit here. The more programmatic church growth experts find a justification at Yoido Full Gospel Church. In addition, cell-based gurus quote this church frequently.[1]

1 I'm reminded of the influence of St. Augustine. He was so deep and sound theologically that both Protestants and Catholics look to him for support.

Perhaps G. L Johnson sums up the sentiment of many when he introduced the 13th annual church growth conference at Yoido Full Gospel Church, 'Dr. Cho's life and ministry have touched the whole world for Jesus Christ. He has inspired more people to fill great churches than any other man alive.' I wholeheartedly agree to his view. Yoido Full Fospel Church has many areas of strength. The following are the strengths of Yoido Full Gospel Church.

1. Cell Groups

Yoido Full Gospel Church's recent 1997 brochure promoting their 16th annual church growth conference read the following.

> In 1980, Dr. Cho inaugurated the annual Church Growth International Conference introducing to the pastors and lay Christians from around the world the principles of church growth and the home cell. Since then, thousands of pastors and lay Christians have been trained, and a multitude of churches have experienced similar church growth in their local churches. Reverend Cho said, '...You will become a believer in this new way of evangelism, care, spiritual maturation, and fellowship. We are talking about a totally different church based on the home cell. The home cell has been the backbone of Yoido Full Gospel Church. Any church, that wishes to implement this concept, has to be completely reorganized into a cell-based church...'. On Sunday, you will also attend one of the main worship services, an experience that will convince you of the power of the home cell... Home cells are run by lay Christian leaders, through training that is provided by a pastor.[2]

My initial impressions about cell ministry were positive. Approximately, twenty-four districts operate throughout the day on Sunday. These districts are clearly geographical.

The desks of the paid sub-district leaders surround the desk of the district leader.[3] Each district has between twelve to twenty-three sub-districts, and each sub-district contains about ten to fifteen sections. Each section contains between five to fifteen home cell groups. Each cell has approximately five to ten households. The vast majority of cell groups are led by women. Karen Hurston

---

2 *The 16th Annual Church Growth International Conference.* (Seoul: CGI, 1997), p.2

3 For some reason, Yoido Full Gospel Church does not use the terms, zone pastor and district pastor. They simply call them sub-district leaders. I was also told that Yoido Full Gospel Church tries to minimize the distinction between district pastor and sub-district pastors.

writes, 'But the most prevalent cell groups – in 1993 numbering 28,000 – remain the women's groups.'[4] During my extensive interview with Reverend Song Ho Lee, district pastor of the Yong San District, he told me that nine out of every cell leader is female.

2. Spirituality

Yoido Full Gospel Church excels in this area of spirituality. The church can be summarized in the phrase 'A spiritual church.' Members wrestle in prayer. Spirituality is taken seriously. The imagery of solider and warrior best describes this church. What a thrill to walk by the grottos at prayer mountain and hear the cries and pleas of Korean saints, ascending like incense to the throne of God. I was told that 1,000 prayer warriors pass through the prayer mountain every day.

So many of these dear saints of God are dedicated to personal prayer as well as corporate prayer. There are daily corporate morning prayer services and evening worship services. At 5 a.m. in the morning, I witnessed thousands of people in the main sanctuary fervently praying. In fervent pleas to God, these believers rock back in forth while seated in the pew. Loud cries can be heard throughout the sanctuary as the believers pray in unison. This church is alive with spirituality. Although spirituality is clearly the emphasis at Yoido Full Gospel Church, this is not to say that there is no place for theological scholarship. There are several theological schools including a four year theological university for those desiring to enter the ministry and a Pentecostal Training School for all members. Normally, the early morning prayer begins with a time of reflection upon the Word of God.

3. Vision, Dreams, & Goals

Yoido Full Gospel Church is the result of the dreams and vision of one man of God – Rev. Cho. As I strolled along the Han River and looked at at the towering structure called Yoido Full Gospel Church, I felt compelled to praise God for the vision that God placed on this one man. Reverend Cho is a dreamer. He lives in visions and dreams. He has personally lifted me to a higher understanding of

4 I don't know where Hurston got her figures. Perhaps she is counting the branch churches. Hurston also mentions that only five percent meet at the work place as opposed to the home. I will discuss this issue of a weaknesses of a cell system based on women's groups at another place.

vision and leadership. His flaming vision has now been passed on to thousands of leaders. Reverend Cho says,

> Everything starts from visions and dreams. Before you worry about giving birth to a child you must first become pregnant. Likewise, as a cell leader, you must become pregnant with your cell system and about soul winning… Thus, a clear goal and goal-led visions and dreams are very, very important. When people do not have visions, they do not believe. And they do not work.[5]

4. Excellent Organization and Use of Modern Techniques

Reverend Cho syas, 'If you don't get organized, then people will not work.'[6] The organization of this church is outstanding. Although these people are 'Spirit-led', they also are excellent planners. Flow charts hang on every wall – complete with photographs and colors representing positions. Computers and other high-tech equipment are utilized with great effectiveness. Everything is modern at Yoido Full Gospel Church – the elevators, the vending machines, the furniture, the buildings, etc. Goals are posted in most district offices.[7] Buses run almost every hour (precisely on time) from the church to the prayer mountain. Those at Yoido Full Gospel Church are not afraid to take advantage of modern technology to enhance the work of God.

5. Missions

Yoido Full Gospel Church takes missionary work seriously. There are hundreds of missionaries sent out from Yoido Full Gospel Church. Yoido Full Gospel Church supports these missionaries until they can become independently stable. Along with their World Mission Department, I noticed a mission agency (from Yoido Full Gospel Church) to China, and various other missionary organizations in the church. One entire skyscraper building is entitled 'Administration and World Mission Building.'

Cell Groups at Yoido Full Gospel Church

Explosive growth is taking place in this church. Although many rea-

---

5 *Church Growth* Manual No.7. (Seoul: CGI. 1995), p.22.

6 ibid, p. 18.

7 We were told during the 'debriefing time' after the morning worship service that Yoido Full Gospel Church has an annual budget of $100,000,000.

sons for this growth could be listed, one key reason is the cell system.

1. Development of the Cell System[8]

It is important to mention that Reverend Cho's initial dependence on women continues to influence the cell structure at Yoido Full Gospel Church. This trust in women cell leaders functioned as a main driving force of developing the cell system as it is today. I used to think that Reverend Cho used women leadership because they were the 'preferred option.' However, I realize more and more that, at one time, they were Reverend Cho's 'only option'. I also thought that women led both men and women, but that is not the case. Almost exclusively, women lead women, and men lead men.

According to Karen Hurston, in January, 1994, there were 32,000 cell groups.[9] In another place, Hurston mentions 28,000 women's groups,[10] one thousand youth cell groups,[11] many children's home cell groups.[12] However, according to the more recent statistics of Kannaday, there are 19,704 women's cell groups, 3,612 men's cell groups, and 569 children's cell groups.[13]

It's amazing to think that there are only 3,612 male cell groups to care for a congregation of some 253,000 attendees![14] Yet, Reverend Cho does not flinch at those statistics. He turns them into a positive blessing. He states,

> Most of our cell leaders are women... 70 percent of them are women. Men are very slow to hear from the Lord. Women are a treasure in the church. In the Western culture, they are not using women very much, and that is a curse in society. However, in our church we are using women freely and wholeheartedly.[15]

---

8 Here, I would not explain in detail about the development of the cell system. Many writings dealt with the calling by God of Reverend Cho, Yonggi to cell ministry, initial establishment of sections, and the progress of cell ministry (Hurston 1995 pp. 81-88, Cho, Yonggi 1981).

9 ibid., p. 88.

10 *Church Growth* Manual No. 7. (Seoul: CGI, 1995), p. 91.

11 ibid., p. 91.

12 ibid., p. 91.

13 Kannaday, P. L., ed. *Greetings to the 13th Annual Church Growth Conference.* The Last Frontiers. (Seoul: CGI, 1995), p. 139.

14 If 7.5 men were added to each men's group (Kannaday 1995, p.130), only 27,142 men would be cared for in the cell. This would imply that the cell system truly isn't the base of the church among the male population at Yoido Full Gospel Church.

15 *Church Growth* Manual No.7. p. 31.

2. *Cell Administration*

The administrative structure is geographical. The homogeneity of the groups fit four categories: men, women, youth, and children. The children's cell groups are organized under the Christian education department – they are not administered through the twenty-four geographical districts. Neither is there a separate youth district. The youth cells fall in line under normal sub-district/section groupings. Like the adult groups, the youth are divided into female and male cells.

Leadership is divided into district pastors, sub-district pastors, and section leaders. Over all the entire cell ministry and under the direct leadership of Pastor Cho is the director of Pastoral Care Department. This pastor oversees the district, sub-district, section leaders, home cell leaders, and assistant home cell leaders. According to the literature that I received in April, 1997, there were twenty-four district leaders, 449 sub-district leaders, and 2,077 section leaders. The director, district leaders, and sub-district leaders are all full-time staff.

Since I was told that there were 700 staff pastors at Yoido Full Gospel Church, this would mean that out of the 700 full time staff, 474 or about 70% of full time pastors are directly connected to the cell ministry. The cell groups of Yoido Full Gospel Church moves from one home to the other every week. Cell groups rotate from house to house on a weekly basis at Yoido Full Gospel Church. The reason for this rotation is both Scriptural (house to hosue) and practical (it blesses a variety of homes). However, the '... unwritten rule is that no home should host a group more than once a month.'[16]

3. *Female Cell Leadership*

As of March, 1995, there were 3,612 male home cell leaders as opposed to 19,704 female home cell leaders.[17] This means that there are more than five times as many women's groups as men's groups. Interestingly enough, of the 719 full time pastors, 433 of them are women, yet very few women (if any) occupy higher levels of leadership. Women hold the positions of cell leaders, section leaders, and sub-district leaders (paid), but the positions of district leader, director of Pastoral Care Department, all elders, and all preaching pastors are male. This fact reveals to me that female leadership is a necessity due to effectiveness of reaching other women. However,

I6 ibid.. p. 90.

17 Kannaday. op.cit., p. 139.

Biblical and cultural norms of patriarchal leadership are guarded at higher levels of leadership.

4. Various Additional Departments

The church is primarily administered by cell groups, but there are plenty of other departments and programs in the church. Reverend Cho wrote,

> In the main church, of course, you must have Men's Fellowship, the Youth Movement, and other organizations. In the church, you have all the traditional departments so they can enjoy having fellowships with one another.[18]

In the same context, Reverend Cho makes the point that the cells are the base of the church. However, we have already noted that a large percentage of males in Reverend Cho's church do not regularly attend a cell group.

5. Strict Hierarchical Control

The strict hierarchical control of the Jethro system fits smoothly with the norms of Korean culture. Everyone has a place in the system. For example, Reverend Cho writes, 'The sub-district leaders are constantly questioned and encouraged by the large district pastor- If you do not work properly, you will be punished.'[19] Such Language would certainly not be acceptable for leadership structures in the United States. Yet, in a hierarchical society like Korea, leadership flows from top to bottom. The leadership structure at Yoido Full Gospel Church can be even diagramed by a pyramid – Reverend Cho at the pinnacle while each other shepherd under one another makes up the funnel.[20]

Growth of Cell Groups of Yoido Full Gospel Church

How has Yoido Full Gospel Church raised up so many cells and cell leaders? How have they successfully multiplied their cell groups? First of all. a goal of cell groups is set. It is clear that Reverend Cho asks each leader to dream God's vision and to think God's thoughts for the cell group. Goals are written down and then meditated upon. When the goal is reached, the cells are divided. And through

---

18 *Church Growth* Manual No. 7. p. 17.

19 *Chunch Growth* Manual No. 7. p. 17. ibid.

20 Kannaday. op.cit., p. 137.

this division and subsequent multiplication, the church grows. It seems that the mother-daughter method is primarily utilized as opposed to cell planting from scratch in order to prevent problems of dividing the cell group.

One of the district pastors at Yoido Full Gospel Church said,

> When a Home Cell has 12-15 members, it is divided into two. At that time, the section leader encourages and trains a new Home Cell Leader to be courageous to carry out a new Home Cell Leader's duties.

However, it appears that there are varying degrees of intensity. K. Hurston's research points to and focus on aggressive evangelism by some cell leaders while other groups multiply more slowly.[21] She wrote,

> I made one random sample survey of 340 cell groups from eight different districts. Those groups reported that people from 472 families had been born again and applied for church membership during that past year. However, a little more than half did not report any new people in their groups being born again and applying for church membership.[22]

It was very enlightening to find out from a district pastor that cell multiplication takes place in his district when there are ten people per group. I questioned him several time on this area, and he seem to confirm this fact.[23]

Cell Leadership of Yoido Full Gospel Church

The largest church in the history of Evangelicalism has successfully nurtured, trained, and employed thousands upon thousands of lay Christian leaders. The very reason, that the cell system of Yoido Full Gospel Church was successful, was, I conjecture, the leadership of cell leaders. It is important to analyze how Yoido Full Gospel Church has accomplished the successful cell leadership.

1. Leadership Requirements

There are various qualifications to become a cell leader. A district Pastor said, 'The qualifications to become a Home Cell Leader are a regular attendee of church services, faithful in giving tithes, of being

---

21 *Church Growth* Manual No. 7. p. 92-93.

22 Hurston, op.cit., p. 218.

23 Pastor Lee could speak a little English, but most of the time he preferred to speak to me through the interpretor.

filled with the Holy Spirit, and of having devotional posture.' In an in-depth interview with another district pastor, I learned that a potential leader must first attend the church for more than three years, be baptized in water and in the Spirit (with the evidence of speaking in tongues), and attend the worship services faithfully.

From K. Hurston's observations, only section leaders are required to speak in tongues.[24] She also notes that to become a section leader, one must be a cell leader for at least two years.[25] Interestingly enough, she told me that there were no educational requirements for cell leaders. I learned that the educational training at Yoido Full Gospel Church are for everyone. This district pastor told me that it is preferred that all potential cell leaders receive Christian education at Yoido Full Gospel Church, but it was not mandatory to become a leader.

2. *Leadership Emergence*

Normally a cell leader emerges naturally from among the group itself. Mr. Kim, a cell leader of Yoido Full Gospel Church, said,

> The new cell leader is chosen among the same Home Cell Group Members. If necessary, the existing Home Cell Leader or a section leader recommends an appropriate member capable of leading the new Home Cell.

K. Hurston emphasizes five qualities of cell leadership essential at Yoido Full Gospel Church: contagious enthusiasm, clear testimony, dedication, access to time and money, and the Holy Spirit-led life.[26] Reverend Cho believes that the first and most important characteristic to form in the life of a potential cell leader is the capacity to dream big dreams.[27] After each cell leader catches the vision to dream God's vision, Reverend Cho encourages them to write the vision down on paper. From the piece of paper, he then encourages the leaders to look at the vision and live in the vision.[28] Afterwards, he teaches his leaders to think positively and not to allow negative thoughts to sway them,[29] to speak the Word of God,[30] and to work with the Holy Spirit.[31]

---

24 *Church Growth* Manual No. 7, p. 76.
25 ibid,. p. 75.
26 ibid., pp. 73-74.
27 ibid., pp. 21-27.
28 ibid., p. 27.
29 ibid., pp. 27-32.
30 ibid., pp. 32-37.
31 ibid., pp. 37-43.

3. Leadership Mobilization

Reverend Cho believes that only ten percent of the lay people will ever be mobilized for ministry. After years of endeavoring to reach 100 percent mobilization, he is now content with ten percent. He says,

> So far I have only succeeded in mobilizing 10 percent of my congregation. I have tried every way I know. I have pushed, I have pulled, and I have tried to scare them. Still only 10 per cent have been mobilized.[32]

4. Cell System Versus Church System

There are various levels of leadership at Yoido Full Gospel Church. On one hand, leadership meets at the cell level, while on the other hand leadership functions around the deacon-elder paradigm. As of March, 1995, there were 2,990 senior deacons, 21,169 junior deacons, 3,712 senior deaconesses, 54,596 junior deaconesses, and 919 elders.[33] This becomes confusing to me because there are two leadership branches at Yoido Full Gospel Church.

One works through the cell system (some are paid staff) while the other is volunteer lay leadership that works within and outside of the cell system. At first I thought that they were separate entities, but there does seem to be some overlap. One district pastor says,

> Each sub-district has 1-5 elders, 15-25 senior deacons and deaconesses, 15-20 section leaders and 80-100 Home Cell Leaders. Elders oversee the sub-district and Home Cells, helping the sub-district pastors.
>
> Senior deaconesses are well distributed to the Home Cells.[34]

From this quote, it seems to me that the elders and senior deacons actually oversee districts. Might there be authority conflicts? This district pastor assured me clearly that the various leaders submit to one another and various leaderships are in harmony with each other.

Duties of a Cell Leader

The cell leaders of Yoido Full Gospel Church have the following important duties.

---

32 ibid., p. 13.

33 Kannaday. op.cit., p. 139.

34 ibid., p. 128. re-citation.

1. Visitation

There is a heavy emphasis on visitation at Yoido Full Gospel Church. K. Hurston strongly emphasizes this aspect of cell leadership.[35] One of the district pastors at Yoido Full Gospel Church recently said,

> The District Pastor supervises the sub-district pastors. Every day he visits the homes of the sub-district members in turn with the sub-district pastor and he preaches the Word of God... Every month he goes up the Osan-Ri Chihashil Memorial International Fasting and Prayer Mountain... The District Pastor sets a goal for growth for the District and encourages the sub-district pastors to reach the goal by the end of the year.

According to a 1987 survey of 400 lay Christian leaders, the average cell leader visited between three and five households each week.[36] From my observation, district pastors and sub-district pastors spend the majority of their time in visitation. In fact, the only required weekly report is the number and type of visits that each district pastor has accomplished. Discipleship training of new believers at Yoido Full Gospel Church is intimately related to cell visitation.

The sub-district pastor and the section leader visit the new convert. They share testimonies and the new believer prays once again to receive Christ. These new converts are placed in the most appropriate cell (based on age, social status, and location) in that his/her section of the city.

2. Setting Growth Goals

The above quote also tells us that the District Pastor sets a goal for growth for the District, which is then carried on by those under him. It seems that goal projection is a key activity for cell leaders at Yoido Full Gospel Church. Reverend Cho, Yonggi says,

> Many people criticized me because I was giving goals to my people then encouraging them to accomplish the goals. But if you don't give them a goal, they will have no purpose for being in the cell.[37]
>
> Many churches are failing in their cell system because they do not give their people a clear goal and remind them constantly of their goal. If they have no goal, then these people will gather

35 *Church Growth* Manual No. 7. pp. 95, 109-120.

36 Hurston, op.cit., p. 218.

37 *Church Growth* Manual No. 7. p. 18.

together and just have a grand fellowship.[38]

These quotes stir me up with passion because I have also noticed that the most radical, effective cell ministries today are the most goal oriented.[39]

3. Making Personal Contact

The growth goals are meaningless unless the cell leader is willing to reach out and touch his or her neighbors. Reverend Cho, Yonggi says,

> I have found the only definite way to increase church membership is through personal contact, and personal soul winning. If you know the person, it is better. Since you are personally touching your neighbors, through the cell system, it is far easier to win them to the church.[40]

Personal contact does not only involve evangelism. Cell leaders distribute gospel literature as well as meet their material and physical needs.[41]

4. Prayer

Prayer is a way of life and is the reason for life at Yoido Full Gospel Church. I believe that it is the key behind the success of this great church. K. Hurston relates several illustration of cell group victories through the ministry of prayer.[42]

5. Leadership Training

Reverend Cho says,

> We have a Cell Leaders' Bible School and Cell Leaders' Bible College. We have a quarterly Cell Leaders' Conference to give them intensive training. At this conference leading ministers from around the world are invited to lecture to our tens of thousands cell leaders.[43]

---

38 ibid., p. 18.

39 In Reverend Cho's church the goal is for each cell group to win one family to Christ every six months. If the group does not accomplish that goal, Reverend Cho encourages them to pray. (1995, p.18).

40 *Church Growth* Manual No. 7. p. 19.

41 ibid., pp. 102-105.

42 ibid., p. 102.

43 ibid., p. 20.

In addition, Karen Hurston makes reference to a eight week Cell Leader's College in which potential cell leaders receive training on such topics as the responsibilities of a cell leader and Bible lesson preparation.[44]

The one aspect of specific cell training that both Karen Hurston and several district pastors affirm is the quarterly cell leader's seminar. Normally, Dr. Cho speaks at these seminars. However, I learned that well-known outside speakers may also speak at these events. The section leader also holds a monthly leadership training meeting in his/her home.

Hurston points out,

> ...there is a monthly leaders' meeting in each sub-district when the group leaders of that area meet with their staff pastor in the home of the section leader for prayer and ministry.[45]

The Cell System Mind of Reverend Cho, Yonggi

Up to now, I have examined the cell system as the main strength of Yoido Full Gospel Church. I have been studying the Pure Cell model for the last five years. I have concluded that Yoido Full Gospel Church is the mother of most of the other cell churches around the world. Although other churches have perfected their cell ministry beyond that of Yoido Full Gospel Church, the original formula was born right here. Yoido Full Gospel Church continues to base its church philosophy on the cell system. This quote by Cho is revealing,

> If you don't want to change the structure of your church, do not go into the cell system. It will only be an added burden to you, and it will die.[46] Many people come to me saying, 'The cell system is working in Korea, but not in America and other parts of the world. It is only according to the culture, isn't it?'[47]

Reverend Cho goes on to replay and gets more specific by saying,

> It is not a cultural thing... if you want to organize a cell system, you must restructure your church. You must get your church totally involved in the cell system. First, divide the city into districts, sub-districts, sections and cells, and get everyone involved in the system[48]... If you are not going to change the basic structure of your church, then don't even dream of planning a cell system.[49]

---

44 ibid., p. 75.
45 ibid., p. 76.
46 ibid., p. 17.
48 ibid., p. 18.
49 ibid., p. 19.

The following table highlights some of the basic characteristics that not only characterize Yoido Full Gospel Church but other Pure Cell churches around the world. Yoido Full Gospel Church is unique in that it was the forerunner of the cell church design.

FOUNDATIONAL PRINCIPLES	PURE CELL MODEL
LEADERSHIP TRAINING	Potential leaders receive some sort of pre-training before leading the cell group and a great deal of ongoing training while leading the group.
GEOGRAPHICAL DIVISION	Cell groups are divided into geographical districts. In far away districts, regional chapels are built for worship services and to control the cell system.
JETHRO SYSTEM	Top leadership is raised up to pastor cell leaders under them. There is normally a cell leader, section leaders, sub-district leader, and district leader.
MULTIPLICATION	The cell group gives birth to another cell group and the process continues.
EVANGELISM	Evangelism is more of a group activity than a personal with the goal of multiplying the church.
CENTRAL PLANNING	Cell group planning takes place on a centralized level in district offices and relayed to each cell.
CELL LEADER CARE	Cell Leaders are cared for by district pastors, sub-district pastors, and section leaders.

TABLE: Yoido Full Gospel Church: DISTINCTIONS OF THE CELL STRUCTURE

Yoido Full Gospel Church is the forerunner of all cell churches and the modern cell movement started from Yoido Full Gospel Church.

Yoido Full Gospel Church is an organization, in which not only the 'church growth group', i.e. cell groups, but various departments and their activities are oriented to growth. Because this Church is so diversified, I believe that it is best to place it in the 'church growth camp' rather than into a strict cell-based model. The cell system of Reverend Cho, Yonggi has provided great inspiration for church revival and growth to numerous churches.

Bibliography

1997 *The 16th Annual Church Growth International Conference* CGI: Seoul, Korea. Cho, David Yonggi.

1993 *Church Growth.* Manual No. 6. Church Growth International: Seoul, Korea.

1995 *Church Growth.* Manual No. 7. Church Growth International: Seoul, Korea.

1997 *Why Tiny Singapore Is at the Top of the Class* L.A. Times (Sunday, Feb. 23). Crowther, Geoff and Choe Hyung Pun.

1991 *Korea* 2nd ed. Lonely Planet Publications: Hawthorn, Australia. Egli, Jin.

1993 *North Star Strategies* Special Report #5. Urbana, Illinois. Johnson, G. L.

1993 *Greetings to the 13th Annual Church Growth Conference. Church Growth.* The Last Frontiers. Manual no. 6. Church Growth International: Seoul, Korea. Kannaday, P.L., ed.

1995 *Church Growth and the Home Cell System.* Church Growth International: Seoul, Korea. Keating, Kevin.

1997 *Land of the Morning Calm.* International Travel News. March. Yoo, Cheong-mo.

CHAPTER 3

The Effect of Rev. Cho's Sermon Style for Church Growth on the Development of Theology

DR. MA, WON-SUK

The purpose of this paper is to analyze the sermon of Reverend Cho, Yonggi from the perspective of the Pentecostal theology and to discuss its theological merits. I would like to stress in this writing that Reverend Cho, Yonggi's sermon has resolved creatively the tension between transcendence and immanence, that surface in any religion and has contributed greatly to church growth. In any religion tension is created between transcendence and immanence. Transcendence is a phenomenon manifested in an advanced religion. The emphasis on transcendence makes it almost impossible to approach by manifesting their highest god greater. In order to approach god the function of religious profession, such as a monk, clergy man and priest, etc. is important. On the contrary, in an inferior religion, gods and spirits are not so almighty and affect only some people. Of course, these gods are easy for the worshipper to approach and answer the prayer of the worshipper. Things or needs of everyday life are the reason for the worship or religious rites.

In any religion, there exists a dilemma between transcendence and immanence. Religious dilemma of Christianity often appears in the history of churches. Especially, during the Middle Ages, Christianity which was in control by the Roman Catholics, stressed the transcendence so much that any religious acts were impossible without the presence of a religious professional. It speaks for itself that they insisted on Latin translation, the Vulagate, so that only a priest could read the Bible. Thus, the Reformation made the Bible accessible to the general public.

It should be highly regarded as it recovered the truth of Christianity of the High Priest for everyone by obstructing the one sided trend of developing transcendence of Christianity. Nevertheless, the reformed Christianity also keeps the element of transcendence to perform a religious service in the church only by trained elite groups (theologians or ministers).

The sermon of Reverend Cho, Yonggi follows basically the tradition of the Pentecost. However, his sermon proclaims the message that appeals to the life of general public by the power of the Holy Spirit. Thus, it overcame the transcendence of traditional Korean Christianity and contributed to church growth. Now, I will discuss these points by analyzing the characteristics of Reverend Cho, Yonggi's sermon.

The Characteristics of Reverend Cho, Yonggi's Sermon

1. Bible-centered

The sermon of Reverend Cho, Yonggi is very much Bible-centered. Reverend Cho bases his sermon on the traditional Pentecostal understanding of the Bible. The scribes of the Bible are accepted as a matter of fact, without any doubt. In this respect, the Pentecostals have been accustomed to the text analysis and criticism like fundamentalists.[1] However, the Pentecostals have absolute loyalty to the authority of the words of God. They believe the power of God which recreates the past miracles in everyday life of the saints today. The sermon of Charles Parham in his early days of ministry sums up this point very well.

> Many teachers will acknowledge that all the prophecies about the Coming of Jesus Christ has been accomplished literally. However, they understand the prophecy about the Advent of Christ spiritually. Why don't these teachers, who believe in the words of promise about the Justification and Sanctification to be realized completely today, believe in the promise of healing?[2]

Thus, the words of God and its authority become very important

---

1 William W. Menzies, Non-Weslyeyan Origins of Pentecostal Movement, *Aspects of Pentecostal-Charismatic Origins*, edited by Vinson Synan (plainfiled, NJ: Logos, 1975), p. 85, This book suggests a strong connection between the Pentecost and the Fundamentalism.

2 Charles F. Parham, *The Sermons of Charles F. Parham* (New York/London: Garland,1985), p. 42.

in the Pentecostal sermon.[3] Likewise, applying the words of God to modern situation, transcending time and space has a direct implication in the saints' faith. It is the same God who performed miracles for the saints in the past, looks after today's saints. Therefore, the intervention of God is freely proclaimed and hoped for in the sermon of Reverend Cho, Yonggi on this Biblical basis.[4]

Another distinguishing feature of a Pentecostal sermon is frequent use of narrative resources. This is not due to theological reason only as the stories in the books of Luke and the Acts are used to illustrate the Pentecostal dogmas. On a higher existential dimension, the characters of the Bible are often regarded the same as today's Christain life. This narrative theology is very importantly contained in the Pentecostal spirituality as testimonial stories manifest the Pentecostal faith.

This historical and theological Pentecostal understanding of the Bible and sermon is shown ostensibly in Reverend Cho, Yonggi's use of the Bible. Since Korean churches generally keep the conservative tendency, the theology of Yoido Full Gospel Church can be thought of as a part of conservative theology. However, his sermon makes the characters of the Bible realistic or shows the spiritual transition of today's Christians into the Bible conspicuously.

This realistic feeling, that is demonstrated in Reverend Cho's sermon, has a great theological contribution in that it transcended the high obstacles of time, space, and culture, to make the Bible our story of today.

2. *Experience-centered*

Reverend Cho, Yonggi's sermon is experience-centered. This is in big contrast with the tradition of Reformism that put too much emphasis on the word of God. Of course, the reformed theology also stresses the religious experience, which is metaphysical, and it

---

3 Guy P. Duffield, *Pentecostal Preaching: The L.I.F.E. Bible College Alumni Association Leadership on Preaching for 1956* (New York: Vantage, 1957), pp. 38-58; Ray H. Hughes, The Uniqueness of Pentecostal Preaching, *Azusa Street and Beyond*: Pentecostal Missions and Church Growth in the Twentieth Century, edited by L. Grant McClung, Jr. (South Plainfield, NJ: Bridge, 1986), p. 91; Sung-Hoon Myung, Spiritual Dimensions of Church Growth as Applied in the Yoido Full Gospel Church (Ph.D. dissertation, Fuller Theological Seminary, 1990), p. 206. Dr. Myung, Sung-Hoon says that the sermon of Reverend Cho, Yonggi is based on the Bible.

4 John Goldingay, *Approaches to Old Testament Interpretation*, updated edition (Downer Grove, IL: Inter-Varsity, 1990), pp. 66-96.

is in a very dimension from the realism (or materiality) of Pentecostal theology. It is hoped that People have fellowship with God through praise, testimony, and prayer; that is to say to experience the presence of God. The sermon intercedes and continues this anticipation. Experiencing the presence of God can mean many things such as emotional excitation, baptism by the Holy Spirit and healing. The Transcendant God is looked as a person, who indwells in His people. McGavran says the following.

> The Pentecostalists believe that God is speaking to us through our intuition and dream and that God is knocking at the door of our heart and is next to us. The Pentecostalists believe that God, the Father in Heaven, is God of power who works in us. This dogma is believed in by other Christian sects, but the Pentecostals also believe in it.[5]

Reverend Cho, Yonggi's sermon deals with problems that are directly related to our life such as disease, poverty, family problem, business trouble, and interpersonal relationship, etc.[6] We need to remember that the Pentecostal Christians are traditionally from the lower social class.

They felt the need to ask help from God more than the saints of other main denominations. Today's treand of secularism is in good contrast to the Pentestal movement of early churches, which regarded them as the eschatological entity.[7] This reflects the second Pentecostal movement in the form of a charismatic movement. This point is manifested in the altar call. This invitation is an important part of the sermon, and it provides opportunity for the people to respond to the message of the preacher. The most frequent invitation is for salvation and healing, devotion and the baptism by the Holy Spirit, prayer on the life's problems, blessing, business, children, marriage, etc.

The illustration or the testimony of how the Biblical truth was applied in one's life makes up the important part of Reverend Cho,

---

5 Donald A. McGavran, What Makes Pentecostal Churches Grow?, *Azusa Street and Beyond*, p. 122.

6 Sung-Hoon, Myung, *Spiritual Dimensions of Church Growth as Applied in the Yoido Full Gospel Church* (Ph.D. dissertation, Fuller Theological Seminary, 1990). Dr. Myung, Sung-Hoon says the seemingly different characteristics of Reverend Cho's sermon is because it is closely related to our daily lives.

7 The Garland Series, *The Sermons of Charles F. Parham*. These are collection of Reverend Parham's sermons. About half of these 20 sermons are dealing with eschatological themes such as Future of Nations, United States in Prophecy, The Bride, The Millennial Age, The Judgment Age, etc.

Yonggi's sermon. His sermon relays the theological point of being able to experience the presence of God very persuasively and leads to experience the love and power of God and His goodness by telling the real story of saints. This practice has a merit, in that, it makes the saints experience and recognize God, as well as forming active and experiential faith.

The fact that Reverend Cho, Yonggi's sermon is experience-centered, is based on his spiritual experience. As Duffield said, all sermon starts from the preacher himself/herself. The Pentecostal preachers are more than having loud voices or passionate looks, the posture to move front and back of the platform, variety of gestures or the capability to preach without the manuscript.[8] The characteristics of a true Pentecostal preacher comes from a unique spiritual experience called the baptism of the Holy Spirit. In fact, only those, who have this Pentecostal experience, can proclaim the message passionately and with firm conviction.[9] The reason that Reverend Cho, Yonggi preaches a sermon emphasizing spiritual experience is because he, himself, experienced the power of being baptised by the Holy Spirit.

3. Holy Spirit-centered

The theology and sermon of Reverend Cho, Yonggi emphasizes the baptism by the Holy Spirit after conversion. The dogma of the baptism by the Holy Spirit characterizes the Pentecostals at their best. This is one of the changes that comes in one's life after conversion.[10] In many cases, this important faith in baptism by the Holy Spirit is shown through Pentecostal sermons. He/she stresses, without any hesitation, that baptism by the Holy Spirit is a special gift of God to all believers. It is necessary for the people of God to live a successful and victorious life on this earth and a necessary condition to be a witness for Christ. Thus, in the worship service led by him/her, a prayer for experiencing the fullness of the Holy Spirit is never left out.

---

8 Duffield, p. 24.

9 Duffield, p. 26. Won-Seok Ma, The Spirit of God upon Leaders of the Ancient Israelite Society and Igorot Tribal Churches, *Pentecostalism in Context: Essays in Honor of William W. Menzies, Journal of Pentecostal Theology Supplement Series 11* (Sheffield: Sheffield Academic Press, 1997), pp. 291-316.

10 Grant Walker, Wild Theories and Mad Excitement, *Pentecostals from the Inside Out*, edited by Harold B. Smith, Christianity Today Series (Wheaton: Victor, 1990), p. 21.

The Pentecostals believe that all spiritual experiences flow from the experience of baptism by the Holy Spirit.[11] The experience of baptism by the Holy Spirit is the watershed of Pentecostal life. From my experience, it is a sudden highly enhanced spiritual feeling and cognizance. After the experience, I heard the voice of God in various ways including a firm faith through strong impression and words in my mind and vision. In this manner, many people experience spiritual charisma mentioned in the Bible. From this experience, many people encounter physical healing, emotional freedom, answer to prayer, many kinds of miracles, calling for ministry to save souls, etc. From the experiential perspective, the baptism by the Holy Spirit is a floodgate event. Although the sermon is not directly related to the baptism by the Holy Spirit, we can see often that the preacher invites the people for the baptism by the Holy Spirit to finish his/her sermon. This invitation is also for the saints, who have been attending the church for a long time but need to be filled with the Holy Spirit again as a recharge. The faith of Yoido Full Gospel Church and the sermon of Reverend Cho, Yonggi speaks for this tradition of Pentecostal theology very well.

This theological point can be made not only through a sermon but also through a testimony. The theological cognizance, that the baptism by the Holy Spirit after the conversion, is the gate to lead to a miraculous and blessed life by epoch-making change in one's life of faith.

4. *Indwelling of Transcending God*

The sermon and theology of Reverend Cho, Yonggi is a good example of creating a high degree of process for situational adaptation.[12] His sermon has led many Christians to welcome the indwelling and nearing of transcending God. This success is believed to be influenced by modern ministry of Pentecostal movement. I will now suggest three roots for this success here.

Firstly, it is faith that God can intervene in the life of a human. As

---

11 Robert P. Menzies, Spirit-baptism and Spiritual Gifts, *Pentecostalism in Context*, pp. 48-59, Robert Menzies concluded that the baptism by the Holy Spirit is the passage of special charisma. These special charisma means the supernatural and prophetic gifts of the Holy Spirit. (pp. 58-9)

12 Allan Anderson, 'David Yonggi Cho's Pentecostal Theology as Contextual Theology in Korea', and Hwa, Yung, 'Missiological Implications of Dr. David Yonggi Cho's Theology', These research papers were presented in Youngsan International Theology Symposium that was hosted by Hansei University during 26th and 27th of September, 2002.

aforementioned, it is related to the Pentecostal understanding of the Bible. Secondly, it is the appearance of charismatic movement between the 1960's and 1970's. Unlike traditional Pentecostalism, the second Pentecostal movement united Pentecostal experience and prosperity with miracle performing God.[13] Thirdly, it is the upward mobility of not only developing nations (for example, South Africa and Asia), which have long suffered from poverty, but also Western countries. Many modern Western and non-Western Pentecostal churches have been influenced by this movement. We need to remember that non-Western Pentecostal churches began to appear in the 1970's and afterwards. This phenomenon is not psychological escapism. Hughes pointed out that it is the sermon, which instills the faith.[14] That is the faith of miracle and extraordinary, instantaneous faith, which is instilled with proclamation of the word of God.[15]

In Pentecostal worship, the faith of the saints are often challenged to believe in humanly impossible things.

Reverend Cho, Yonggi's sermon of active faith style was a big contrast to traditional Korean Christianity, which was influenced mainly by the tradition of Presbyterian. The Presbyterian tradition represented mainly the elite reformed theology. In other words, one cannot deny the fact that traditional Korean Christianity was of transcendence. This reflects the faith of early missionaries, especially Puritan faith of Presbyterian missionaries. At the same time, it is related to the concept of korean traditional religion, that places advanced Confucianism and Buddhism, etc. above inferior Shamanism. Naturally, Christianity, which propagates the only almighty God, began to emphasize Yahweh or Christ above all other gods as an almighty and transcending person. This ultimately changed into a form of transcending religion, which places great significance on worship service, clergy men, or religious symbols (for example church building), etc.

Until 1960's, Korean Christians just heard the work of God amidst painful circumstances. Considering the Japanese colonization of the first half of 20th century and communist persecution during the Korean War of 1950's, it appeared that God gave the strength to endure hardships. Reverend Cho, Yonggi described traditional

---

13 Cheryl Bridges Johns, Pentecostal Formation: A Pedagogy among the Oppressed, *Journal of Pentecostal Theological Supplement Series 2* (Sheffield: Sheffield Academic Press, 1993), p. 79.

14 Hughes, p. 93.

15 Hughes, p. 93.

preachers as people, who built an altar on the Mount Sinai to preach the judgment for these people.[16] On the contrary, Reverend Cho calls his sermon a message of hope. When Reverend Cho preached 'I can do', they attacked him severely with the accusation of promoting humanism and even shamanism.[17] Despite these criticisms, Reverend Cho will be long remembered as a pastor, who made a new image of God, among Korean Christians.

His thought on blessing of God is wholistic including spiritual welfare, health. and comfortable living based on 3 John verse 2. In other words, it does not minimize the image of transcending God and was a theological task to approach God as a good God, whom humans can experience nearby.

The Contents of Sermon for Immanence of Transcending God

Traditionally, the Korean Christianity was very reluctant to accept the immanent work of God. This can be viewed as the influence of theological trend of existing mainline denominations in Korea. At the same time, Korean religious orientation of cultural tradition was influenced by existing confucianism, and Korean Christians thought they have to follow Christianity as an advanced religion with strict format, order, and procedure. In this respect, most form of immanent faith was left to so called backdoor spirituality such as prayer house or revival assembly. When Yoido Full Gospel Church introduced expressive and experiential spirituality in the worship service, there were many criticisms. However, in the course of time, these cry of criticism subsided, and on the contrary the preachers and churches, which adopted these worship formats increased more and more with time. The sermon of Reverend Cho, Yonggi is based on the fivefold gospel, and this makes the transcending God a person, who we can experience in our life. Here, I will deal with the message of divine healing and blessing to assist the immanence of transcending God.

16 Paul Yonggi Cho, The Secret Behind the World's Biggest Church, *Azusa Street and Beyond*, p. 102.

17 Harvey Cox, *Fire from Heaven: The Rise of Pentecostal Spirituality and the Reshaping of Religion in the Twenty-first Century* (Reading, MA: Addison-Wesley, 1995), pp. 224-6. Harvey Cox asserts that Reverend Cho, Yonggi's sermon is strongly associated with Korean traditional shamanism.

1. Message of Divine Healing

Traditional Pentecostal faith is also called apostolic faith. This was so called because the supernatural elements of Christianity of early churches such as various charisma and miracles, etc. were restored and reclaimed. Of course, in the same context, it is also called restorationism. As we can see in the Bible or modern Pentecostal movements, there is a few phenomena as touching as divine healing among supernatural events. Form the perspective that this could happen to himself/herself, relatives, or a close acquaintances, its emotional, spiritual impact and result is very significant.

For example, after Christ proclaimed the He was the Messiah, He healed and drove out demons as a proof. (Luke 7:22) Also, in the gospel of Matthew, after explaining the kingdom of God, a way to proclaim its coming was to drive out the demons and heal the sick. (Matthew 4:23). Thus, the divine healing became an exemplary means to prove the presence of God and His power explicitly. This tradition was set in the Old Testament already. Naaman. a commander of the Army in Aram (Syria), was cured of his leprosy, and he swore that there was no God in all the world except in Israel (2 Kings 5:15), proving the superiority of God of Israel. The divine healing was often manifested as a sign of the power to defeat and control the death, a curse for humans. The function of divine healing is very important in the relationship between religious transcendence and proximity, because it is an example of the power of our transcending God in the most explicit manner.

The sermon of Reverend Cho, Yonggi does not end with testifying the word of God. In some respect, the proclamation of the words of God is only the first half of the sermon in Pentecostal churches. It is regarded as most important to experience the presence of living God based on the proclaimed words.

Here, I mean it is the same context that Western Pentecostal churches always have an altar service. During this time, it is hoped and proclaimed that the healing and answering of God is manifested as a direct and explicit experience. Prayer for the sick at Yoido Full Gospel Church is very expressive. Every saint lays their hand of faith upon the place of pain and suffering to seek the healing by Christ. It is not just a requisition, but it reminds of spiritual warfare to rebuke and drive out the demon that brings the sickness, in the name of Christ. It shows an active faith by proclaiming words of God such as 'the punishment that brought us peace was upon him, and by his wounds we are healed.' (Isaiah 53:5) and 'If you can?' said Jesus. 'Everything is possible for him who believes.' (Mark 9:23) Through this process, Reverend Cho, Yonggi proclaims that certain diseases are healed through his spiritual charisma. And, a special religious experience, that almighty God is satisfying the most practical needs of people so as to show His immanence and proximity simultaneously, is exhibited. In the ministry and sermon of Reverend Cho, Yonggi, the divine healing is functioning as a sign of God's kingdom that is present among us.

2. *Message of Blessing*

Pentecostal understanding of blessing is not so different from the understanding of traditional Christianity. Nevertheless, Pentecostals, especially Korean Pentecostals, are different from traditional Christians in two aspects. Firstly, they believe God is actually blessing them here and now. Secondly, they believe God blesses them not only in spiritual matters but also physical, material, and relational matters as well.

In this respect, the Pentecostal understanding of blessing is very similar to the concept of Shalom in the Old Testament. (Judges 6:24, Jehovah-Shalom, The Lord is Peace) When they beseech to God, they believe and hope God will intervene and give them visible blessing. In other words, The Pentecostal faith has two dimensions of hope and experience in their life. In the Pentecost, there are numerous testimonies of people, who were blessed by God. The journals (or magazines) such as Charismata and Pentecostal Evangel routinely print articles on miraculous healing. Shinanggye is one of the best selling monthly magazine, that is published by Yoido Full Gospel Church. The magazine contains stories on blessing of God, answer to prayer, and testimonies on miracles.

Reverend Cho, Yonggi's theology of blessing surpasses the theory on the Holy Spirit and begins with the theory of Salvation. The reason that humans are cursed is because of their sins, and they believe the children of God, who had a forgiveness of their sins through the blood of Christ, are already free from the curse of poverty and disease. It is the same point of view that Christ's redemption includes the divine healing. Thus, the range of blessing includes all dimensions of every daily thing, physical and spiritual. (3 John verse 2). Of course, there is some room for a theological debate in that the completion of the kingdom of God is yet of the future. Nevertheless, it makes sense that people of God in this world is hoping for the blessing now as a guarantee of the kingdom of God.

Especially, the emphasis of blessing that is shown through Reverend Cho's message is based on the true nature of God, that He is good. God promises to bless His people in accordance with your sincerity. God's blessing means experiencing God in our daily life. This experience is not only transcending but also immanent, practical and experiential.

For this reason, the Pentecostals do not hesitate in asking for God's such blessing. This kind of experience enhances the relationship with God. It makes people go forward to get nearer to God and have a deeper faith.

Reverend Cho, Yonggi's Sermon and Church Growth

Another distinguishing feature between traditional Christian sermon and Pentecostal sermon in Korea can be found at the missionary nature of the Pentecostal movement. Pentecostals have believed that experiencing the presence of God as a consequence of the baptism by the Holy Spirit was the essence of the Pentecost from the beginning. And this experience was regarded as an empowerment by God for their evangelism. (Acts 1:8) In other words, mission is the reason for the Pentecostal existence. Thus, in a Pentecostal church, the sermon on baptism by the Holy Spirit is important. A dynamic evangelism is only possible after the Christians are empowered by the Holy Spirit.

Therefore, it is a theological misunderstanding to regard the passion of Yoido Full Gospel Church for salvation of the soul as a mere program for church growth. The theological meaning on evangelism is very well explained in the mesaage of Reverend Cho, Yonggi.[18] The message of Reverend Cho challenged and gave the motive to the Christians to evangelize their neighbors actively. Naturally, this resulted in reaping the fruit of church growth. Because of this aspect, Dr. Peter Wagner asserts that the Pentecost believe in not only the power of miracle but also the power to save the soul.[19]

The theological basis of this evangelism and mission is a unique Pentecostal missionary understanding of the baptism by the Holy Spirit as aforementioned. It is because of a clear theological purpose that the power of the Holy Spirit will reach to the ends of the earth to make people witnesses for Christ.

On the contrary, the theory on the Holy Spirit of traditional Christianity is usually based on Paul and John's views on the Holy Spirit, and they have stressed the work of the Holy Spirit on the

18 Myung, p. 206. Dr. Myung, Sung-Hoon views this type of sermon as a mission-oriented sermon.

19 C. Peter Wagner, Characteristics of Pentecostal Church Growth, *Azusa Street and Beyond*, p. 129.

dimensions of Salvation (Paul) and saint's life (John). In this respect, the theory on the Holy Spirit of Korean Pentecostal theology, represented mainly by Reverend Cho, Yonggi, made a theological advance of all believer's prophethood, taking one step further from all believer's priesthood. The Pentecostal faith, that emphasizes the passionate and experiential dimension on the evangelism, has done more than its share. Thus, the sermon of Reverend Cho, Yonggi has contributed greatly in bearing the fruit of church growth and evangelism.

The Theological Contribution of Reverend Cho, Yonggi's Sermon

The excellence of the Pentecostal faith is in harmonizing the profound transcendence of God and affectionate immanence. And the place to experience this harmony is our daily life. The Pentecostals are having continuous immanent meeting with the ultimate transcending God. The catalyst for this seemingly uncomfortable harmony is a unique Pentecostal experience so called the baptism by the Holy Spirit. The Pentecostal sermon is one of several effective methods that this unique Pentecostal harmony is taught, proclaimed, remembered, cleansed, and elaborated. Since the Pentecostals expect the real presence of God in their daily life, the sermon becomes the means to relay this hope. Through worship and sermon, the awesome presence of God becomes actualized. God remains as the almighty and ultimate transcending entity, who is never depreciated. However, this God becomes immanent and down-to-earth in our life.

Reverend Cho, Yonggi's sermon and pastoral theology is rooted in the traditional Western Pentecostal pattern. However, this was rooted and immersed in a unique environment of Korean religion, culture and society so as to have an interaction with each other. When Korean Christianity was maintaining traditional theology and worship pattern, Yoido Full Gospel Church never tried to hide the color of the Pentecost and adopted it fully. When the traditional theology was holding onto the transcendence of God, Reverend Cho, Yonggi proclaimed the living and presence of God boldly and courageously. This is because of a firm conviction of good God, who has shown him experience and miracles during Reverend Cho's faithful life. Reverend Cho's sermon, which is Pentecostal and yet adapted to Korean situation, teaches us that theology should not overlook God, who is working in this real world. His fivefold gospel compelled many Korean people to meet the living God. Theology will always deal with the meeting of gospel (the Bible) and everyday life (the mission field). In this respect, the sermon of Reverend Cho has contributed greatly in suggesting an important model for situational theology.

The influence of Reverend Cho, Yonggi and Yoido Full Gospel Church on the growth of Korean churches are well known all over the world. However, his theological contribution and influence of his leadership requires further future research. As suggested in this writing, the impact, influence and contribution of Reverend Cho's theology and sermon on the churches in Korea and around the world is very unique and important. This influence will continue to make the waves to contribute positively on the future of Korean churches. I hope that the tasks to theorize these aspects and to analyze its contribution to theology will continue rigorously and energetically in the future.

CHAPTER 4

A Study of Rev. Cho and the Growth of Yoido Full Gospel Church

DR. PARK, MYUNG-SOO

Yoido Full Gospel Church is the world's largest church. There are not many fields such as politics, economics, and general societal milieu that Korea is proud of as the world's largest or the best. However, no one questions that Yoido Full Gospel is the world's largest church. Then, how could Yoido Full Gospel Church grow as the world's largest church? Many scholars have studied this. Scholars are investigating the return to the Pentecostal faith of the early churches as the cause for the astonishing growth of Yoido Full Gospel Church. For example, the baptism by the Holy Spirit. divine healing and benedictions, etc. I totally agree on this point. Among all the churches in the world, I think the reason for the remarkable growth of Yoido Full Gospel Church is its Pentecostal faith. I believe this point can not be overemphasized.[1]

However, I also think that the growth of Yoido Full Gospel Church can not be explained by the spiritual reason alone. Reverend Cho, Yonggi, who has built and developed the church from the beginning, says he adapted himself to the changing environments of our time constantly. Behind the growth of Yoido Full Gospel Church, many situational elements have contributed greatly. Yoido Full Gospel Church has grown along with the industrializa-

---

1 Here the most extensive research in this point is Sung-Hoon Myung, 'Spiritual Dimensions of Church Growth as Applied in the Yuido Full Gospel Church' (Ph.D. dissertation, Fuller Theological Seminary, 1990). Besides this research, there are more references on this point; Sung-Hoon, Myung, *Spiritual Dimension of Church Growth* (Seoul: Seoul Logos Inc., 1992, Korean); C. Peter Wagner, *Church Growth through Spiritual Battle*, Korean translated by Na, Gyum-Il (Seoul: Love Together Publishing Co., 1998), etc. For revival of primitive religious Christianity that emphasizes spiritual aspect, refer to Dana L. Robert. 'Shifting Southward: Global Christianity since 1945, *International Bulletin of Missionary Research* (April 2000).

tion and urbanization of Korea.

We can see two aspects of Yoido Full Gospel Church at the same time. One is a primitive religion that is represented by the Pentecostal faith. Here is a strong faith on supernatural reality and a definite hope for the miracle as well as a passionate and self-absorbing worship.

Nevertheless, in Yoido Full Gospel Church, many modern technology and equipments are mobilized at the same time. They have an ultramodern building, and state-of-the-art broadcasting facilities and satellite broadcasting are used as well as worship pattern that fits with the modern culture.

I conjecture there are two elements present in the Pentecostal faith simultaneously. One is the motive for restorationism to return to the early churches. To them, the Acts of the New Testament is the home for all Christians to return to. From the outside perspective, this tendency is very similar to shamanism that is deeply rooted in Korean culture. However, from the perspective of true nature, the Pentecostal movement emphasizes the work of the Holy Spirit, the Spirit of God. In this respect, the Pentecostal movement is different from the aboriginal shamanist faith.

The other is that the Pentecostal movement is a modern religious movement that started in the 20th century. I think the Pentecostal movement of the 20th century is more open to the culture of the 20th century. They are less negative to modern civilization and try to be in harmony with it. In other words, since the Pentecostal movement does not have a long historic heritage, it adapts to modern culture better. This can be seen in the church structure. Yoido Full Gospel Church has some similar aspect with a modern enterprise that has a strong, propelling power to move forward with a clear purpose rather than a traditional church structure. I regard these characteristics as the signs of modernity in Yoido Full Gospel Church.

Then, how could Yoido Full Gospel Church with its Pentecostal faith of the early churches be a modern church that adapts to the 21st century?

The model society is no longer only for the elite. Now is the age of politics of the general public, economics of the general public, and culture of the general public. This general public likes a simple culture better than a complex culture. The religion which fits in the age of the general public, is the Pentecostal movement. The Pentecostal movement is a primitive religion in the sense that it believes in miracles but is also modern in the sense that it is a religious movement for the general public.

I will now return to the issue of the growth of Yoido Full Gospel

Church to Reverend Cho, Yonggi, with these two points in the back of the mind. Firstly, I will examine how the Pentecostal faith appeared in the churches of Korea and how Reverend Cho, Yonggi adapted to it in the historic context. Secondly, I will analyze how Reverend Cho grafted this Pentecostal movement to Korean society with his leadership. And lastly, I will present my study of how the ministerial strategy of Reverend Cho, Yonggi is related to the emergence of the mega-city of Seoul.

Reverend Cho, Yonggi and Pentecostal Faith

1. The Beginning of Korean Pentecostal Movement

The Pentecostal movement in Korea can be traced back to the entry of a female missionary, Mary Rumsey, into Korea in 1928. However, the Pentecostal movement during the colonization of Japan was not so vigorous. The vivacity of Pentecostal movement in Korea started with the entry of missionaries from the Assemblies of God during Korean War. The United States Assemblies of God sent out a missionary, Arthur B. Chestnut, who was ministering in China, to Korea in 1952. From that point on, the Pentecostal movement of Korea progressed while connected to the Assemblies of God, the world's largest Pentecostal denomination.

Korea was undergoing an extreme confusion during its liberation from Japan in 1945. To put salt in the wound, Korean War broke out in 1950, and all people of the Republic of Korea had no one to console and comfort them. In this regard, the traditional Korean churches could not suggest any special solution. The Korean churches were all disputing with each other, and a division rather than a consolidation seemed to be their goal. The largest denomination in Korea, the Presbyterian, was divided by alumni pastors of Gorye Theological School on the issue of commemorating the dead Japanese soldiers of World War II in a temple. It was further divided on the issue of the authority of the Bible. The Methodist churches were also in conflict with each other over the issue of some pastors, who have taken a friendly stand with Japan during the colonization. In addition, many competent pastors were involved in politics and took important positions in the government. To them, taking care of the saints was put on the back burner, and politics was their main conern. These Korean churches could help the suffering saints for one reason or another.

Thus, many people were falling into heretic religions while Korean churches could not deal with their mission. The Korean churches in the 1950's were facing the strongest heresy in the history of Korean churches. It was the Unification church and Evangelism Center. After the Korean War, Park, Tae-Seon of Evangelism Center called himself the 'olive tree of the last days'. He built the village of faith and led divine healing assemblies. About the same time, Moon, Sun-Myung of the Unification church lured people by saying that the first Advent of Jesus had failed and that he called himself the Jesus of the second Advent to finish what Jesus could not complete. The Korean Christianity was facing a great danger in keeping the pure faith.

We need to look at the message of the Evangelism Center and the Unification church here. They knew what the despondent Korean public wanted through the Korean War. They suggested a millenium kingdom called the village of faith to the poor public, healed the sick, and filled the religious needs of the general public by saying that Korea is the country to which Jesus will return. The essence of their message was divine healing, the Advent, and blessing.

At the same time, the worship service, which they led, were filled with passionate ecstasy. Succinctly speaking, their religion had the image of primitive religion. Most Koreans were not interested in the eradication of the Japanese influence or dispute over dogmas, that Korean churches at the time thought of the importance. They needed consolation, comforting, hope, and healing. It was not the existing religion but heretic sects, which provided for these needs.

2. *Characteristics of Korean Pentecostal Movement*

In my opinion, it was the Pentecostal movement, which did not drift far away from the realm of traditional Christian faith while satisfying the religious needs of the general public in this situation. The Pentecostal movement confesses the Apostle's creed. acknowledge the authority of the Bible, and accepts the Trinity. In this regard, the Pentecostal movement should be included in the realm of historical Christianity. However, the Pentecostal movement maintains the image of the most primitive religion among all Christian sects. In fact, the Pentecostal movement has a strong desire to return to the early churches. So, they often explain their religion with the word, 'primary'. The Pentecostal movement strongly challenges the modernism, which attempts to explain the gospel of Christianity with reasoning and eradicates any supernatural elements of Christianity. In the Pentecostal movement, there is a strong religious experience and a message of divine healing, eschatology, and blessing. These are the elements that are lacking in the Christianity of illuminism. It can be safely said that the

Pentecostal movement, which started in America, has been applied very well to Koreans, who pursue elements of primitive religion.[2]

3. The Leadership of Korean Pentecostal Movement

When Reverend Cho, Yonggi started his ministry in Daejo-Dong, he clearly propagated this Pentecostal faith. He learned the faith Tent church in 1958 of Christianity early from a Pentecostal missionary. experienced divine healing, and worked for a long time as an interpreter of missionaries. Especially, the experience of being cured of tuberculosis in the last stage was the turning point in his faith. To him, Christianity was not a just a formality, it was a reality to solve the most pressing problems in one's life. Even while he was studying at Full Gospel Theological School, he interpreted the lecture of a Pentecostal missionary. In doing so, he not only experienced the Pentecostal faith but learned about it theoretically. This made him remain as a Pentecostal for life, and a leader of the world Pentecostal movement.

I think it was Reverend Choi, Ja-shil, who assisted Reverend Cho, Yonggi in recovering the primitive Pentecostal faith and in having it take root as a Korean faith. If Reverend Cho, Yonggi developed a deep relationship with the world Pentecostal movement through his excellent English speaking skills, it was Reverend Choi, Ja-Shil, who connected the Pentecostal faith to the religious minds of Koreans. She led Reverend Cho to the Mount Samgak payer house early to have him meet with the Korean and Pentecostal faiths. Reading the non-fiction, 'I was a Hallelujah lady', many primitive religious stories, that are hardly written by Western theologians, are found. For example, there is a story of the killing of a huge serpent, which was believed to be a guardian of a shaman's house. The purpose of the killing of the snake is to free the entire town from shamanic faith, and introduce Christianity. There is also another story of fighting spiritually with a local shaman in the name of Jesus.[3] To Reverend Choi, Ja-shil. the supernatural world was not

2 On this point, I have a different opinion than Kim, Heung-Soo. Kim, Heung-Soo views the appearance of Pentecostal faith after the Korean War as a distortion of true Christian faith in *Korean War and Research on the Spreading of Undulating Faith* (Seoul: Center for Korean Christian History Research, 1999). However, I would like to view the appearance of Pentecostal faith as the restoration of original gospel to return to the early church.

3 Choi, Ja-Shil, *I was the Hallelujah lady*, (Seoul: Youngsan Book Press, 1982). pp. 238-244.

another world view, but it was an actualization.

It is thought that Reverend Cho, Yonggi encountered traditional and primitive Korean faith through his partner and mother-in-law, Reverend Choi, Ja-shil.[4]

The person, who led Reverend Cho, Yonggi to this primitive Pentecostal faith, was a Pentecostal missionary, J. W. Hurston. Actually, there was an ostracizing movement among the Korean Christian sects, because he continued divine healing assemblies at his tent church in Daejo-Dong. At this time, even the ministers of the Assemblies of God thought of the practice of divine healing as superstitious and refuted it. At this time, it was this missionary, Reverend Hurston, who encouraged Reverend Cho and explained that divine healings and miracles are not superstitious but Biblical, they express the true nature of the Pentecostal movement, that was sweeping the world. Hurston missionary had worked in Liberia, Africa for 8 years earlier and had witnessed so many works of the Holy Spirit and the results of divine healing.[5] Reverend Hurston introduced Reverend Cho to world-class Pentecostal leaders including Reverend Oral Roberts, and Reverend Cho accepted the 'primary' Pentecostal faith through them.

In fact, this primitive faith was in Korea earlier. The Holiness church, that was introduced to Korea in 1907, had this primitive faith pattern. So, many people called the worship of the Holiness church (originally, it was called Gospel Evangelism Center) as leaping sorcery troupe, Southern sorcery troupe, or exorcising troupe. This Holiness church also emphasized the gospel of divine healing with zeal. This primitive faith was well accepted in the downtown Seoul, the home of the aristocratic classes. Thus, many Presbyterians converted to the Holiness church. A case in point is Lee, Myung-Heon, the first graduate of Gyungseong Bible School (presently, Seoul Theological University).[6] In other words, the Holiness church satisfied the primitive religious needs, that Presbyterian and Methodist church could not satisfy at that time. And it achieved a noticeable growth even during the period of colonization by Japan.

Regarding this point, Kwak, Ahn-Ryun, a Presbyterian mission-

---

4 Myung, Sung-Hoon, *Church Growth and the Holy Spirit: Centered on the Work of the Holy Spirit in Yoido Full Gospel Church* (Seoul: Seoul Book Center, 1992), pp. 38-39.

5 Karen Hurston, *Growing the World's Largest Church* (Springfield, MI: 1994), pp. 22-29; 212, n. 3.

6 Lee, Myung-Jik, *Brief History of Holiness Church of Chosun Yasogyo Asian Mission* (Gyungsung: Board of Directors of Holiness Church, 1929, Korean), p. 51.

ary, speaks the following.[7]

> Some small religious sects broke off from Presbyterian in Korea, because they felt the church was too 'cold' for them. The Holiness church applauds, shouts, dances in the platform during the worship, and it absorbed several hundred members of Presbyterian church. To some individuals, having a vision, experiencing the tremble, and healing the disease by laying hands on were happening frequently.

Nevertheless, the Holiness church could not maintain such passion that it showed during the colonization period. After the liberation, the Holiness church wanted to belong to the main stream churches in Korea, emphasized the faith of balancing knowledge, humanity, and righteousness, and attempted to exclude divine healing from their dogma at one point in time.[8] Amidst this turmoil, it was the Pentecostal movement, which could satisfy the religious minds of Koreans.

Reverend Cho, Yonggi of Yoido Full Gospel Church told me that the growth of Full Gospel Church is due to the reason that the Holiness church of Korea did not propagate the Full Gospel soundly. To recapitulate, the Holiness church of Korea did not emphasize Full Gospel after the liberation, and in fact it switched back to take the Presbyterian stand. Reverend Cho said his Full Gospel Church took over and filled the gap for further development of evangelism in Korea. The Pentecostal movement grew bigger than any imagination because it gave the discouraged, confused and frustrated Koreans after the liberation consolation, comfort, and hope not through faith of speculation or formality but through Biblical primitive faith.[9]

4. Theological Basis of Yoido Full Gospel Church

Many scholars hold the view that today's growth of Yoido Full Gospel Church is because Reverend Cho, Yonggi compromised the gospel of Christianity with shamanism. And they believe it is a sit-

---

7 Kwak, Ahn-Ryun, *Korean Church and Neighbors Mission Policy,* Korean translated by Park, Yong-Gyu (Seoul: Korean Christian Books, 1994), p. 341. cf. 369.

8 Minutes of General Assembly for the Revival of Christian Chosun Holiness Church' (1995, Korean) cf: 'History of Korean Holiness Church', *Korean Christian Holiness Church* (Seoul: Holiness Church Press, 1992), p. 404.

9 During the converation at CCMM building in Yoido on September 27, 2002, he confessed that he cherished the theological heritage of fourfold gospel of the Holiness Church.

uational adaptation of Korean Christianity. Scholars like Harvey Cox and Walter Hollenweger are two examples of this opinion.[10] However, I do not think so. I believe the American Pentecostal movement was introduced to Korea by the missionaries, and it appealed to the religious minds of Koreans very well. Here, if we forget that the American Pentecostal movement was the origin, it is to forget the important root of Full Gospel Church. This American Pentecostal movement coincided with the religious desires of Korean public and thus created today's Yoido Full Gospel Church.

In the early Pentecostal movement of Korea, Full Gospel faith and shamanic faith were not in a compromising relationship but in a state of war. There was always a warfare with its strongest enemy, shamanic faith, waiting wherever Pentecostal faith was introduced. This would be appropriately called a spiritual warfare today. Reverend Cho, Yonggi always worked on the ministry of driving out the demons in the name of Jesus Christ. In this respect, although it may look from outside as if there may be a similarity between them, there is a clear difference between them. Reverend Cho, Yonggi not only did not make the gospel of Christianity shamanic but drove out shamanism by the gospel of Christianity. This was an act of faith for the Pentecostal movement, and taking after the ministry of Jesus at the same time. The ministry of Jesus was the ministry of driving out evil spirits.

Reverend Cho, Yonggi's Leadership and Growth of Yoido Full Gospel Church

According to a research by Dr. Hong, Young-Gi, the biggest reason that the saints of a Korean church prefer a mega-church is because of their fondness for the senior pastor.

The attraction to the senior pastor makes them to attend his/her church. The research of Dr. Hong, Young-Gi reveals that the rates of choosing a church on the basis of senior pastor alone were 58.5% for mega-church, 42.4% for large church, and 37.1% for medium-sized and small church. The saints consider what is the type of the church or who is the senior pastor in choosing a church for them, and this

10 Harvey Cox, *Fire from Heaven: The Rise of Pentecostal Spirituality and the Reshaping of Religion in the Twenty-First Century* (Reading, MA: Addison-Wesley Publishing Co., 1995), p. 328; Walter Hollenweger, *Pentecostalism: Origins, Developments Worldwide* (Peabody, MA: Hendrickson Publishers, 1977), p. 100, n. 2.

factor becomes more important for larger church.[11]

1. Charismatic Leadership

The most important factor in explaining the growth of Yoido Full Gospel Church is Reverend Cho, Yonggi. Without the charismatic leadership of Reverend Cho, Yonggi, today's Yoido Full Gospel Church can not exist. The leadership of Reverend Cho, Yonggi is a typical charismatic leadership. As it is known widely, he received Jesus Christ at the end of his life While he was suffering from the last stage of tuberculosis he experienced the grace of divine healing. This makes many poor people find another self in Reverend Cho, Yonggi, look themselves as the same as Reverend Cho, Yonggi, and identify with Reverend Cho, Yonggi.

However, the true nature of Reverend Cho, Yonggi's leadership is that he is a messenger of the spiritual power, that God is working through him. Reverend Cho, Yonggi led the divine healing assemblies from the beginning, and it became a trademark for his assembly. To many people, Reverend Cho, Yonggi was known as a 'empowered pastor', and this perception was the main reason for people to come to his church from all over. Literally, people thought that God's charisma is conveyed through him. This perception again distinguished Reverend Cho, Yonggi from other common pastors, and it acted as the main driving force to overcome hardships in his church.

According to Max Weber, a charismatic leader provides a spiritual and material benefit to his/her followers through his/her power and keeps his/her charisma. In this respect, it can be said that Reverend Cho, Yonggi have successfully kept his charisma.[12]

2. Outstanding Team Ministry

However, I think Reverend Cho, Yonggi did not rely on this charismatic leadership alone. In fact, Reverend Cho, Yonggi is an excellent team minister. He started the Daejo-Dong church with Reverend Choi, Ja-shil from the first. Reverend Choi, Ja-shil (a junior pastor at

---

11 Hong, Young-Gi, *Korean Mega-Churches and Charismatic Leadership* (Institute for Church Growth, 2001, Korean), pp. 179-180. This book is the first pioneering research that studied the relationship between the leadership and Korean mega-churches.

12 Max Weber, *Economy and Society*, eds., G. Roth and C. Weber (New York: Bedminster, 1968), p. 1112.; Hong, Young-Gi, *Mega-Churches and Charismatic Leadership*, p. 100.

that time) started her church and brought Reverend Cho, Yonggi as a preacher. They used to evangelize as a team since their days at Full Gospel Theological School. This relationship developed further when they started a pioneering church together. Their team was a very ideal team. Reverend Cho, Yonggi delivered a young, fresh, and forceful sermon, and Reverend Choi, Ja-shil served the church with a visitation and prayer, following typical Korean ministry style. Here, we can see a Korean model of team ministry. Reverend Choi, Ja-shil thought a sermon was not her realm. She wanted to work together with Reverend Cho, Yonggi as a preacher from the beginning. Here we can see a division of tasks.

The reason that this team ministry was possible was because one was in the motherly position, and the other was in a position like a son. From this perspective, these two people were not rivals but in a cooperating relationship. The relationship between the two developed into a mother-in-law and son-in-law relationship, and this made an Asian team ministry that can not be seen anywhere else. There is an adage in Korea, 'the love for a son-in-law is mother-in-law's'.

Reverend Choi, Ja-shil could watch her son-in-law on the path to a successful ministry with a joyful mind. Many people think the American team ministry is ideal, but Reverend Cho, Yonggi and Reverend Choi, Ja-shil grew Yoido Full Gospel Church through an Asian family team ministry.[13]

Reverend Cho, Yonggi was also involved in another team ministry in a different sense. It is an international ministry with foreign missionaries. From the first, Reverend Cho, Yonggi worked with missionaries. he cooperated with missionaries as an interpreter, and the missionaries helped his pioneering church. Especially, Reverend Hurston influenced him greatly. Reverend Cho, Yonggi could delve into the Pentecostal faith deeply through him. Additionally, Reverend Hurston became the director of Seodaemoon revival center with the subsidy of Assemblies of God. At that time, he invited Reverend Cho, Yonggi as a partner minister and handed over the directorship to Reverend Cho, Yonggi soon enough.[14] Afterwards, he worked on the ministry along with Reverend Cho, Yonggi for a

---

13 The cooperative ministry of Reverend Cho, Yonggi and Reverend Choi, Ja-Shil are well written in the biography of Reverend Choi, Ja-Shil, *I was the Halleluiah lady*.

14 Hurston, *Growing the World's Largest Church*, p. 212, n. 6.

long time. He did a brief stint in Vietnam for a mission ministry between 1970 and 1975 and came back to Korea to make Church Growth International program, which trained overseas ministers visiting Yoido Full Gospel Church. Through this development process, Yoido Full Gospel Church began a worldwide ministry.[15] In fact, the international activity of Reverend Cho, Yonggi was made possible because he was working with these missionaries.

Here, Reverend Cho, Yonggi has a strength that most Korean ministers can not catch up. It was his international network. After the liberation form Japan, Korean Christianity was influenced by the United States in many ways, and the fact that Reverend Cho, Yonggi was working in an international ministry was a strength that other ministers could not dare to imitate.

He taught the growth secrets of Yoido Full Gospel Church overseas through his international network and led numerous Pentecostal revival assemblies in many third world countries. In this manner, he became the best known Korean in Christian world. After the liberation and through the 1970's, most denominations refuted missionaries to insist on nationalism. However, Reverend Cho, Yonggi was on the way to world mission with foreign missionaries. Here, it may be due to missionaries, who helped him humbly, but it was also due to Reverend Cho, Yonggi's attitude to work together with them.

3. Leadership for Mobilizing Lay Christians

The decisive contribution of Reverend Cho, Yonggi's leadership is that he mobilized all congregation members in evangelism through cell organization. A leader is not one, who works by himself/herself, but is the one, who leads people to work. Reverend Cho, Yonggi fainted on a day in 1964. His church was growing rapidly, and he was bombarded with tasks that accompanied the rapid growth. Thus, his health could not handle all the work. From that time and on, he organized districts and cells. Through the cell system, Reverend Cho, Yonggi began to move and manage this humongous church. Reverend Cho, Yonggi instilled a mission motive to district and cell leaders and managed it systematically. Yoido Full Gospel Church is actually a mega-church composed of tens of thousands of cells. Without this cell organization, his church

15 Hurston, *Growing the World's Largest Church*, p. 192.

could not grow so strong.[16]

Harvey Cox is viewing the secret of growth of Korean Pentecostal movement as the absolutely dazzling organizational genius.[17] He mentions that Peter Drucker, a guru in modern administrative science, is focusing on how leaders of non-profit organization are instilling the motive and vision to their members to reach a certain, planned objective. He continues to mention that Reverend Cho, Yonggi is excellent in this area. Donald McGavran of Fuller Seminary had evaluated Yoido Full Gospel Church as 'the best organized church in the world'.[18] I think the genius of Reverend Cho, Yonggi is not in his theology but in his adaptability to changing situations and organizational power that fits in with change.[19]

The strength of Reverend Cho, Yonggi's cell system is in making lay Christians evangelists. He provided so many lay Christians the opportunity to participate in the work of church, and in turn this gave them the meaning of life. However, the function of cell leaders of Yoido Full Gospel Church is a little different from recent disciples training. If the disciple training puts emphasis on studying the Biblical truths in a relation of a teach and a student, the cell worship emphasizes the spiritual aspect of sharing the problems of the saints and praying together. In this respect, the first responsibility of the cell leader is not to teach its members but to pray for the saints and assist in solving the problems of the saints.

Another strength of a cell organization is that it enables all people to have fellowship, that is hardly found in a mega-church. Many people criticize Yoido Full Gospel Church for being too big to function as a community. However, this is a serious misunderstanding.

Of course, there is no fellowship for entire saints to get together at the same time. However, it is not that there is no fellowship. Another kind of fellowship is provided. So to speak, it is a new type of fellowship through numerous small groups. Since this fellowship community was successful, today's Yoido Full Gospel Church could exist.

---

16 Cho, Yonggi, *Church Growth, do you really want it?* (Seoul: Seoul Book Center, 1995, Korean), pp. 221-242. For zone structural ministry, there are the following resources written in English; Paul Y. Cho wlth R. Whitney Manzano, *More Than Numbers* (Waco, Texas: Word Books, 1984); David Yonggi Cho with Harold Hostetler, *Successful Home Cell Groups* (Seoul, Korea: Seoul Logos, 1997), etc.

17 Cox, *Fire from Heaven*, p. 231.

18 Hurston, *Growing the World's Largest Church*, p. 192,

19 Cox, *Fire from Heaven*, pp. 234-237.

4. Leadership That is Full of Hope

I will not write about the theology of Reverend Cho, Yonggi here. Already, I have dealt with Reverend Cho, Yonggi's theology elsewhere.[20] What I would like to mention here is the meaning of Reverend Cho, Yonggi's message in an industrial society. In fact, the position of Reverend Cho, Yonggi in modern Korean society is that he instilled hope and courage to poor and discouraged people in the industrializing Korean society. He did not spread traditional message as it was, but he spread the words of God according to the situation of the society. Of course, this new type of message is not his creation. He relayed the messages of Pentecostal activists or people stressing positive thinking by adapting it to situations in Korea. Thus, he could spread a new message of hope to industrializing Korean society. On this point, as Harvey Cox pointed out, the growth of Yoido Full Gospel Church and economic growth of Korea are of the same context.[21]

The leadership of Reverend Cho, Yonggi is in the same place as the former president of Korea, Park, Jung-Hee in politics and Jeong, Ju-Young, the former president of Hyundai Enterprise in economics. All these people are goal-oriented. They all led people with a strong leadership. We call this time the age of developmental dictatorship. At one time, we had a very negative evaluation of Park, Jung-Hee.

However, a recent survey showed that the most respected person by Koreans was the former president Park, Jung-Hee. According to a study by Korea Gallop on 1,154 Korean adults. they chose Park, Jung-Hee (20.1%), the great King Sejong, Admiral Yi, Soon-shin, and Kim, Gu, the leader of independence movement during the colonization by Japan in that order as the most respectful person in Korean history.[22] If the leadership of Park, Jung-Hee in politics was very important, I believe the counterpart in religion is Yoido Full Gospel Church. he gave the courage and hope to Korean people, who were struggling in poverty and despair.

The Reverend Cho, Yonggi's message of hope has its significance clearly when it is compared to the progressive people's movement then. At that time, the minjung (people) movement viewed that all societal problems were in the positional structure, which created the

---

20 Park, Myung-Soo, 'Pentecostal Movement and Reverend Cho, Yonggi's Theology', *Research on Korean Preachers* (Seoul: Korean Church History Research Institute, 2000, Korean), pp. 17-56.

21 Cox, *Fire from Heaven*, p. 230.

22 *Chosun Daily News* August 26, 2002.

conflict between the rich and poor. Since this was a structural conflict, they viewed that the solution could be found in the change of societal structure.[23] So, they tried to solve this problem through many political upheaval. Compared to this radical movement, Reverend Cho, Yonggi taught that the solution is to try hard with a hope through the power of the Holy Spirit. Through his message, many people preferred the ethics of diligence of a reformed church to a fight between different social classes. The Pentecostal faith did not understand this world as a place to escape but understood it as a place to be blessed. This thought reoriented the solution for the conflict between the classes from a fight to nurturing of a sound middle class. From this perspective, the Reverend Cho, Yonggi's gospel of blessing contributed greatly to making of Korean middle class.

We are learning through the history that the Puritans emphasized diligence to contribute to the forming of Western Capitalism and that John Wesley of the Great Britain contributed to forming the middle class in England through diligence, also. However, Reverend Cho, Yonggi's threefold blessing contains something that surpasses this diligence.

It is the gospel of hope and courage. He cried out everything is possible in the power of the Holy Spirit so as to transpose the power of the Holy Spirit as the energy in the life. This Reverend Cho, Yonggi's message gave many poor people the hope and made them have a dream of success. Capitalism only works in the place where there is a hope for success.

Along with this point, Reverend Cho, Yonggi's influence on the

---

23 Some scholars attempt to view the Pentecostal theology and Minjung (populace) theology as the same kind. (Lee, Hong-Jung, 'Minjung and Pentecostal Movement in Korea', *Pentecostals after a Century: Global perspective on a Movement in Transition*, ed., Allan Anderson and Walter J. Hollenweger [Sheffield: Sheffield Academic Press, 1999], pp. 138-163) It is because these two movements are mainly geared to Minjung (populace or general public). However, I think this analysis is not historically correct as a matter of principle nor theoretically correct. In fact, when the Minjung theology gained the popularity during 1970's and 1980's, the Minjung theology and Pentecostal movement did not have any connection to each other. Historically, they didn't have any connectivity, and they were separate events. Additionally, whereas Minjung theology wants to achieve its purpose through confrontation between different socio-economic classes, the Pentecostal movement stressed an important virtue of diligence to live a diligent life day by day through the power of the Holy Spirit. These two movements are totally different theoretically, also.

development of Korean economy is his understanding on materials. In traditional Korean society, where the scholarship is valued, materials are often viewed negatively. Although there was a Holy Spirit movement centered on the Holiness church before the Pentecostal movement as aforementioned, this Holy Spirit movement still regarded the material blessing negatively. However, Reverend Cho, Yonggi refuted this negative understanding of materials and taught that God is 'Good God', who wants to bless us. This Reverend Cho, Yonggi's message was subject to many criticisms. However, if materials are not regarded as a positive thing, the economic development is hard to achieve.

This can be compared to what Calvin did. He did not denounce the interest, instead he understood the interest as a new economic system to enable Western Capitalism. At the end of the Middle Ages, the Catholics refuted the interest, and the financial business could not develop. However, Calvin taught that the interest of commercial society is similar to land rent of agricultural society and made today's Capitalism possible.[24] Likewise, Reverend Cho, Yonggi did not regard the wealth negatively. By regarding it positively instead, he suggested a strong Biblical basis for economic participation of Korean Christians.

The Development of the City of Seoul and Urbanized Ministerial Strategy of Reverend Cho, Yonggi

What we often forget in explaining the growth of Yoido Full Gospel Church is the relationship between a mega-city and mega-church. In fact, Seoul is a very rapidly developed city, and a mega-church with hundreds of thousands members can appear only in this environment. Reverend Cho, Yonggi understood this urbanization and adapted to it well.

Many scholars assent that urbanization and religious revival go against each other. Since the city is a symbol of modernity and a religion is of old ages, they thought that a religion can not revive in a city and a religion can be kept only in the rural area. However, this hypothesis is wrong, because the world's largest churches are almost always located in a mega-city.

Harvey Cox thought that urbanization and traditional religion could not coexit. The reason is that the city will be secularized and the traditional religion will lose its place. However, Harvie Conn of

24 W. J. Busma, *Calvin*, Korean Translated by Lee, Yang-Ho (Seoul: Nathan, 1991), pp. 447-470.

Westminster Graduate School of Theology refutes the statement of Harvey Cox by asserting that secularization is one but not all aspect of urbanization and it is a phenomenon of the rural area as well. According to Harvie Conn, a religion is not disappearing in a modern city but returning within a modern city on the contrary to Harvey Cox's assessment.[25]

1. Meaning of Urbanization

Then, what is urbanization? Urbanization means that populous people live together in a small space.[26] This urbanization was made possible by several factors. In the first, political reasons such as administration and military base were the main factor at first, but commercial reason became the main factor.

Industrialization began in the 18th century, and there were many factories built in the city. Additionally, numerous people in the rural area moved to the growing cities. From this point, the urbanization in a modern sense started. From this context, industrialization and urbanization are often regarded as a synonym.

However, this industrialization continued further with the development of traffic and communication, and many small cities formed around a big city to form a metropolitan area. This metropolitan area is composed of a big city and satellite cities or big cities are connected by satellite cities. These metropolitan cities were first formed in the East coast of the United States. New York has several satellite cities, and it is connected to Boston and Baltimore by the satellite cities in between.

2. Urbanization in Korea

Then, how did Korean society go through the process of urbanization? After the liberation, Korea experienced a rapid urbanization. Compared to other countries, it took 100 years for England, 80 years for the United States, and about 45 years for Japan to increase the rate of urbanization from 20% to 60%. In contrast, Korea spent only about 30 years (1949-1980) for this rate of urbanization. The rate of urbanization in Korea was 15% right after the liberation, 37% in the

---

25 Harvie M. Conn, 'The Secularization Myth', *Evangelical Review of Theology*. volume 12 (January 1988), pp. 78-92.

26 Lee, Se-Il, 'City', *Britannica World Encyclopedia* (Seoul: Britannica/Dong-A Daily News, 1993, Korean), 5: pp. 92-97.

1960's, 50.2% in 1970, and 69.4% in 1980. With a rapid industrialization since 1970's, 77.3% of all Korean population now live in a city.[27]

According to professor Park, Heung-Soo, the urbanization in Korea can be classified into 4 steps or stages.[28] The first stage was between 1946 and 1955. People, who came back abroad and escaped the North Korean communist regime, gathered in the cities to increase the population in the cities.

The second stage was between 1955 and 1965, and during this time the urbanization continued with typical population increase of a developing nation and population transfer from economically depressed rural areas to booming cities. The third stage was between 1965 and 1975, and there a massive influx of rural population into the cities due to rapid developing industrialization. During this time, the urban population surpassed 50% of total Korean population. The last stage was after 1975, and the urban population continued to increase with the fourth national 5 year economic development project. During this time, policies to control urban concentration of the population and to build new cities were devised and implemented. About this time, Seoul was already a metropolitan city.[29] The most clear case of urbanization in Korean society can be seen in Seoul and its metropolitan area. The population ratio of the metropolitan area to all Korean population was 20.8% in 1960, 28.3% in 1970, 35.5% in 1980, and 42.7% in 1990.[30]

3. *Growth Stage of Korean Churches*

Looking at the growth of Korean churches through this process of urbanization, exemplar churches, that were formed in the first

---

27 Kim, Young-Seob, Cho, Yong-Hyo, 'Population Projection in Seoul Metropolitan Area and the Alternatives', *College of Social Science* (Hanyang University), N. 2 (1983), p. 109; Kang, Cheol-Gu, 'Comparison Study on Urbanization Process of Seoul Metropolitan Area within the Boundary of the Han River' (Masters Thesis, Graduate School, Seoul City College, 1991, Korean), p. 8.

28 Park, Heung-Soo, 'Excessive Urbanization and Population Dispersion Policy', *Social Science Research Collection*, Yonsei University, no. 13 (1982, Korean), p. 80; Kang, Cheol-Gu, 'Comparison Study on Urbanization Process of Seoul Metropolitan Area', (Korean) p. 29.

29 Choi, Jin-Ho/Lee, Jeong-Yeol, 'Characteristics of Suburbanization around Seoul and the Alternative Policy', *Research on National Land*, vol. 11 (1984, Korean), pp. 34-51; Kang, Cheol-Gu, 'Comparison Study on the Urbanization Process of Seoul Metropolitan Area', (Korean) p. 9.

30 Lee, Se-Il, *City*, p. 97.

stage, would be Youngrak and Choonghyun church. These churches have the characteristics of being the church for the refugees. However, Yoido Full Gospel Church does not have any special connection with the refuges. Yoido Full Gospel Church was not built by the refugees but by poor and alienated people in the city.

In this respect, Yoido Full Gospel Church is a church of the second stage. At first, Yoido Full Gospel Church started in a tent church in Daejo-Dong. However, it moved to Seodaemoon.

This was accomplished by the mission strategy of the Mission Department of the Assemblies of God. At that time, the Assemblies of God was planning a mission program called global conquest. The plan was to build Full Gospel Revival Center in important cities in the world for concentrated urban evangelism. At that time, Maynard Ketcham, the Chief of Asia Mission Bureau of the Assemblies of God, decided to start the global conquest program in Korea.[31] Then, Seodaemoon was a place of gathering, and people attended zealously the assemblies led by the Pentecostal evangelists.

4. Urbanization and Mega-Church

The Full Gospel Church at Seodaemoon grew beyond any imagination. At first, the 600 members of Daejo-Dong church moved along with their church, but new members continued to increase day by day. So, the Seodaemoon Full Gospel Church with a seating capacity of 1,500 grew to have 3,000 members in 1964. It was far beyond the seating capacity at that time. What Reverend Cho, Yonggi introduced was to have a sevearl Sunday services. And there were four Sunday services in 1964.[32] I believe this option contributed greatly for the church to grow into a mega-church. When the number of congregation members increase exponentially due to urbanization, the way to accomodate them is to utilize the space fully. I do not know when the churches in Korea began to have a multiple Sunday services, but I can say this option was a new change to adapt to a mega-city.

Here, we need to think about urbanization and the public society.

31 Park, Myeong-Soo, 'Reverend Cho, Yonggi and World Pentecostal Holy Spirit Movement', Youngsan International Theological Symposium, (2002); Maynard L. Ketcham, *Tigers that Talk* (Charlotte, NC: PTL Television Network, 1979), pp. 99-111.

32 *40 Years History of Yoido Full Gospel Church* (Yoido Full Gospel Church, 1998, Korean), p. 109.

Many people understand urbanization in terms of modernization. However, urbanization is closely related to the appearance of public society, and it brings forth public culture.[33] And this public society makes public religion possible. A city is a group of multitudinous public. Here is not the society, which is governed by a few elite, but the city is the place to satisfy the desires and tastes of the public. This publicity changes existing religion. In other words, it creates a new religion, which fits the needs and desires of the public. I believe this is the reason that this city of great public society created a mega-church.

As mentioned above, urbanization was in its spurt between 1965 and 1975. Many small factories were built around Seoul, and a big industrial complex was built in Youngdeungpo, Seoul. At this time, Yoido Full Gospel Church attempted an important change. That was to move the church from Seodaemoon to Yoido. After 10 years of ministry at Seodaemoon, a worship service was first held at Yoido in 1969. After all kinds of hardships, finally, a dedication worship service was held at the completed Yoido Full Gospel Church in August, 1973.

I think the center of Seoul moved from Gangbuk (North of the Han river) to Gangnam (South of the Han river) in the 1970's. During this time, starting a new church at Yoido has a very important significance. Yoido was at first used as an airfield by the United States Air Force after the liberation from Japan. However, a development in this area started in 1968, and the Mapo Grand Bridge was completed in 1970, connecting Yoido to other parts of Seoul (Yoido is a triangular delta island in the middle of the Han river). This infrastructure was the foundation to develop a new city town. Yoido became an important location for transportation, connecting Gangbuk (North of the Han river) and Youngdeungpo. And in Youngdeungpo, numerous factories were set up along with the industrialization of Seoul. Yoido Full Gospel Church was now located in an important place to evangelize people, moving into Seoul because of the industrialization.

Additionally, the time for Gangnam (South of the Han river) opened since the later half of the 1970's. Yoido is not next to Gangnam, but it is connected to it directly through the riverside road (also known as the 88 Olympic freeway). This geographical

33 Park, Myeong-Soo, 'Evangelism and Public Christianity: An Analysis', *Holiness Church and Theology* (Holiness Church History Research Center, Seoul Theological University, Spring, 2002), pp. 10-38. In this article, I explain the Pentecostal movement as public Christianity.

location meant that Yoido Full Gospel Church had positioned itself very well for Gangnam area, new residential place for the middle class, as well as for the industrialization.

5. Yoido Full Gospel Churches Rapid Growth

Yoido Full Gospel Church grew exponentially during this time period. Especially, the growth rate after moving to Yoido is just unbelievable. As shown in the following table, the growth rate at Yoido far surpasses the growth rate during the days at Seodaemoon. This is because of its strategic location connecting it to traditional saints in Gangbuk (North of the Han river), people in the industrial complex of Youngdeungpo and the middle class at Gangnam (South of the Han river).

Table 1: Growth of the membership at Yoido Full Gospel Church (1967-1979)

Year	1967	1972	1973	1974	1975	1976	1977	1978	1979
Membership	7750	10970	12556	19856	22992	35794	48975	75361	100930

data source: '40 years history of Yoido Full Gospel Church', p.166

Yoido Full Gospel Church became a church for all classes of people, to accommodate the middle class and the poor at Youngdeungpo. This is in contrast to other successful churches. The Youngrak Church is mainly for the refugees, and most churches of Gangnam area mainly serve the middle class. However, Yoido Full Gospel Church is for the lower-income class and yet has been successful in accommodating the middle class as well, thus overcoming class barriers in a church.

Reverend Cho, Yonggi still makes an effort to evangelize the lower-income class, and at the same time he also established Full Gospel Businessmen's Fellowship Union, Full Gospel Medical Profession Missionary Union, ect. to outreach the middle class and professionals. He has succeeded in overcoming the class barrier in the church.

Since the 1980's, the government started building neighboring cities to solve the housing problem of Seoul. A full development of Gangnam was accomplished, and a grand housing complex was built in Gangbuk at Nowon-Gu. Also, new cities at Boondang and Ilsan started to form, and the neighboring cities around Seoul began to boom suddenly. The model city is Bucheon. The Bucheon city was a small town of Kyunggi-Do (Province), but it has grown to be a big city with over 1 mllion population now along with the development of metropolitan area development.[34]

Yoido Full Gospel Church began to reorganize its structure to follow this new pattern. Many saints at Yoido Full Gospel Church used to live in Seoul but now had moved to the outskirt of Seoul. They continued to worship at the mother church using the means of public transportation. However, this created many uncomfortable situations. They had to leave the house early in the morning to attend the Sunday service. To solve this problem, Yoido Full Gospel Church began to build branch sanctuaries.

It was 1983 when Yoido Full Gospel Church built the first branch sanctuary. During this year, branch sanctuaries at Incheon, Bucheon, and Seongnam were established. These sanctuaries are all located in the outskirt of Seoul, and it is understood that the intention was to keep in step with the growth of Seoul metropolitan area. However, branch sanctuaries were continuously built. And during the 1980's, other branch sanctuaries were built at Euijeongbu, Wondang, Elkanto, Gangnam (the second sanctuary), Gangdong, Nowon, Goori, Boopyung, etc.

This process continued in the 1990's to build Songpa, Gangbuk, Dobong, Kimpo, Boondang, Elim, Sangdong, Poongjin, Ansan, Dongbu, Joongdong, and the fifth sanctuary. Some branch sanctuaries become independent as a church in the 1990's. First of all, Incheon, Bucheon, Seongnam sanctuaries became branch churches. Next, Elkanto, Wondang, Goori, Nowon, Samick, Euijeongbu sanctuaries also developed into branch churches. In my opinion, this is due to the fact that an appropriate policy was prepared in the context of the populace dispersion policy of Seoul city and new city development in the metropolitan area.

This system of branch sanctuaries and churches is made possible largely because of the development of internet and satellite broadcasting system. Since 1995, the worship service scenes of Yoido Full Gospel Church have been broadcasted to all branch churches and sanctuaries all over Korea. This new church system is not possible without the development of science and technology and was made possible because Yoido Full Gospel Church's modernism, transcending the traditional ecclesiology.

---

34 Kang, Cheol-Gu, 'Comparison Study on Urbanization Process of Seoul Metropolitan Area', pp. 69-70.

When we look at it from the perspective of church history, the early churches had one bishop in one city, and all the other churches around it were under the authority of the one bishop. The church, where the bishop resided, was called the episcopal church, and the other churches were under its directorship. The priest, who was in charge of this branch church, was called a presbyter.[35] Yoido Full Gospel Church is a modern episcopal church and is in the position to oversee the branch sanctuaries. This is surely a new church form, that is difficult to find in a reformed church.

Coexistence of Tradition and Modernity

We have seen that the old thing to return to the Pentecostal faith of the early churches and the new thing to adapt to the flow of modern society are coexisting in Yoido Full Gospel Church. The reason that Yoido Full Gospel Church became the world's largest church today is because it kept the good old as well as the new things. Many people are correct in understanding the growth of Yoido Full Gospel Church in its spiritual dimension. However, it is beneficial to see how Reverend Cho, Yonggi has applied it to the modern society along with this point.

This double sidedness can be understood in terms of the so called post modernism. The past Enlightment understood that primitivity and modernity could not coexist. Thus, most social scholars thought that the primitivity would fade as the modernity progressed. However, this hypothesis was wrong. On the contrary, the form of ancient religion is being developed further as the modern civilization is developed. This is a phenomenon that is often observed in the United States, Japan, and China. The United States is a country of the state-of-art science, but evangelists, who emphasize the miracle of divine healing, are appearing in TV everyday at the same time. Although Japan is proud of its development in Asia, many traditional religions are reappearing. After the communism collapsed and capitalism was introduced in China, numerous new religions are appearing in the country. This shows that modern civilization and ancient religion can coexist in the 20th century. In fact, it is so called later modernism, which was introduced to explain these two contradictory phenomena. According to this theory, the world can not be explained by reason and logic alone.

When we meet Reverend Cho, Yonggi, we can feel that he is

---

35 Walker, Williston, 'A History of Christian Church', Korean translated by Song, *In-Seoul* (Seoul: Christian Digest, 1996), p. 116.

breathing in the modern culture of the 21st century. When we explain the growth of Yoido Full Gospel Church in the future, we should look for how he identified the characteristics of modern society and applied the characteristics to his ministry as well as Reverend Cho, Yonggi's Pentecostal spirituality.

Up to now, I have analyzed the growth of Yoido Full Gospel Church in the context of history, organization and society in connection with Reverend Cho, Yonggi. However, in order to understand the growth of Yoido Full Gospel Church more comprehensively, a further research in many areas such as the development of mass-media, the change in the inner structure of the church, worship service style for the public, etc. is needed. I hope the research in this direction will continue in the future.

CHAPTER 5

The Influence of Rev. Cho's Church Growth on Korean Society

DR. HONG, YOUNG-GI

The purpose of this paper is to analyze the effect of Rev. Cho's church growth on Korean society. To speak in more detail, it is to study his theological perspective and his ministry on church growth with respect to its positive effect on Korean society. My purpose is related in a wider scale to the effect of a religion on the society.[1] The traditional theory has claimed that a religion can not promote societal change.[2] For example, Marx thought religion existed only in people's mind and ideal realm. Thus, he regarded it as a dependent variable that is determined by the influence of society. However, Max Weber asserted that the function of religion for societal change is not uniformly predetermined. He thought that the religious ethics and ideas contributed significantly in developing modern capitalism. That is to say that a religion has had a power to change a social system as well as to maintain it.

Contemporary sociology of religion maintains the view that a religion can influence public affairs.[3] Especially, the past terror incident at the world trade center on September 11, 2001 reminds us that a religion can effect the realms of politics. A religion provides society comprehensive standards and mental dynamics to act in accordance with such standards. It often acts as an independent variable by retaining great material and human resources. Thus, we have to acknowledge the fact that Christianity has influenced a change in Korean society, and Reverend Cho's church growth has to be analyzed in this context.

---

1 Berger, Peter L., 'Religion and Society' (Chongro Books, 1993, Korean).

2 Oh, Gyung-Hwan, 'Sociological Theory of Religion' (Seokwang-Sa, 1990, Korean)

3 Yamane, David, Secularization On Trial: In Defense of a Neosecularization Paradigm, *Journal for the Scientific Study of Religion* (36(1), 1997), pp. 109-122.

This article analyzes the range of social reform that was effected by Reverend Cho's church growth conception, reviews the effect of his church growth on Korean society, and afterwards addresses the future tasks that need to be carried out for the development of Korean society.

Systematic Power of Church Growth and Societal Change

Where does this systematic power of Christianity to cause a societal change come from? Kim, Nyung[4] presents that such systematic power of the church to cause a societal and political change is the power by the standards or the norms, by the organization, and by behaviours. The normative power refers to biblical prophetic calling and offering of the ideology. The organizational power includes a variety consolidation, the organizational size, the wide range of influence (periodicals, mass media, school, etc.), international network, material resources, and human resources. Behavioural power refers to the ethical authority of the church and societal recognition of the public trust.

Reverend Cho's church growth movement has its foundation mainly on the organizational power. The international network, periodicals, mass media and the organizational size, etc. of Yoido Full Gospel Church greatly enhanced the influential power of his church growth movement. Yoido Full Gospel Church had a small beginning but experienced an explosive growth with time. The Korean chruches and society did not pay much attention to Reverend Cho's vision and message for church growth at first. Then, after seeing the explosive growth of his church, they began to have much interest and attention. This progressive power is much related to the influential power of the Pentecostal churches in Latin America. The Pentecostal movement had explosive growth among the poor and the alienated and appeared in time as a strong power that could cause a societal change.[5]

One factor, that we have to carefully observe in the systematic power of Reverend Cho's church growth influencing Korean society, is the normative element. The normative element includes the mind-set and ideas that can make people react. These ideas have the power to change the awareness and behavior of people in the long

4 Kim, Nyung, 'Korean Politics and Church – National Conflict' (Sonamoo *Pine Tree*, 1996, Korean).

5 David Martin, Tongues of Fire: The Explosion of Protestantism in Latin America (Cambridge, MA: Basil Blackwell, Inc., 1990)

run. Max Weber concentrated more on the religious ideas than on the religious organizations in explaining the societal change. He correctly viewed that the ethics and conceptions of the reformed churches could greatly influence a societal change. In the case of Reverend Cho, his views on the ministry and message influenced significantly the patterns of people's lives. The lifetime message of Reverend Cho's ministry can be summarized in the fivefold gospel and threefold blessing.[6] This is the essence of the Christian gospel and his theology of church growth as he understands it. Then, what dimension of societal change is immanent in his theological perspective on church growth?

The Societal Changing Dimension of the Fivefold Gospel and Threefold Blessing

One of the criticism that Reverend Cho has encountered so far is that his message encourages a selfish faith of receiving personal blessing while it does not have any contribution to make to societal change. I believe that this criticism is not justified. Reverend Cho's theological perspective contains a strong power for a deep societal change. His fivefold gospel is the result of grafting the historical and theological doctrines of the methodist and holiness church to Korean aboriginal context. That is, it includes the baptism by the Holy Spirit and Sanctification in the gospel of the fullness of the Holy Spirit. It also extracted the gospel of 'blessing' from the conception of blessing for the salvation of the whole man as the result of Jesus Christ's redemption. Therefore, the fivefold gospel refers to the gospel of regeneration (the new life attained by believing in Jesus Christ), the gospel of the fullness of the Holy Spirit (living the holy life by being filled with the Holy Spirit after believing in Jesus Christ), the gospel of divine healing (curing the satanic disease), the gospel of blessing (to be free from the curse of poverty and to live abundantly as well as to be blessed to give and serve others), and the gospel of the Advent (the Advent of our Lord, Jesus Christ, and the hope for the Advent of the Kingdom of God).

First of all, Rev. Cho's gospel of regeneration inspired many people of Korean society the sense of self-identity and the hope of life. Jayakumar,[7] in his insightful study says that Dalits, the Indian populace, embraced the modernity and rapid societal change.

---

6 Cho, Yonggi, *Fivefold Gospel and Threefold Blessing* (Seoul Logos Inc., 2000, Korean)

7 Samuel Jayakumar, 'The Impact of Modernity on the Dalits of India', *Transformation* (17(2), 2000), pp. 75-80.

Furthermore, he stresses that it was the Christian faith that made people control their lives in the sense that the poor began to understand themselves anew and found new hope through their faiths. I believe this point applies to Reverend Cho's message and ministry. Reverend Cho helped the poor in Korea to find a new identity in Jesus Christ (and this help resulted in social transformation of the poor).[8] For this reason Hwa Yung[9] states that Reverend Cho's Pentecostal movement could influence the societal and political change more powerfully than Minjung theology. Reverend Cho's gospel of regeneration contributed greatly to planting Christianity among the alienated class.[10]

The gospel of the fullness of the Holy Spirit empowers the people, who have been regenerated by the gospel of regeneration, to live the life of following God's will. Full Gospel contains powerful elements for the awareness of the poor and the oppressed.[11] The 1998 Brussels Declaration of the World Missions Bureau of the Assemblies of God declared that Christians filled with the Holy Spirit could proclaim the gospel's reforming power and could and should testify to it.

Douglas Peterson holds the view that it is the dispensation of the Holy Spirit that made the societal doctrine of the missionary movement Pentecostal.[12] When Christians are empowered by God's authority, they are equipped to perform the mission work of God's kingdom despite the life's hardships and needs. Reverend Cho's gospel of the fullness of the Holy Spirit provided the dynamics for Christians to perform societal service and to experience the inner transformation by feeling the power of the Holy Spirit in everyday life.

---

8 Hong, Young-Gi, 'Reverend Cho, Yonggi's Theology Expanding the Implications of the Gospel: Comments on a Research Paper of Dr. Hwa, Yung Presented at 2002 Youngsan International Theological Symposium', Youngsan International Theological Symposium, Hansei University (September 26-27, 2002), p. 154.

9 Hwa. Yung, 'Missiological Implications of Dr. David Yonggi Cho's Theory', A Paper Presented at the Yongsan Interntional Theological Symposium Held by Hansei University, 26-27 September 2002.

10 Lee, Young-Hoon, 'The Influence of the Pentecostal Movement on Korean Churches', *Pentecostal Theology Research Platform* (No. 1, Pentecostal Theology Research Center, Hansei University, 1998), pp. 116-117.

11 Hong, Young-Gi, 'The 21st Century Pentecostal Missiology', *The Holy Spirit and Theology* (No. 18, 2002, Korean), pp. 352-377.

12 Douglas Peterson, 'missions in the Twenty-first century: Toward a Methodology of Pentecostal Compassion', *Transformation* (16:2, 1999): pp. 54-59.

The gospel of divine healing proclaims the wholeness of the inseparable spirit and body. Namely, it is the message of proclaiming the presence of God and salvation of the whole man by divine healing. Reverend Cho's divine healing ministry enabled many Koreans to experience the power of the living God and provided them the light of life. The dispensation of divine healing does not just end with healing of the individual disease, but it causes a reform in the community. When the experience of divine healing is sublimated in the Holy Spirit, the social changing power of the divine healing ministry can surface. Reverend Cho's gospel of divine healing has profound implications for the individual, community and the societal change.

The Gospel of Blessing was conceived due to a situation of crisis in Korea. Reverend Cho professed that the Gospel of Blessing was a theological necessity right after the Korean War, during which time many people were suffering from extreme poverty and hurt.[13] Hwa, Yung[14] points out that Reverend Cho's preaching on material blessing was misunderstood. That is to say that his preaching was equated with the American gospel of prosperity which regarded prosperity to mean money. Reverend Cho taught that poverty is not the will of God and that we can live the life of threefold blessing when we have God as the highest priority.

Reverend Cho, Yonggi says that the gospel of blessing has to be interpreted anew as the korean society changes.[15] Blessing is the will of God, and people, who are blessed, should devote themselves in sharing this blessing. The Full Gospel message of Reverend Cho, Yonggi stressed blessing up until middle of 1980's. Since the economic development of late 1980's, he emphasized the practice of blessing and love. The Reverend Cho, Yonggi's gospel of blessing has a very recondite societal dimension. The gospel of blessing gave hope to hungry and poor Korean people and many poor countries. And the missionary sharing of the blessing contributed positively to the social reform, because it could increase the social influence and trust of the Christian gospel.

The gospel of the Advent shows the purpose of preaching the gospel. Since the Pentecost understood the calling of the Holy Spirit eschatologically, the characteristics of the world mission of the

---

13 Conversation at a farewell dinner of Youngsan International Theological Symposium, September 27, 2002.

14 Hwa, Yung, op. cit.

15 Conversation at a farewell dinner of Youngsan International Theological Symposium, September 27, 2002.

church was also eschatological.[16] The eschatological hope for the Coming of the Holy Spirit and the Advent of Jesus Christ in the Acts inspired the mission of the church, and it was two experiential entities, which mobilized the 20th century Pentecostal movement with zeal for the world evangelism.[17] Reverend Cho, Yonggi not only preached the eternal, futuristic kingdom of God but also testified that the eternal blessing of the kingdom of God can be experienced here on the earth right now. Reverend Cho, Yonggi brought the eschatological concept of the kingdom of God to the present, seeing that the presence of God 'here and now' was very important in relation to the wholistic salvation.[18] Thus, since Reverend Cho, Yonggi's gospel of the Advent implies the eschatological hope and the desire for the will of God to be actualized on this earth, it has a dimension of social reformation.

The threefold blessing is a fruit of the fivefold gospel and includes a healthy life, the life of wellbeing and the happiness of the soul. This blessing is to proclaim the wholistic salvation of the Christian gospel for us. The dogma of 'threefold blessing' is unique in that it can not be found in the traditional Pentecostal church. This is a theology that is based on the Korean situation between the 1950's and 1960's. The threefold blessing shows that it is a message of wholistic salvation to include the spirit, soul, body, and all universe. This message of Reverend Cho, Yonggi refutes the dualism that distinguishes the spirit and body, the world and church, etc. The fivefold gospel and threefold blessing of Reverend Cho, Yonggi may not entirely have been practiced soundly in the reality of Korean society, but they have a clear significance for social reform.

The Influence of Reverend Cho, Yonggi's Church Growth Movement on Korean Society

Some critics have regarded the traditional Pentecostals, conservative and other-worldly in their theological orentation and have assumed that the Pentecostals do not have a concern for what's going on in the society. However, Douglas Peterson stresses that recent studies on the Pentecostal movement make such assumption

16 Hong, Young-Gi, 'Church and Mission: A Pentecostal Perspective', *International Review of Mission* (No. 358, July 2001), p. 299.

17 Murray W. Dempster, 'Social Concern in the Context of Jesus Kingdom, Mission and Ministry', *Transformation* (16(2), 1999), p. 45.

18 International Theological Research Center, *Introduction to Full Gospel Theology* (Seoul Logos Inc., 2002, Korean), p. 90.

doubtful.[19] During recent decades, the world Pentecostals have increased their interest in the social problems from the perspective of their mission. Although the ministry of Reverend Cho, Yonggi has been criticized for not having an interest in social problems, I believe the importance of his ministry has to be evaluated again. So, let's examine how the church growth movement of Reverend Cho, Yonggi has influenced the reform of Korean society.

1. Change in the Minds for Positive Life and Hope

Many scholars, who study democracy, point out that it is in the mind of people. In other words, democracy belongs to the citizens, who obtain the culture of democratic politics rather than the laws of human rights or liberty.[20] This shows that one of the most important tasks for developing the Korean society is to reform the the minds of its citizens. The message of Reverend Cho, Yonggi affected the attitudes of many people who were suffering from poverty and disease.[21] The collection of Reverend Cho, Yonggi's sermons (21 volumes, 780 messages) reveals that they deal with faith, trials, victory, prayer, happiness, and growth, etc. This shows clearly what kind of blessing and life the poor and suffering people should live in yhe realities of life. The Reverend Cho, Yonggi's message was the language of faith on the dream and hope of God.[22]

Reverend Cho, Yonggi himself answers that it is the most important influence of his ministry on the Korean society that he instilled 'the dream and hope for the positive life'.[23] If most people are trapped in despair and despondency, what kind of society would that be? Myriad of people, who gathered in the Full Gospel, could renew their identity and light the flame of hope again.[24] The author also thinks it is the most meritorious point of Reverend Cho, Yonggi's ministry that the reformation of the mind by the Gospel

---

19 Douglas Peterson, *Not By Might Nor By Power: A Pentecostal Theology of Social Concern in Latin America* (Oxford: Regnum International, 1996), p. 147.

20 Pae, Sung Moon, Korea *Leading Developing Nation: Economy, Democracy, and Welfare* (Maryland: University Press of America, 1992), p. 167.

21 Interview, Park, Deuk-Hoon (Editor, News & Joy 2002.10.27); Interview, Ko, Jik-Han (President, Young 2080, 2002.10.27).

22 Cho, Yonggi. *The Fourth Dimension* (Seoul Logos Inc., 1996).

23 E-mail Interview (correspondence), Cho, Yonggi (Senior Pastor, Yoido Full Gospel Church, 2002. 10. 24).

24 cf. Myung, Sung-Hoon, *Spiritual Dimension of Church Growth* (Seoul Logos Inc., 1993), pp. 256-257.

and the change in the value system contributed to the development of the Korean society. It is a very noticeable change in recent Korean society that Reverend Cho, Yonggiís message altered the attitude of the general public.

2. *Function for Social Integration*

Up until now, we have understood the functions of progressive and conservative churches as confronting structures in Korean society. However, we have to acknowledge that each has contributed to the society. Whereas the progressive church has enhanced the social trust of the church by making prophecies on the society, the conservative church has assisted numerous people, who were in despair under unstable political and social circumstances, aggressively through the message of hope and consolation and visitation. Until the 1980's, Reverend Cho, Yonggi's ministry was mainly geared to the function of social integration rather than the function of social reformation in Korean society. The function of social integration means that religion provides a sense of community to its members and justifies the society's important value and ethics to contribute to the order and stability of the society.

Reverend Cho, Yonggi's ministry could serve the function of social integration in the context of religious social studies by uniting Christians in community by the experience of the Holy Spirit in faith along with a povitive look on life.[25] Whereas the progressive Christianity absorbed people by participating aggressively in the resolution of social conflicts, Reverend Cho, Yonggi's ministry provided a sense of stability to a class of people who were trapped in cultural deprivation, and the alienated class, who were trapped in economic deprivation.[26]

3. *Redemption and Lift*

Many Koreans recently had to endure war and division, poverty and disease, and mental anguish.

Naturally, lots of Koreans pursued some value, which can overcome the poverty in mind. Reverend Cho, Yonggi's ministry result-

---

25 International Theological Research Center, *Introduction to Full Gospel Theology* (Seoul Logos Inc., 2002, Korean), p. 212.

26 Yoon, Seung-Yong, 'Investigation on Religious Reaction Types to Societal Changes – Centered on Korean Society after the Industrialization', Ph.D. dissertation, Religious Studies, Seoul National University, 1992, (Korean), p. 186.

ed in healing of disease and receiving of material blessing of many people, who were suffering from the disease and poverty by coming to the church. Reverend Cho, Yonggi's message of 'let's live well' along with the slogan of 1970's new village movement, strengthened positive and productive attitude and contributed to the economic development and modernization of Korea. His ministry provided a practical opportunity to people to produce the effect of economical and social benefits. Reverend Cho, Yonggi's gospel of blessing contributed greatly in enlarging the middle class of Korea and instilled hope to the general public. This positive and active attitude of life bred faith, and many people became 'the have's' socially, economically, and spiritually. We can call this phenomenon, redemption and lift.

As Murray Dempster mentioned, each saint's redemption and lift can become the main driving forces for social reformation and devotion for the missionary ministry.[27] Redemption and lift begets the testimonial theology. In the Full Gospel Church, the testimonies of people, who were healed of disease, met God amidst despair, and received material blessing while in poverty, continues. These testimonies unify the community and make the theology of the community lively. Thus, redemption and lift have a social significance, and it is a continuing task of Reverend Cho, Yonggi's ministry to sublimate the meaning.

4. Cultural Reform

Reverend Cho, Yonggi's ministry has often been criticised as being shamanic. However, this is a misunderstanding. Although Reverend Cho, Yonggi's ministry has a seedbed of shamanic environment, his ministry of healing and blessing by the work of the Holy Spirit does not mix with the shamanism. Allan Anderson[28] or Hwa, Yung,[29] etc. indicate that it is wrong to say Reverend Cho, Yonggi's ministry as shamanic. They understand that Reverend Cho, Yonggi's ministry has an interplay with shamanism. There is a big difference in shamanism and reciprocal action with shamanism.

---

27 Murray W. Dempster, 'Evangelism, Social Concerns and the Kingdom of God', *Called and Empowered: Global Mission in Pentecostal Perspective*, Byron D. Klaus and Douglas Peterson (Peabody, MA: Hendricks, 1991), p. 27.

28 Allan Anderson, 'David Yonggi Cho's Pentecostal Theology as Contextual Theology in Korea', A Paper Presented at the Youngsan International Theological Symposium Held by Hansei University, pp.. 26-27, September 26-27, 2002.

29 Hwa, Yung, op. cit.

The latter is clearly Christian contingency in shamanic culture.

Reverend Cho, Yonggi's healing ministry is carried out by the power of the Holy Spirit. His emphasis on blessing is to proclaim 'the Good God' to people in despair. This has an important implication on the relationship between the gospel and culture. It changes the value and life pattern of people by delivering the gospel message of Christianity appropriately in the context of people in the shamanic background. Reverend Cho, Yonggi church growth theology has to be understood in relation to the Korean context, that produced such theology. His ministry's dimension on cultural reform needs to be illuminated anew.

5. Leadership and Social Change

The Pentecost has been the place for the alienated and women to come to the church in order to reclaim their feeling of self-existence and to practice their leadership. Douglas Peterson says this point is an important social expression of the Pentecost.[30] All new believers in the Pentecostal church are given a task regardless of their social or economic status as soon as they convert. They participate in numerous small group and missionary activities voluntarily as well as giving other voluntary service and evangelizing. Through these activities, the new believers are given the opportunity for the leadership, and they are trained to be successful leaders.

Reverend Cho, Yonggi's ministry changes the new believers into devoted persons through the experience of the Holy Spirit. He gives them the opportunity for voluntary service and leadership development.

One thing to notice carefully in Reverend Cho, Yonggi's ministry is the function of women. In Korean society, where women were traditionally not recognized in the society, Reverend Cho, Yonggi recognized their value to engage them in church leadership. This leadership development and practice is based on the Pentecostal dogma of spiritual gift. Women, who were deprived of the opportunity to put their spiritual gift into action, have now received the leadership opportunity with the responsibility for evangelism and nurturing. Reverend Cho, Yonggi's ministry enhanced women's social value and contributed to the development of human resources in Korea.[31]

---

30 Douglas Peterson, *Not By Might Nor By Power: A Pentecostal Theology of Social Concern in Latin America*, p. 121.

31 Ma, Won-Suk, 'The Work of the Holy Spirit in a Societal Dimension', *International Theological Research Center, Christian Sanctification by the Work of the Holy Spirit* (1997, Korean), p. 161.

6. Reciprocal Reaction with Modernity of Korean Society

The characteristics of modernity is based on the faith of advancement, science and technology. Capitalism, urbanization, knowledge sector (e.g. college), mass-media, etc. can be viewed as important carriers of modernity. James Hunter[32] said the characteristics of the Pentecost was an anthropological protest against modernity. This describes the unique, dual nature of the Pentecost in regard to the modernity; it resists the spirit of modernity, but it utilizes its technology. Reverend Cho, Yonggi has dealt with the important passage to the modernity, college and mass-media, etc., in his ministry. The Pentecostalists in the early days have built many schools as a means to change the life of people in the process of causing a social change.[33]

Reverend Cho, Yonggi has exerted his unsparing effort to develop the talented through Hansei University, Bethesda University, and Full Gospel School of Theology, etc.

Reverend Cho, Yonggi also used TV and radio broadcasting as a missionary means. *Invitation to the Happiness* was the first TV broadcasting ministry in Korea. This program contributed greatly to evangelism by suggesting true (Biblical) way to happiness regardless of the faith. From 1996, Yoido Full Gospel Church started satellite mission policy through the first Korean communication satellite, Moogoonghwa (the rose of Sharon). Since the 1990's when computers were widely distributed, Yoido Full Gospel Church has established Internet Broadcasting Department to live-broadcast the worship service, and the sermons of Reverend Cho, Yonggi are provided to the netizens (cyber-place people, who use the internet for many activities of life) through VOD (Video on Demand). These cases shows that Reverend Cho, Yonggi's ministry does not refute social values but utilizes it fully for the effectiveness of Christian gospel.

Thus, we can see that it is a wrong viewpoint to think Full Gospel is mainly of the other-worldly spirituality. Reverend Cho, Yonggi's ministry not only has been influenced by the modern social development of Korea but also has had an active interaction with the modernity. Grant Walker once described the Pentecostal movement

---

32 James D. Hunter, 'The new religions: demodernization and the Pretest against modernity', Bryan Wilson (ed.) *Impact of New Religious Movements*, pp. 1-20, New York: Rose of Sharon Press, 1981.

33 Douglas Peterson, *Not By Might Nor By Power: A Pentecostal Theology of Social Concern in Latin America*, p. 121.

as 'the garden of Eden equipped with a satellite dish'.[34] And this description is applied well to Reverend Cho, Yonggi's ministry. Furthermore, Walker's description shows symbolically well the spirituality of the Full Gospel, which is grafted to the modern technology of Korean society.

7. Diligent Social Service Activities

Traditionally, the Pentecostalists have been very active in helping the needy.[35] This devotion can come from the mind touched by the Holy Spirit. If Reverend Cho, Yonggi's message influenced the mental aspect of Korean society mainly until the late 1980's, it began to effect the structural aspect of the society since the late 1980's. This is well revealed in the practice of social ethics and service of Yoido Full Gospel Church. The social service of Yoido Full Gospel Church has largely been underestimated by other Christian denominations in Korea and Korean society in general.

Yoido Full Gospel Church has started 'love in practice movement' ardently since the 'sharing movement' headquarters was established in 1982. This movement continued until 1987, and 320,000 pieces of life's necessities were collected to be distributed to the orphanage, an asylum for the aged (nursing home), slum areas around a city, churches in the farming and fishing community, and Sorokdo (Sorok island) asylum for the patients of Hansen disease (leprosy), etc. Since 1992, old clothes and paper are collected and handed out to the unfortunate neighbors as an act of warm love. Additionally, the blood donation drive of love has started actively since 1988, and 56,030 people have participated in it as of 2001. Also, the love bread movement has helped the unfortunate neighbors by collecting the coins from the saints' piggy banks. Yoido Full Gospel Church opened a new chapter in Christian social welfare activities by building the Elim Welfare Town in Gunpo-Si (city) of Kyngki-Do (province) in 1988 for promoting a healthy and bright society. There are technical school, nursing home, and a relaxing quarter in honor of the aged, etc. Those, who enter this technical school, are provided all tuition and dormitory expenses free of charge. After they obtain the second grade certification of national technological license, all of them are offered a full time job. Those, who become a

---

34 Grant Walker, 'Searching for Eden with a Satellite Dish: Primitism, Pragmatism, and the Pentecostal Character. Hughes, Richard (ed.) *The Primitive Church in the Modern World*, Urbana and Chicago: University of Illinois Press, 1995, pp. 139-166.

35 Ma, Won-Suk, 'The Work of the Holy Spirit in a Societal Dimension', p. 165.

resident of the living quarters in honor of the aged, are offered all medical benefits and other welfare services free of charge until they pass away.

The typical Yoido Full Gospel Church's practice of love is free operations for the heart diseased people since 1984. In the beginning, it was for the children mainly but later included infants and adults as well. The heart disease operation expanded overseas, and now the children of the Republic of Uzbekistan, Nepal, Cambodia, and Ukrain can be the beneficiary. By the year of 2001, the number of free heart operations reached 3,000 with the total cost of 4,140,000,000 Won (about 3.6 million US dollars).[36] On May 3, 1996, Reverend Cho, Yonggi of Yoido Full Gospel Church received the highest medal given to a citizen by the Republic of Korea, Moogoonghwa medallion. The contribution of Reverend Cho, Yonggi in supporting the movement for the free heart operations was thus recognized. These cases reveal that Reverend Cho, Yonggi's ministry does not privatize Christian faith but contextualises it. A delicate balance of spirituality and social sensitivity is important in a creative church leadership.[37]

8. Establishment of Kookmin Daily News and Its Social Influence

By establishing Kookmin Daily News in 1998, Reverend Cho, Yonggi began to influence Korean society with Christian gospel. From the viewpoint that Kookmin Daily News is the first Christian daily newspaper in Korea established with Christian spirit, its historical meaning is very significant in the ministry of the Full Gospel and Korean society. The Kookmin Daily News set the mission slogan of 'love, sincerity, and human', and it was established to illuminate all areas of the society with a viewpoint of Christianity and to create a righteous society. From its beginning, the Kookmin Daily News has promoted the movement to change the minds of people to have more interest for the alienated citizens by the Korean society. From January 29, 1989, it has helped thousands of boys and girls head of the household.

Since 1992, it has propagated the blood donation drive of love along with the headquarters of love-practice movement to induce thousands of churches in Korea to participate in the blood drive. Additionally, it has engaged in a campaign for 'kind neighbor,

36 Full Gospel Family Newsletter, February 24, 2002.

37 Hong, Young-Gi, 'Modernity, Tradition, and the Korean Church: Church Growth and Pastoral Leadership', *Asian Journal of Mission* (September 2001b, 3(2)): pp. 185-211.

bright society' and kindness movement for all people in Korea. 1,300 social organizations participated to contribute in the movement to change the mind into kindness as a way of life. Besides, this movement also donates wheelchairs for the handicapped, worked to improve the burial culture, to send calandar of love, etc. it has made a sincere effort to make the Korean society bright and healthy.

The Kookmin Daily News has carried out the task of providing affordable medical care for the poor with the foundation of voluntary medical service corps of love under the support of the Ministry of Health and Welfare since May 23, 1998. Through 400 free medical care activities, it has treated 36,447 and performed 145,903 medical examinations. Above all, the Kookmin Daily News published articles on the alienated and lowly people of society to draw the love and interest of people. The Kookmin Daily News visited the famine fields and reported it vividly. The coverage received a wide concern and support for the cause. It has helped many refugees with the donation. Additionally, it reported the famine in the third world countries and AIDS along with the World Vision to put the love movement of Christian spirit into action. Also, the campaign of bone marrow donation resulted in many participating to vitalize the sharing of love and life on the occasion of its 14th anniversary.

The editing counsels of Kookmin Daily News endeavor to infiltrate Christian view of the world. It made a religion corner in the daily newspaper, Kookmin Daily News, so that the general public would not feel an aversion for Christianity. The tesimonies of well-known people are published to influence non-Christians to have a positive perception for Christianity. In 2001, as an annual project, it compared the donation culture of the global village to urge systematic improvement of the donation environment through *together with sharing* article.

It promoted the view to propagate the sharing movement by analyzing the donation culture of the United States and Korea. It pointed out the fact, that Koreans donate 0.8% per capita income on the average and it is the level that one would be hesitant to call it donation, and urged a change in the heart. The special project article on the society corne, entitled *good neighbor, good world* or *the living story of this person* dug up and reported the story of people serving the unfortunate neighbors to make the Korean society brighter and better. These articles are permeated covertly with Christian world view so as to influence Korean society.

The Kookmin Daily News has undoubtedly influenced the Korean society greatly as a communication channel of Christian culture and as a speaking platform of Korean Christianity to the society. Now, the future task of the Kookmin Daily News is to infiltrate the Christian world view throughout all the newspaper deeply and to develop further the professionalism as a press of Christianity.[38] It is very important to reanalyze and guide all areas of Korean society, politics, economics, and culture, etc. with a Biblical and gospel point of view.[39] The powers of Korean politics and society can not ignore the influence of Kookmin Daily News now. Thus, it is very important for the Kookmin Daily News to spread the Christian values with necessary kind of eyes for the society.

9. Christian NGO Activity

The social activities of evangelists of Korean church spread widely at the 1990's. The most important merit of Korean evangelical Christianity in the 1990's is its contribution to the civil movement.[40] The civil society is volutary, self-supporting, self-content, and self-governing (from government, politics, and economics) organization.[41] The civil society has greater interest in public purpose than that in private purpose, and it does not pursue an employment in the civil service or power from the country although it deals with the matters of the nation.

On the contrary, it demands concession and benefits, policy change and responsibility, etc. from the nation. Thus, the civil society pursues public good rather than power. Healthy civil movement signifies vision and devotion for healthy society.

The fact that Reverend Cho, Yonggi's ministry started a relationship with the civil movement has a great significance theologically and socially. The NGO (Non-Government Organization), *Good People*, with chairmanship of Reverend Cho, Yonggi, that was established in 1999 is a typical example. An incorporated body, Good People, is the first church NGO in Korea, that started from Yoido Full Gospel Church, to work for the poor and suffering neighbors in

---

38 Interview, Hahm, Tae-Gyung, (Reporter, Religion Department and International Affairs Department, Kookmin Daily News, October 19, 2002, Korean).

39 Interview, Kim, Sang-Gil, (Head, Religion Department, Kookmin Daily News, October 27, 2002, Korean).

40 Hong, Young-Gi, 'Evangelical Christians and the Democratization of Korea Since 1987', A Paper Presented at the International Conference on *Evangelicals and Democracy in the Third World* held by the International Fellowship of Evangelical Mission Theologies in Washington, D. C., pp. 28-30, July 2002.

41 Larry Diamond, 'Toward Democratic Consolidation', *Journal of Democracy* (5(3), 1994): p. 5.

the global village, relying on the words of the Lord, 'Go and do likewise.' (Luke 10:37), to transcend race, national boundary, religion, and ideology. The Good People explains their establishment purpose as follows. (www.goodpeople.or.kr)

1. It is the purpose of *Good People,* a corporation, to support the mission to the unreached third world countries effectively and to flow the love and righteousness of God on this earth.
2. We support them until they are self-supporting to be able to deal with their lives fully not just by giving them daily provisions but also by supporting their education and development as well as providing emergency relief and medical care in the places of famine, disease, and disaster.
3. It is the result of collapsed Christian love that the egotism, lust, rage and conflict between social classes, and suffering and confusion are flooding the modern people. In this life spot, it is a practice of true love and furthermore a way to revive the society that we reach out the unfortunate neighbors.
4. For this purpose, *Good People* desires to be the light and salt for the world by training and nurturing good Samaritans, who have the world view in love following the truth of Christ, by putting the love for the alienated neighbors into action.

Good People have continued various activities since its inception. As an education and supporting ministry, it hosted and supported children's choir, the movement to help the poor neighbors, sales of Christmas cake, offering of free corn porridge, etc. in 2002. Additionally, Good People have been sending corn seeds and fertilizer, meals for North Korean children and roasted rice powder, and medicine for the tuberculosis, etc. every year to North Korea.[42] Moreover, it has continued the ministry of helping the refugees for freedom to settle in Korea through Good People College, unfortunate neighbors, foreign laborers, and operating Good People service corps of love as well as undertaking hospice works. Especially, the Good People college is the first private organization established for offering career training and helping the new business for the freedom refugees (North Korean expatriation) to settle in Korea. This college offers a two week course of hands-on training annually to provide a basis for self-supporting of the freedom refugees centering on cultural orientation of South Korean society, counseling and healing of personal and family issues, and nurturing of job skills and business ownership, ect. The Good People College

42 Good People, 'Good People White Paper 2000' (Yoido Full Gospel Church, 2000).

received favorable response from Korean presses. Many presses have evaluated the one year course of Good People College as a model ministry of the NGOs.[43]

The overseas ministry of Good People include rebuilding of Talegaon school in India. medical care for the third world, support for Vietnam, Nanai tribe of Russia, clothing assistance for the third world, medicine for tuberculosis patients in the Philippines, prevention of AIDS in Kenya of Africa, etc[44] Emergency relief is also an important ministry of Good People. It quickly reaches anywhere there is suffering due to disasters with relief supplies and medical care. It sends out relief personnels to Kosovo, Turkey, Afghanistan, etc. Especially, Good People and Yoido Full Gospel Church have hosted vigorous relief activities through special offering of all congregation members to help the flood victims, who were suffering from the worst flood in recent Korean history because of the typhoon, Rusa, that struck all over Kŏrea in the late August, 2002.

The 'flood disaster relief corps', that was founded by an NGO, Good People and Yoido Full Gospel Church, delivered about 740,000,000 Won worth of money and supplies with an annual manpower of 1,000 volunteers.

The vision of Good People is 'building of global village that all people live together in harmony and the world filled with God's love and righteousness'. This vision of God's kingdom is dreaming of reformed world in gospel as an eschatological vision of Full Gospel faith. Since Good People is a NGO of Yoido Full Gospel Church, it has the advantage of acquiring various service resources including human and material resources. However, for the development of Good People with a history of three and a half years and Reverend Cho, Yonggi's citizen movement, it requires the task of developing holistic theological system about the citizen movement, sharing of Gospel mind on the citizen development, and organizing Christian NGO network. Then, it can expand its realm to social and international Christian NGO, maintaing the identity rooted in the spirituality of Full Gospel.[45]

---

43 Kim, Jin-Ho, 'Don't Make the Second Class Citizens Anymore' (*ShinDongA* June 2002); Park, Seong-Won, 'What is re-tech?' (*Newsweek*, Korean edition, August 28, 2002); Hong, Dae-Sun, 'Guidance for North Korean Refuges to Settle in South Korean Society' (*Hangyerye Daily News*, February 26, 2002), so forth.

44 Good People, 'Good People White Paper 2000'

45 Interview, Cho, Seok-In (General Secretary, Good People, October 27, 2002).

10. Participation in the Environment Movement

The environmental problems in Korea is becoming more and more important. It is the general view of scholars to regard the 20th century as the century of economic concern and the 21st century as the century of environmental concern.[46] Reverend Cho, Yonggi and Yoido Full Gospel Church established Christian environmental movement mission division in 1995 to honor the calling of the stewardship for the environment and nature.

Under the motto of 'nature love, nation love', it has been in the forefront of the environmental preservation movement to spread the campaign for guiding the reform of national mind on the preservation of the environment.

Good People, having the concern on environmental issues, started the project of ecological garden on the side stream of the Han river in Yoido of Seoul under the support of the city of Seoul and Green Seoul Citizen Commission. The purpose of this project was to provide ecological education program to the visitors by observing the ecological park and developing educational resources, that are appropriate for this park. During this project, a full time staff was placed in the park for continuous monitoring, and the result of this monitoring greatly helped the production of the educational resources and development of the educational method. A total of 8,685 visitors experienced the nature through the ecological schools, developed by this project, for the environmental and ecological education such as the weekend seasonal ecological school, weekday ecological school, ecological school for the handicapped and boys and girls, teachers invitational ecological school, ecological schools for preschool and primary school children. The important contribution of this ministry is to suggest a model for the operation and management of an ecological park in the city. Various experts and civil servants of the city participated together in this project and suggested a cooperative system policy for the urban ecological park.

As the Priest of Jesus Abbey, Dae, Cheon-Duk, stressed, the main concern of the 21st century will be ecology. The environmental ministry of Reverend Cho, Yonggi and Yoido Full Gospel Church is an importance example of holistic mission for the society. Grant McClung, a Pentecostal theologian,[47] suggested evangelism, ecu-

---

46 Ahn, Gi-Hwoi, 'Environmental Education for New Millennium', *Environmental Education*, (12(1), 1999): p. 1.

47 McClung, L. Grant, Try to Get People Saved: Revisiting the Paradigm of an Urgent Pentecostal Missiology, Dempster, Murray W, Klaus. Byron D, and Peterson, Douglas (eds.) *The Globalization of Pentecostalism: A Religion Made to Travel* (Oxford and Irvine: Regnum, 1999).

menism, eschatology along with ecology based on the words of God and the Holy Spirit as a paradigm for the future mission. The mission of the kingdom of God is very holistic and includes the environmental problems.[48] We have to remember that Reverend Cho, Yonggi's ministry is dealing with holistic problems. Reverend Cho, Yonggi stresses the responsibility of the church to give the hope of salvation and love to people, who are facing despair, poverty, and suffering. More and more people are suffering and are being alienated today than ever before despite changes brought about by science.

The Future Task to Serve the Korean Society Better

Up to now, I have dealt with the positive influence of Reverend Cho, Yonggi's church growth movement on Korean society. Now, I will suggest the following for future development of his Christian ministry for Korean society.

Firstly, we need to emphasize the societal significance of the Holy Spirit in the future. The personal inner change through the experience of the fullness of the Holy Spirit needs to be developed to affect the broader societal and communal change. In the 1990's, the fact that Reverend Cho, Yonggi preached sermons more on Christian ethics can be interpreted more positively in this sense. The Full Gospel Church has to strive to investigate the task of changing the threefold blessing of Full Gospel spirituality, that has been stressed on a personal level, into a societal level with qualitative and structural methods.[49] In other words, we have to broaden the effect of the gifts of the Holy Spirit from the mere speaking in tongues or healing at a personal level to the communal and societal dimensions. The societal value of the gospel of the Holy Spirit has an important significance on how the church should function in a society.[50]

Secondly, the sharing movement should be developed further. Yoido Full Gospel Church has made so many contributions in this regard. However, numerous brother and sisters are receiving the minimal benefits of housing, clothing, food, education, sanitary,

---

48 Hong, Young-Gi, *Vision Project for the Kingdom of God* (Korean Christian Books Society, 2002, Korean), pp. 185-196.

49 International Theological Research Institute, *Introduction to Full Gospel Theology*, p. 234.

50 Hong, Young-Gi, 'The 21st Century Pentecostal Missiology', *The Holy Spirit and Theology* (No. 18, 2002, Korean), pp. 362.

and medical care to keep them barely alive.[51] In this time, the systematic development of Reverend Cho, Yonggi's ministry of sharing movement can be an important passage for the Full Gospel to contribute to the Korean society by enhancing the social trust on the church and developing the theological identity of the so called 'gospel of blessing'.[52]

The spirituality of sharing will become a more important ministry in this age of globalization and widening gaps between the rich and the poor.[53] The continuous sharing movement will be able to prevent the potential danger of redemption and lift through voluntary downward mobility.

Thirdly, it is important to develop the theology of social participation. The message of Full Gospel, that Reverend Cho, Yonggi proclaims, has an implication for a powerful social and political change. Nevertheless, it is the current situation that lacks the theological work on a political reform. The framework of Minjung (populace, general public) Theology in the past can not explain meaningfully the Christian political participation in today's changed Korean society. Since Yoido Full Gospel Church has already started to participate in the civil movement actively, it needs to develop a comprehensive project, which can include the issues from the service and participation for Korean society to social justice. This project should include practical social participation and theological task (the consolidation of theory and practicality). People will sincerely think twice about Christian message when Full Gospel churches develop evangelical civil movement, suggest Christian alternatives for social issues, and contribute to democracy of Korean society.[54]

At last, social leadership should be cultivated. The most important means that Christianity can influence Korean society is to nur-

---

51 David Bundy, Problems and Promises: Pentecostal Mission in the Context of Global Pentecostalism, A paper presented at the 29th Annual Meeting of the Society for Pentecostal Studies, March 16-18, 2000, in Kirkland, USA, 2002, p. 21.

52 cf. Hong, Young-Gi, 'Nominalism in Korean Protestantism', *Transformation*: An International Evangelical Dialogue on Mission and Ethics, 16(4), 1999, pp. 136-141.

53 Hong, Young-Gi, 'Progress and Pitfalls: Globalization and the Korean Church', A Paper Presented at the International Conference on *Reinterpreting East Asian Christianity* in Shanghai University of China, October 10-12, 2002.

54 Hong, Young-Gi, 'Evangelical Christians and the Democratization of Korea Since 1987'.

ture Christian leaders in all fields of Korean society.[55] Until now, Reverend Cho, Yonggi has nurtured so many talented people. However, in order to bring about a long-term reform of Korean society, a more systemic and long-term project for leadership development is needed.

That is to develop leaders, who are equipped with both ability (professionality) and faith (spirituality) in each field of politics, economics, sociality, culture, education and church, etc.[56] Thus, we have to grow people of faith, who have critical eyes and acting power for a healthy society, to send them into Korean society.[57] Although it takes time to grow and train people, it will develop the social leadership of Full Gospel in the long run and promote social reform by the gospel.

Toward the Kingdom of God

I think the influence of Reverend Cho, Yonggi's ministry on Korean society has been underestimated so far. His emphasis on the message of fivefold gospel is ultimately oriented toward the kingdom of God, that will be completed through Jesus Christ. Thus, we have to find the most important theological basis for Reverend Cho, Yonggi's ministry to reform the society in the kingdom of God.[58] Reverend Cho, Yonggi's ministry has contributed greatly in actualizing the vision of kingdom of God in Korean society.

His great achievements signify that he is in a position to influence Korean society tremendously in the future as well. In this respect, his ministry of social reform based on the fivefold gospel should be evaluated again, and its continuous development should be ensured. If his ministry continues its self-renewal by the power of the Holy Spirit in the future, it will contribute greatly in reforming Korean society and churches around the world. I hope God, Who has blessed Reverend Cho, Yonggi's ministry up to now, continues to utilize him greater in the future. And through his ministry, I pray earnestly for the Coming of the Kingdom of God upon Korean society. 'Amen, Oh, Lord Jesus, be upon us.'

---

55 Hong, Young-Gi, 'Revisiting Church Growth in Korean Protestantism: A Theological Reflection', *International Review of Mission* (April 2000, No. 353), pp. 190-202.

56 Interview, Myung, Sung-Hoon (Reverend, The Second Sanctuary of Yoido Full Gospel Church, October 27, 2002).

57 Interview, Park, Deuk-Hoon (Editor, *News & Joy*, October 27, 2002).

58 cf. Hong, Young-Gi, 'Vision Project for the Kingdom of God'

